Being Creative
in Primary English

SAGE was founded in 1965 by Sara Miller McCune to support the dissemination of usable knowledge by publishing innovative and high-quality research and teaching content. Today, we publish over 900 journals, including those of more than 400 learned societies, more than 800 new books per year, and a growing range of library products including archives, data, case studies, reports, and video. SAGE remains majority-owned by our founder, and after Sara's lifetime will become owned by a charitable trust that secures our continued independence.

Los Angeles | London | New Delhi | Singapore | Washington DC | Melbourne

Being Creative
in Primary English

Adrian Copping

Los Angeles | London | New Delhi
Singapore | Washington DC | Melbourne

Los Angeles | London | New Delhi
Singapore | Washington DC | Melbourne

SAGE Publications Ltd
1 Oliver's Yard
55 City Road
London EC1Y 1SP

SAGE Publications Inc.
2455 Teller Road
Thousand Oaks, California 91320

SAGE Publications India Pvt Ltd
B 1/I 1 Mohan Cooperative Industrial Area
Mathura Road
New Delhi 110 044

SAGE Publications Asia-Pacific Pte Ltd
3 Church Street
#10-04 Samsung Hub
Singapore 049483

Editor: James Clark
Editorial assistant: Robert Patterson
Production editor: Nicola Marshall
Proofreader: Kate Campbell
Indexer: Silvia Benvenuto
Marketing manager: Dilhara Attygalle
Cover design: Naomi Robinson
Typeset by: C&M Digitals (P) Ltd, Chennai, India
Printed and bound by CPI Group (UK) Ltd,
Croydon, CR0 4YY

Adrian Copping © 2016

First published 2016

Library of Congress Control Number: 2016932128

British Library Cataloguing in Publication data

A catalogue record for this book is available from
the British Library

ISBN 978-1-47391-565-7
ISBN 978-1-47391-566-4 (pbk)

At SAGE we take sustainability seriously. Most of our products are printed in the UK using FSC papers and boards.
When we print overseas we ensure sustainable papers are used as measured by the PREPS grading system.
We undertake an annual audit to monitor our sustainability.

Contents

About the Author

Adrian Copping has been working in teacher education for the last twelve years. At present, he is Primary PGCE Programme Leader and Senior Lecturer in English and Literacy based at the Lancaster campus of the University of Cumbria. Previously, Adrian worked at two contrasting schools in Lancashire, as class teacher and leader. Adrian's particular interests are the use of teacher-in-role and other drama techniques to develop children's writing and understanding of text and also the impact of creative thinking on children's writing. Adrian has presented work on this at various national and international conferences. In his teacher education work, Adrian continues to develop close working relationships with primary schools, which have enabled him to keep abreast of current practice as well as develop his areas of research interest.

Acknowledgements

I would like to acknowledge, with immense gratitude, the many teachers, student teachers and children who have wittingly and unwittingly contributed to this book. Particularly, I would like to thank Kate Skellern from Stramongate Primary School, Kendal, Cumbria, for her support with Chapter 5 on the Early Years Foundation Stage (EYFS).

I would also like to thank my wife, Ceridwen, for her proof-reading and attention to detail, and also to thank our children, Kezziah, Arron and Tirzah, for allowing me to sit in my study during holiday time and write this book. I appreciate your patience and your insights into learning, teaching and school.

Introduction

A case for creativity

Whenever I use the word 'creative' to describe someone or talk about the concept of 'creativity', I usually receive a variety of responses. Some might say, 'I'm not creative' or 'I haven't got a creative bone in my body.' Others connect the word to certain subject disciplines or artistic skills or talents: 'I'm not creative, I can't draw' or 'I am very creative I'm good at displays.' This is not to suggest that these responses might be in any way wrong, but I do wonder what assumptions the responders are making about creativity and what their conceptual understanding of creativity is.

Unpacking 'creativity'

Vernon (1989) suggests that, in order to be creative, one must demonstrate some level of originality. He goes on to discuss this in terms of restructurings and inventions that are of scientific or technological value. In the National Advisory Committee on Creative and Cultural Education's (NACCCE) report, *All our Futures*, Sir Ken Robinson (the Committee's chair) goes further, suggesting another three characteristics of creative processes. These are: thinking or behaving imaginatively … that this imaginative activity is purposeful … and that it must be of value in relation to the objective' (1999: 30). Anna Craft (cited in Desailly, 2012: 13) terms this imaginative activity 'possibility thinking'. Asking questions such as, 'What if …?' and

'What would happen if …?' allows the thinker to suggest many possible outcomes and alternatives.

Creativity is not tied in to a particular subject. It is not to do with any particular set of skills or talent. It is about thinking. Guilford (1967) developed this idea by identifying two different dimensions of thinking: convergent and divergent. Razouminkova defines convergent thinking as a process that: 'uses stereotyped mental operations that converge on only one task solution' (2000: 11). In other words, convergent thinking is about getting the job done and there is one of way doing it, or one answer. Teachers, usually subconsciously, can play a game with children called 'Guess What's in my Head', where they have one answer in mind and so the questions they ask are designed to elicit this one particular answer. This would be quite an extreme form of facilitating convergent thinking but illustrates the point. With respect to divergent thinking, Razouminkova goes on to state that: 'during divergent thinking many new ideas on some mental task are generated, implying that not only one solution may be correct' (2000: 11). In other words, the focus moves from getting the job done to the process of getting the job done as the focal point. In this sense, the journey to completion is where the learning takes place and the end product may well be of secondary importance as there will be many ways of completing it, all of which have equal value and merit discussion, debate and consideration.

Maisuria (cited in Craft and Jeffrey, 2008) suggests that, for teachers who want to foster creativity, there is an impossible tension. This tension arises because, whilst teachers' are encouraged during their Initial Teacher Education and into their newly qualified teachers (NQT) years to innovate, take risks and foster creativity, they are on the other hand subject to targets, moderation, accountability, results and published league tables. There is also the threat of poor results leading to an Ofsted inspection. As Craft and Jeffrey go on to say, the Department for Education (DfE) in England 'has now established a significant performativity culture to achieve its improving standards policy through national testing, target setting and national inspections alongside the publication of league tables' (2008: 579). One of the issues I will be exploring in this book, perhaps not explicitly but certainly implicitly, is whether creativity and the performativity culture are necessarily polar opposites. Does there have to be a tension? Does this need to be a dilemma for teachers? Within these questions is the hypothesis that developing creative thinking – and the other facets of creativity that I will be exploring in a small way in this Introduction and developing in Chapter 1 – leads to higher achievement and higher attainment. It is a very brave Year 6 teacher who does not do lots of practice for the Standard Assessment Tests (SATs) from January preparing for the tests in May. However, I wonder whether it is the high-stakes nature of the tests in terms of a performativity culture, rather than the tests themselves, that are viewed with hostility by many in the education profession?

Teaching creatively and teaching for creativity

First, let's get one thing straight: teaching creatively does not mean having to dress up as a certain character and flamboyantly dance around a room. It could, but it doesn't have to. Again, when I mention creative teaching to my students, they start reaching for the dressing-up. Why is that? Who knows, but it could provide some interesting research!

Sue Cowley describes the creative teacher as someone who: 'lights a fire within his or her children: making the whole process of learning seem worthwhile and exciting' (2005: 58). She goes on to provide a list of 16 attributes of a creative teacher, which I think all relate to being child-centred, responding to the children in your class and meeting their learning needs. There is no blueprint for how to do it, and Cowley does not offer her readers a creative teaching toolkit which will work; instead, she encourages teachers to put children first, to put their learning first and to engage them in enjoying learning and see it as a worthwhile use of their time. She encourages teachers to explore, discover, play, adventure, imagine, question and challenge.

Whilst teaching for creativity is clearly linked to teaching creatively, there are some subtle differences. Craft and Jeffrey suggest that teaching for creativity is about '*learner empowerment*' (2004: 77). This could be seen as giving learners more control over their own learning and therefore giving children more opportunity to be innovative and express themselves. It might involve giving them opportunities to pose questions, identify challenges and work together to offer a variety of possibilities for resolution.

The National Curriculum: straitjacket or safety blanket?

I consider myself to be privileged to have undergone my initial teacher education during the early mid-1990s, when the National Curriculum seemed to be changing every year. Many of my school-based mentors cursed this new thing that had taken their freedom away. However, for me as a new, inexperienced teacher, having a curriculum was very helpful because it presented some key statements relating to skills, knowledge and understanding that I had to cover. I was an English subject leader during the late 1990s when the National Literacy and Numeracy Strategies were introduced and cursed the myriad of specific objectives and seemingly end-less lists of curriculum coverage. However, my undergraduate initial teacher education students in the mid-2000s fell on this like starving vultures upon a carcass, ready to feast on the safety of having specific objectives for their year group. What is a straitjacket for some is a security and safety blanket for others. National Curriculum 2013 at first sight felt like a straitjacket. I scrolled down to the English section and saw on second look, opportuni-ties amongst what looked like an overbalance towards transcription and technical aspects of reading such as word recognition. These opportunities arose from the fact that the wording of the programmes of study are very clever in that there is freedom within them to be creative, foster creativity, engage learners and make learning exciting and worthwhile for children. There is space and scope within the National Curriculum to adventure into new areas, to explore favourite texts and approaches and to enthuse chil-dren about the literature that you are enthused about.

What can creativity provide? Why do it?

Juliet Desailly (2012) argues for the benefits of creativity and what it can give children and their learning. One key point she makes is that children do tend to remember things better if they are learned in creative and inter-active ways. My family is involved in English Civil War historical re-enactment. As a result, we are often invited into local schools in our 'kit' with the various accoutrements of our period to do some teaching. Children can touch armour, swords, try on costumes, examine musket balls and have a go at doing some basic training in musket, sword and pike. Children can explore artefacts 'hands on' and it provides a relevant context for them, especially when they see a seventeenth-century map of their local area and we take them on a walk showing them what the land was like 360 years ago. Weeks later, I may go back into the school for another reason and children come up to me and talk about what they remember and some of the key learning points – admittedly, usually the gory bits.

This also demonstrates another of Desailly's key points that creativity can cater for children's learning styles. Children will engage with a subject or topic in different ways and it is our role as teachers to facilitate them to do that, rather than expect all children to learn in the one way we may ordain through our plans. Both Cowley (2005) and Desailly (2012) state that crea-tivity can make learning more fun and it can also make the teacher's job more enjoyable. In preparation for a university seminar, I asked a Year 4 class what they thought a good teacher was and what they wanted from a teacher. One child said: 'look like you enjoy it … better still, actually enjoy it'. Children want their teachers to enjoy teaching them, to be excited about what they are doing and what they are teaching. In an interview in 2009 with the National Association of Head Teachers (NAHT), talking about 'All our Futures 10 Years On', Sir Ken Robinson supports this. He states that:

> When head teachers are prepared to take creative risks they can truly trans-form the nature of their school. And the thing is that the dividends and the benefits come to everybody. Teachers feel that they are doing a better job … Head teachers … find their jobs becoming easier and more fulfilling. (Robinson, 2009)

Learning should be about discovery. I became a much better mathematician through having to teach it to Year 6. When preparing my maths lessons, I would discover new ways of working out the answer, new approaches, and the following day I would run, grinning, Archimedes-like into the classroom, shouting, 'Eureka, I've found it!' excited to have discovered something and then experiencing the joy of sharing it with my classes. I'm not sure if they were impressed or just playing along, but I hope for the former. Exploration leads to discovery, which leads to excitement and enthusiasm, which then leads to further exploration and learning. This learning is authentic and meaningful because it is something the children wanted to find out or know. My son, aged 12 at the time of writing, loves chemistry at school. Why does this lesson stand out for him above the others? He says that the practical element where, in his words, 'you get to find out stuff yourself, not just copy off the board', motivates him. Not surprisingly, this is the subject where he experiences the greatest achievement and attainment.

Desailly (2012) goes on to say that creativity is useful. Whilst arguably not valued as much by the English education system, creativity is valued in society. Creative ideas are a key part of many businesses, laboratories and public services. Creative ideas and creativity usually help bring success in reality television shows such as BBC's *The Apprentice*, where young busi-ness entrepreneurs compete in a series of tasks to win a business deal with one of Britain's top businessmen.

In the context of this book, I will be considering the concept of creativity within three distinct areas that do overlap. They are:

- Creative thinking
- Creative teaching
- Creative integration of subjects and ideas – this could also be called 'Creative connections'

In the first chapter of this book, these three areas will be explored conceptually, alongside the question, 'Why should we foster creativity in primary English?' I will then give examples of these in many different ways, for different age groups and literary genres throughout the remaining chapters.

References

Cowley, S. (2005) *Letting the Buggers Be Creative*. London: Continuum.

Craft, A. and Jeffrey, B. (2004) 'Teaching creatively and teaching for creativity: Distinctions and relationships', *Educational Studies*, 30 (1): 77–87.

Craft, A. and Jeffrey, B. (2008) 'Editorial: Creativity and performativity in teaching and learning: tensions, dilemmas, constraints, accommodations and synthesis', *British Educational Research Journal*, 34 (5): 577–84.

Desailly, J. (2012) *Creativity in the Primary Classroom*. London: Sage.

Guilford, J.P. (1967) *The Nature of Human Intelligence*. New York: McGraw-Hill.

Maisuria, A. (2005) 'The turbulent times of creativity in the national curriculum', *Policy Futures in Education*, 3 (2): 141–52.

National Advisory Committee on Creative and Cultural Education (NACCCE) (1999) *All our Futures: Creativity, Culture and Education*. London: NACCCE.

Razouminkova, O. (2000) 'Functional organization of different brain areas during convergent and divergent thinking: An EEG investigation', *Cognitive Brain Research*, 10 (1–2): 11–18.

Robinson, Sir Ken (2009) '*All our Futures*: Interview with Sir Ken Robinson – 10 Years on', National Association of Head Teachers. Available at: www.naht.org.uk/welcome/news-and-media/magazines/features/all-our-futures-interview-with-sir-ken-robinson/ (accessed 3 June 2015).

Vernon, P. (1989) 'The nature–nurture problem in creativity', in J. Glover, R. Ronning and C. Reynolds (eds), *Handbook of Creativity*. London: Plenum Press.

Cracking the concept

Creative thinking, creative teaching, creative integration

Learning outcomes

By reading this chapter, you will have:

- Explored the concepts of creative thinking, teaching and integration
- Understood the differences between critical thinking and creative thinking
- Explored the concepts of creative teaching and teaching for creativity
- Explored some teaching approaches that facilitate these aspects of creativity

Chapter overview

The Introduction makes a case for creativity, drawing attention to some definitions and also to the three key elements of creativity in the title of this chapter. This chapter explores the concepts of creative thinking, teaching and integration in more depth and connects to definitions of creativity. Drawing on seminal work from leading writers on creative thinking, this chapter will explore different models of creative thinking, techniques and possible applications linked to inclusive pedagogy and its benefits for children. The chapter will outline some of the differences between critical thinking and creative thinking and suggest that, although much of how we teach encourages critical thinking, it does not do the same for creative thinking. This chapter will also look to 'myth-bust' creative teaching and explore teaching for creativity as well as presenting models for the integration of subjects, primarily drawing on the work of Robin J. Fogarty. There will also be connections made between the concepts and application of classroom approaches, outlining some different techniques and ideas. The concepts in this chapter are then exemplified by primary English teaching throughout the rest of the book.

Creative thinking: the concept of thinking

First, it is important to say that creative thinking and critical thinking are both equally as important. Fisher (1992) states that the concept of thinking is derived from the disciplines of philosophy and psychology. Philosophy is more concerned with the study of critical thinking, relying on and putting forward the merits of analysis and argument and applying logic to situations, whereas Cognitive Psychology (the study of mental processes and the role they play in how people think, feel and behave) gives more emphases to creative thinking and how ideas are formed in the mind. Thinking involves both these aspects. We cannot make sense of the world unless we think, unless we apply logic to situations, unless we analyse situations. But we cannot pursue ideas, we cannot create new things, we cannot have new ideas unless we allow and imagine them to be formed in our minds. Our thinking, however, is not something that we do in a vacuum. Despite the fact that we may often think by ourselves, I usually do a lot of thinking whilst cycling to and from work, Fisher would argue that our thinking is 'mediated by others' (1992: 4). He goes on to suggest that thinking takes place within a social context; it is shaped by the culture we are operating in and the environment in which we find ourselves.

These are not the only disciplines that facilitate the study of thinking. Our understanding of neuroscience has massively increased over the last decade and our knowledge of how the brain works on a physiological level and what it can do is significantly advanced. Humans have been fascinated by the brain for a long time, however. Phrenology, an aspect of science that focuses on measuring parts of the skull, linking to the brain having separate areas and functions, was a popular hobby during the latter part of the nineteenth century. This led to the search for general laws about how the mind works, looking for universal patterns in, as Fisher states, 'cognitive growth and human knowing' (1992: 5). Fisher also cites the contribution of Francis Galton (1822–1911), who devised a method for ranking human beings in terms of their physical and intellectual attributes. He suggested that genius was hereditary and that if your mind was superior in one aspect, it would be superior in all. If this is the case, then what is the point in self-improvement and learning? These findings led to questions around whether intelligence is part of a child's nature or can it be nurtured?

I have just made a connection above between intelligence and the ability to think – which I must confess has significant limitations. The measure of both is very important. Craft (2000) cites the work of Hudson (1973), who made the suggestion that children who excel in disciplines that look for one right answer also do well in traditional IQ tests. In other words, these children are good at convergent thinking. So, the text that measured intelligence actually measured the ability to find the correct answer. Drawing again on Hudson (1973), Craft (2000) goes on to suggest that children who are good at thinking divergently, tend to excel in the arts-based disciplines. Taking this line of thinking to its conclusion could lead us to arrive at the misconception that thinking divergently is creative and therefore applies to the arts and thinking convergently is not creative and applies to science-led disciplines. However, I want to make very clear that this is a huge misconception, certainly in terms of thinking. Guilford (1967) brought to light the distinction between different types of thinking: convergent, being about looking for the one right answer; and divergent, looking for a myriad of possible answers. These apply to any area and any discipline and should not be pigeonholed in this way. Thinking transcends subject disciplines. I also want to make very clear that I am not suggesting that divergent thinking is in any way better than convergent thinking, it is, however, more creative. Craft states: 'possibility thinking, which is the basis of creativity, is involved in both convergent and divergent thinking' (2000: 7).

Possibility thinking

Possibility thinking is an aspect of divergent thinking. So, what is meant by possibility thinking? Craft puts it 'at the heart of all creativity in young children' (2007: 1) and it is all about generating lots of possibilities. Guilford (1967) asked how many uses could be found for a pen; Craft would suggest that possibility thinking is about going even further and asking 'what if' questions. What if the pen was the size of a house and made of foam? What if it was made of wood and the size of a woodlouse? What if it was rolled out to make a flat surface? How many uses could be found for the pen?

The case study below explores possibility thinking in action in a Year 4 class looking at forces. Note how Josh, the class teacher, encourages his class to suggest and try out different possibilities. Where does the learning take place?

Case study

Josh, a Year 4 teacher, was teaching a unit of work on forces. He was focusing on friction and air resistance. Many of Josh's class were interested in Formula 1 motor racing, so Josh decided to turn his classroom into a Formula 1 pit lane garage as a means of stimulating interest. Josh's challenge to his class was clear. He asked them to design and build a car that would be able to go as far as possible unaided from a downhill ramp start. Josh discussed with his class how they would go forward with this. For Josh, the main focus was learning about friction and air resistance, not about creating a beautifully neat car to show to parents. He was hoping for experimentation and a range of ideas, and that is what he got.

As the project developed, Josh observed a lot of discussion around the car's weight and shape and that more weight would provide more downward force. These were children whom Josh would not have expected to be discussing this kind of complexity. Children were suggesting alternative materials, alternative aerodynamic designs, different widths, lengths, shapes and wheel sizes. What would the children do, however, if something didn't work? Although this hadn't really been planned, Josh found that, in the main, the children worked collaboratively quite effectively and sought support from each other. Billy would help Hannah to alter something to help her car go faster. Mel would ask Michael for help when she didn't know why her car got stuck at the bottom of the ramp. The evaluation of the cars was taking place during the design process – those complex skills of refining and evaluating were happening naturally.

Reflecting on the case study

- How did Josh facilitate possibility thinking?
- What are some of the challenges of Josh's approach? Was there any scaffolding?
- What type of work had gone before for Josh's class to respond as they did?
- What did the children learn, and during which aspects of the project did it take place?
- What will you take from this case study?

Craft states that: 'Possibility thinking, then, essentially involves a transition in understanding; in other words, the shift from "What is this?" to exploration – i.e. "What can I/we do with this?" Fostering possibility in children involves enabling children to find and refine problems as well as to solve them' (2007: 2). It would have been easy for Josh to have provided some aerodynamic cutouts for the children to fold, wood and wheels cut to the right lengths and a neat presentation to show the children how to make the best car. But, where would the learning have been? Possibility thinking for Josh was about the children working out what to do with the problem and then uncovering any issues and dealing with them as the process unfolded. This is helping children develop lifelong skills as well as the enjoyment of practical Science and Design Technology. Of course, there are more effective aerodynamic car designs and materials, but the focus for Josh was not on his class finding the right answer, but on developing, exploring, challenging and creating many possibilities in order to develop their understanding of two important scientific concepts.

Creative teaching

Having read the previous section, it would therefore follow that creative teaching is teaching that facilitates and promotes possibility thinking. Absolutely, but it is much more than that. Joubert (cited in Craft et al., 2001), states that creative teaching is an art. There is no manual, procedure or set of routines that one can use to teach someone else to be a creative teacher. The NACCCE's *All our Futures* defines creative teaching as: 'teachers using imaginative approaches to make learning more interesting, exciting and effective' (1999: 89). Joubert (cited in Craft et al., 2001) goes on to comment that creative teachers are constantly reinventing themselves and their approaches, adapting their teaching styles, resources and strategies to the different contexts in which they find themselves. Craft and Jeffrey (2004) cite the work of Woods (1990), who suggests some characteristics of a creative teacher to be: innovation, ownership, control and relevance.

However, what *All our Futures* (NACCCE, 1999) does – also developed by Craft, Jeffrey and Liebling (2001) and Craft and Jeffrey (2004) is to create a distinction between teaching creatively and teaching for creativity – teaching creatively being ostensibly to do with the teacher, and teaching for creativity being more concerned with the way in which creative teaching develops children's and young people's thinking and behaviour. Joubert (cited in Craft et al., 2001) goes on to explore NACCCE's (1999) three principles of teaching for creativity: encouraging, identifying and fostering. I would encourage a read of Joubert's chapter as it explores these principles very effectively.

To summarise, Joubert explains that teachers should encourage children to believe in their creative selves and engage their minds in having a go; in turn, developing children's confidence that they might explore possibility thinking in an education system that is essentially convergent in terms of how intelligence and success is measured. Joubert states that teachers should be identifying children's talents and creative abilities, rather than leading them down narrow career paths and fostering creativity. Learning is a process of discovery and often occurs through exploration and that wonderful moment where a connection is made and we finally 'get it'. Teachers should encourage children to experiment, play and discover. Children should, as Joubert says, 'Innovate not merely imitate' (2001: 25).

What is a creative teacher?

Woods (1990) has suggested some response to this, as we have previously considered. But, what comes into your mind? As a student teacher in the early to mid-1990s, I was heavily influenced by John Keating from *Dead Poets Society* (1989) played by the wonderful Robin Williams. Keating was different, he displayed charisma, he ripped up the textbook (quite literally), he had boys standing on tables, performing poetry, he enthused his class; his classes were fascinating and slightly unpredictable. Could these be characteristics of a creative teacher? The characteristics which Torrance (1965) came up with are: curiosity, independence, intuition, idealism and risk-taking. Cremin (2015) develops this theme by discussing the pedagogic practice of creative teachers. She draws on previous research by Abbs (2002) and Woods and Jeffrey (1996), who state that: 'Creative teachers' pedagogic practice is seen to be most effective when they help children find relevance in their work either through practical application or by making emotional or personal connections' (Cremin, 2015: 36). In order to do this, teachers need to ask questions, they need to know their children and they need to be able to stand back from their position as teacher and notice what is happening around them. How are the children responding? Are the children responding? Teachers should avoid playing 'guess what's in my head' when asking questions but use open questions that allow children to think, have their say and also express themselves. They should use possibility thinking, which is about meeting the child in their understanding of the world and guiding them to further thinking and development. This is a risky business and not for the faint-hearted. As I observe student teachers, I see many 'safe' lessons where, because they fear things going 'wrong', the lessons are over-planned, predictable, over-scaffolded, almost programmed for a clean and sterile view of perfection. I understand why this happens but I urge student teachers to have a go, try something out. But it is a brave student teacher, or a brave teacher who tries something risky, who tries something different. Why? Because letting go of control is risky. Yet, this is about classroom ethos. What does your classroom ethos say about you? Can children make mistakes? Is that okay? Can they have a go? Do you value process? Or do you expect flawlessly neat work, punish mistakes and overly value the end product. If so, how do children respond? What is it like being in your class?

Teaching for creativity

It does not sit well with me to delineate between teaching creatively and teaching for creativity because the lines are very blurred. But, to reiterate the NACCCE's (1999) distinction from earlier in this chapter: teaching creatively is primarily concerned with the teacher themselves, and teaching for creatively is concerned with how the teaching fosters children's creativity. In order to practically explore fostering creativity, let's return to our case study earlier in the chapter of Josh and his science project on forces.

Josh set up a simulation of a Formula 1 pit lane garage. He did this by bringing in some old tyres, posters of drivers and tools and he wore overalls. He also encouraged the children to bring in and wear any Formula 1 clothing they had. Cowley suggests that simulations are a 'powerful way of harnessing creativity' (2005: 93). Simulations replicate real-life scenarios, providing context and concrete experience for children. Primary classrooms have utilised role play in many contexts for many years and simulations are essentially an extension of these. Not only is Josh being creative here, but the simulation can stimulate questioning, creative thinking and a wider response to the subject, in this case forces. In 'Curriculum Approaches' (Copping, 2012), I present a case study that illustrates this very point. The simulation is to contextualise Alfred Noyes' classic poem 'The Highwayman' and the teacher creates a simulation of a murder scene in the classroom, with atmospheric lighting, music and images. The children in this case study respond with a massive variety of questions and comments, where they are exploring and discussing the myriad of possibilities around what has happened or what could have happened. Teaching creatively can stimulate creativity. In fact, you cannot teach for creativity unless you are teaching creatively.

Josh was also taking part as a learner within his classroom (Cremin, 2015). He was taking a risk, he didn't really know how it would turn out but he knew he wanted to work with the children and help facilitate their thinking. In so doing, he was quite prepared to learn himself. However, one important point to note is that Josh perceived his children as creative thinkers. His view of himself as a teacher and of his children as learners was fundamental to the whole idea. Josh saw himself as a learner and a facilitator, a coach almost. He didn't see himself as the all-powerful fount of all knowledge. He didn't put that much pressure on himself. For Josh, his classroom was the children's classroom, too. He viewed the children, not as empty vessels to be filled with knowledge or wild lions needing to be tamed; he viewed his children as active participants in their learning, who had something to contribute to the learning process. In so doing, as Cremin states, Josh left 'space for uncertainty and the unknown and showed considerable creative assurance in building on unexpected contributions or enquiries, fostering the autonomy of learners in the process' (2015: 40).

Seeing this case study through the lenses of 'teaching creatively' and 'teaching for creativity' demonstrates how interlinked they are. Josh would not have had the questioning, exploratory journey of discovery responses to the project had he not taken a risk and taught creatively. His open questions facilitated the discussions. However, these are not just techniques or tips that Josh has picked up in his career; this approach comes from the type of teacher Josh is and his view of what learning and teaching is. This leads to the ethos he creates in his classroom which drives the pedagogic approaches he uses.

Stop and think

How can you take some risks in your teaching? Have a think about letting go of all the control and allowing your children to explore and develop ideas. Children may not arrive at your right answer, but they may get to a solution that works and they will have learned an awful lot through the process.

Creative integration

I have already stated that the pedagogic practice of creative teachers is about creating relevance and understanding and making connections. I would add that creative practice is also about developing children's conceptual understanding of whatever is being studied. Cowley writes in praise of topic work, which she states: 'offers a way of capitalising on the natural links and connections between various subjects' (2005: 86). Let's be clear, this section is not a treatise suggesting that everything should be integrated and that the only way to be creative is to use topic work. What I am doing is exploring the ways in which curriculum areas can be integrated in order to help make learning more cohesive where it works. It might be interesting to encourage children to consider learning from one subject area, let's say English and non-fiction, and apply it to another (see Figure 1.1). All statements in Figure 1.1 are taken from National Curriculum 2014 Key Stages 1 and 2. This figure illustrates that many non-fiction skills demanded by the National Curriculum are essential to developing learning in history. There is scope for these connections to be made and then taught together as it will make a much more cohesive and purposeful learning experience for the children. It makes much more sense to combine English and history in this context to investigate some sources or interpretations of Queen Elizabeth I, rather than doing an hour of non-fiction English work on, for example, non-chronological reports about tractors in the morning then for history in the afternoon, exploring sources about Elizabeth I. Whilst I agree that there could be a case of teach, practice in English and then apply in history, that does indicate some joined-up thinking. However, where concepts and skills can be aligned, then let's do it because it will make learning more cohesive for the children and they will get a greater sense of understanding and purpose to what they are doing.

In 'Curriculum Approaches' (Copping, 2012), I give some examples, drawing on the work of Fogarty of models of curriculum integration, and Figure 1.1 is a further example of her 'Shared' model. Fogarty and Pete (2009) state that: 'by coupling similar disciplines, the overlap facilitates deep learning of concepts

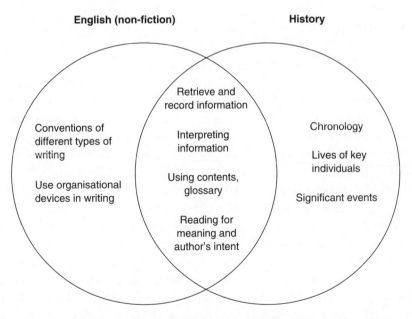

English (non-fiction)   **History**

Retrieve and record information

Conventions of different types of writing

Interpreting information

Chronology

Lives of key individuals

Use organisational devices in writing

Using contents, glossary

Significant events

Reading for meaning and author's intent

Figure 1.1 Skills distinct between and common to both subjects of English (non-fiction) and History

for transfer' (2009: 58). In other words, making connections between skills within two subject disciplines facilitates deep learning.

Why is integrating curriculum areas an integral part of creativity?

The main reason is one I have mentioned before but I do want to unpack it further, and that is making connections. Fogarty says that: 'the brain is a pattern-seeking mechanism and is constantly and continually searching for connections that make sense' (2002: 160). In order to facilitate this, children need to be active in their own learning and they are more likely to be active if they can see a purpose to it and are engaged in it. One way to do this is by giving the learning a context, and a meaningful cross-curricular approach can do that.

This is all about relationships. In the above example, I explored the relationship between elements of two subject disciplines and the notion of relationship is important. Craft (2000) describes a teacher being in a relationship with the subject they are teaching and that creativity is about the dynamic interaction between the teacher, their subject and the values they hold.

In the following case study, this relationship between teachers, curriculum and values for the purpose of context-embedded learning is explored.

Case study

As part of one of their Masters-level modules, PGCE primary student teachers at the University of Cumbria devise, plan and facilitate a creativity week. Throughout this week, student teachers work in teams in primary classes and their task is to run a theme week. As part of that week, students have to teach children to think creatively and to teach creatively themselves as well as teach for creativity and also integrate subject areas creatively. As Elton-Chalcraft and Mills state: 'Children are given opportunities to take more ownership of the learning outcomes through carefully constructed approaches developing their creative thinking (Heilman, 2005). Students are offered a "safe" environment to "take risks" with their teaching and the children's learning' (2013: 2). This case study focuses on a group of student teachers who were facilitating a science week. Each year group team had taken an area of science in which they had experience and planned accordingly. One year group had taken the theme of chemical reactions and had set up a simulation around J.K. Rowling's creation of Hogwarts.

The children had been sorted into groups using a 'sorting hat' and were then ready for a programme of learning that incorporated a lot of high-level science, English and design technology. The classroom had been transformed to look like one from Hogwarts, with cobwebs and 'traditional desks' and one student teacher was performing the role of a 'Rowlingesque' potions teacher quite beautifully. The students had woven the skills from all three disciplines together to create a cohesive and enjoyable collaborative learning experience for the children. Children were experimenting with different powders and chemicals (full health and safety check completed) to discover the effects of mixing certain substances. They were also making an explosion-proof container with which to carry the potions across the playground and then devising a purpose for the potion as part of a task for the 'Hogwarts Apprentice'.

The children were developing skills of negotiation, collaboration and discussion, and also a lot of possibility thinking through 'what would happen if ...' questions, whilst engaging in some high-level science and some resistant materials work in design technology: manipulating materials, understanding properties of materials and using knowledge and understanding to combine various materials together. The skills of marketing their product through persuasive language and market research were developed. The key to its success was that the student teachers had thought very carefully about blending the skills from each subject discipline and which concepts would work effectively with each other. There was nothing random or lucky about how it worked. The connections made and the relationships between all areas made for success.

Reflecting on the case study

- How have you integrated subjects and work in a cross-curricular way? What were the effects?
- What makes for effective curriculum integration?
- What did you notice about how creative thinking, teaching and integration work together?
- What will you take away from this case study?

Elton-Chalcraft and Mills, along with myself and other colleagues from the University of Cumbria, have more recently been engaged in research looking at the impact of creative approaches on children's learning in similar creative themed weeks. The findings of this iteration of the research support the former. The student's approach of exploration, possibility thinking and finding creative connections between subjects facilitated the children to enjoy learning and also have some ownership as they could make decisions around what they did, leading to their delight in exploration and a desire to persevere. Creativity can also facilitate learning resilience. Elton-Chalcraft and Mills state in their findings that:

> teachers, student teachers and children … mentioned the concept of fun or enjoyment and linked this with liberation and time/space to discover. One child said: 'I felt free every day.' This was mentioned in some form or another by several children. (2013: 8)

Try this

Activity 1: Possibility thinking

When you are planning your next piece of teaching, try taking a risk. Ask some open questions that allow for a variety of responses, there may not even be a right answer. If you are not sure, why not ask the children something like: 'What would happen if the sea had no waves?' 'What would it be like if there was no such thing as concrete?' 'Would we still need aeroplanes if we could fly ourselves?' See what responses you get.

Activity 2: Simulation

When you are next planning a unit of work, see if there is a real-life context that you can create in order to engage the children in their learning. For example, if you are studying the Vikings, why not come dressed as one, set up the classroom like a Viking longship or even create what looks like the remains of a fire in the centre of the classroom like a Viking longhouse. It will be fun and engaging and you will enjoy it as much as the children.

Activity 3: Shared integration

When planning, use my example in Figure 1.1 in this chapter. Take two subject areas that you are teaching and do a Venn diagram of some of the skills, knowledge and understanding that are separate from each other and then common to both. Think through how you can teach the common skills, knowledge and understanding together. Try it and evaluate the children's learning as a result.

Summary

Creative thinking is at the heart of creativity. The concept is not really to do with any subject discipline or any particular type of person, creativity is to do with how we think. Pedagogically, it is to do with how we facilitate thought and elicit information. Do we ask children to guess what is inside our head, or do we ask them open questions that could have a myriad of possible responses because we want them to think, to have a go and to develop their understanding of the world? This in turn arises out of who we are as teachers and the ethos we create in our classrooms. It all stems from the crucial question: 'What kind of a teacher do you want to be?' or 'What kind of teacher are you?' Responses to this question drive our teaching approaches. Will we teach creatively by taking some risks and handing over control to our learners? Will we look for imaginative and innovative ways to engage our learners so as to create that joy in learning not just for them but also for us? Out of that desire to give up control and the desire to engage learners comes the desire to foster creativity. Will we be teachers who empower, encourage and develop our children to take more ownership of their learning, to be actively involved, be participants rather than spectators? Finally, as we look to embrace our relationship with the curriculum, how will we respond? We need to be looking for opportunities to make connections between subjects, to encourage children to see how some skills, concepts and understanding can transcend those subject borders whilst others stay firmly rooted within. How will we go about helping our children make learning more real, relevant and contextual?

In the context of the subject of English, my aim for the rest of this book is to do just that. The chapters that follow will explore these creative concepts in the context of English and look at making learning in primary English meaningful, fun, enjoyable and creative.

Further reading

Craft, A., Jeffrey, B. and Liebling, M. (eds) (2001) *Creativity in Education*. London: Continuum.

This text provides a great overview of the concepts explored in Chapter 1. Joubert's chapter on 'The Art of Creative Teaching', is one I have used a lot in this chapter, and all of it is very well written.

Fogarty, R.J. and Pete, B. (2009) *How to Integrate the Curricula*, 3rd edn. Thousand Oaks, CA: Corwin.

This great text explores 10 different ways of integrating the curricula and of exploring advantages and disadvantages of each and gives practical examples of how to use each model and when.

References

Abbs, P. (2002) *Against the Flow*. Abingdon: Routledge.

Copping, A. (2012) 'Curriculum approaches', in A. Hansen (ed.), *Primary Professional Studies*, 2nd edn. Exeter: Learning Matters.

Cowley, S. (2005) *Letting the Buggers Be Creative*. London: Continuum.

Craft, A. (2000) *Creativity across the Primary Curriculum*. London: Routledge.

Craft, A. (2007) *Creativity and Possibility in the Early Years*. Available at: www.tactyc.org.uk/pdfs/Reflection-craft.pdf (accessed 21 December 2015).

Craft, A. and Jeffrey, B. (2004) 'Teaching creatively and teaching for creativity: Distinctions and relationships', *Educational Studies*, 30 (1): 77–87.

Craft, A., Jeffrey, B. and Liebling, M. (eds) (2001) *Creativity in Education*. London: Continuum.

Cremin, T. (2015) 'Creative teachers and creative teaching', in A. Wilson (ed.), *Creativity in Primary Education*, 3rd edn. London: Learning Matters.

Elton-Chalcraft, S. and Mills, K. (2013) 'Measuring challenge, fun and sterility on a "phunometre" scale: Evaluating creative teaching and learning with children and their student teachers in the primary school', *Education 3–13: International Journal of Primary, Elementary and Early Years Education*, DOI: 10.1080/03004279.2013.822904

Fisher, R. (1992) *Teaching Children to Think*. Hemel Hempstead: Simon and Schuster.

Fogarty, R.J. (2002) *Brain-Compatible Classrooms*. Glenview, IL: Pearson SkyLight Professional Development.

Fogarty, R.J. and Pete, B. (2009) *How to Integrate the Curricula*, 3rd edn. Thousand Oaks, CA: Corwin.

Guilford, J.P. (1967) *The Nature of Human Intelligence*. New York: McGraw-Hill.

Heilman, K. (2005) *Creativity and the Brain*. London: Psychology Press.

Hudson, L. (1973) *Originality*. London: Oxford University Press.

Joubert, M. (2001) 'The art of creative teaching', in A. Craft, B. Jeffrey and M. Liebling (eds), *Creativity in Education*. London: Continuum.

National Advisory Committee on Creative and Cultural Education (NACCCE) (1999) *All our Futures: Creativity, Culture and Education*. London: NACCCE.

Torrance, E.P. (1965) *Rewarding Creative Behaviour*. Englewood Cliffs, NJ: Prentice Hall.

Woods, P. (1990) *Teacher Skills and Strategies*. London: Falmer Press.

Woods, P. and Jeffrey, B. (1996) *Teachable Moments: The Art of Creative Teaching in Primary Schools*. Buckingham: Open University Press.

Creative approaches to teaching reading and enjoying text

Learning outcomes

By reading this chapter, you will have:

- Developed an understanding of how to engage children with word recognition creatively
- Developed an understanding of creative approaches to teaching comprehension strategies and higher-order reading skills
- Developed an understanding of how to transfer these approaches to a variety of reading contexts, including fiction and non-fiction
- Developed ways to help children enjoy and be stimulated by literature

National Curriculum links

- The word reading and comprehension elements of all age phases of the English subject section.
- Years 1 and 2 sections focus more on word reading and less on comprehension with that being reversed moving into lower and upper Key Stage 2.
- On p. 4, the importance of using phonics to develop word reading skills is stated and the importance of discussion with the teacher and

reading a range of texts across fiction, non-fiction and poetry in order to develop comprehension skills is also stressed.

DfE (2013)

Chapter overview

This chapter will explore both axes from *The Simple View of Reading* (Gough and Tunmer, 1986; Rose 2006): word recognition processes and language comprehension processes, with more of a focus on language comprehension processes and higher-order reading skills. *The Simple View of Reading* was first developed by Gough and Tunmer in 1986 and then introduced as a framework in an annex to Rose's (2006) *Review of Reading* by Stainthorp and Stuart. The chapter will begin with exploring ways to teach word recognition creatively whilst maintaining interest but also the robustness of a systematic approach. It will then go on to look at ideas to engage children and teachers in other reading foci. This chapter will give theoretical frameworks to develop reading skills such as inference, deduction, authors' viewpoint and social and cultural understanding of texts. It will also consider creative ways to engage children in reading non-fiction skills such as skimming, scanning and bias. The chapter also considers the power of shared and guided reading as techniques, creative ideas and the role that questioning plays in the assessment of reading both formatively and summatively.

Introduction

The teaching of reading has always been a contentious issue in the world of education, but since Sir Jim Rose's *Independent Review of the Teaching of Early Reading* (2006), the debate reached new heights, and the cause, phonics. This has led to the teaching of systematic synthetic phonics becoming statutory through the National Curriculum and the *Teachers' Standards* (DfE, 2011, 2013). There are two recognised approaches to teaching phonics: analytic and synthetic. The analytic approach, in its simplest form, starts with the word and breaks it down into sounds and letters, whereas the synthetic approach uses sounds and blending to build words. As a result, a plethora of phonics schemes and resources have flooded the market and many teachers, in my experience, are following these schemes discretely for 20 minutes each day in their classrooms. So what impact does this have? Johnston and Watson, drawing on statistical data, state that:

since introducing synthetic phonics teaching in England, there has been an increase in the percentage of children reaching the required level in the Key Stage 1 national reading assessments … In terms of decoding ability, in 2012 58% of children in Year 1 passed the new Phonics Check, in 2013 69% passed. (2014: 18)

Taking this statistical data alone within the context of how reading competence is measured, it would appear that more children are able to decode text as a result of discrete systematic, synthetic phonics teaching. Rose's *Independent Review* (2006) uses the theoretical model of the *Simple View of Reading* (see Figure 2.1).

However, Dombey makes it clear that this is not a new idea but that: 'it is intended as a representation of reality that is simplified in order to allow for better understanding of a complex phenomenon and better management of it' (2009: 1).

Teaching word recognition creatively

Cremin et al. (2008) state that the simple view of reading 'encompasses a two-dimensional framework that separates decoding and comprehension which may focus the attention of teachers and young readers on words not meanings, sounds not sense' (2008: 449–50). One of the challenges for readers is to make those connections between the black marks on the page, the

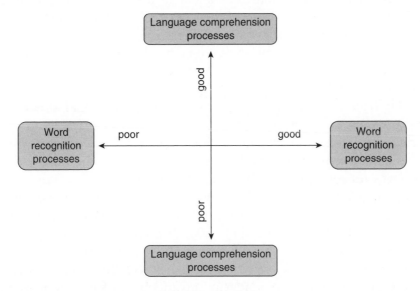

Figure 2.1   The Simple View of Reading. Rose (2006: 53)

sense they make and the meaning they convey. This first section will consider some creative approaches to that. But, let's be clear, whilst the subheading uses the term 'word recognition', I believe it to be unhelpful to separate this from language comprehension and so there will be reference to this, too.

There may be, as Cremin (2009) states, a temptation or even a viewpoint that teaching phonics is the 'antithesis of creative teaching' (2009: 45). There are some instances of phonics teaching which I have witnessed that are indeed that, as there are for science, maths, PE, music and so on. This seems more the case where schools have invested heavily in schemes and teachers are instructed to use the materials verbatim. However, phonics has the wonderful potential to be a hugely creative endeavour. For those of you who have spent many joyful hours grappling with the idiosyncrasies and intricacies of the English language, you have probably come to realise that it is not straightforward. We don't even have to go beyond a simple consonant, vowel, consonant (cvc) word such as 'was' before we hit trouble. Why is the medial vowel phoneme an 'o'? Here we start to hit the creative element of problem-solving. Are there any other patterns? Do any other words do this? In fact, my challenge for you is to re-read this section so far and count how many words do not work phonetically.

So, given the wonderful rich tapestry of pattern and non-pattern that forms the English language, children need, again as Cremin so wonderfully puts it: 'a commitment to the language and meanings of written texts if they are to make phonics work for them' (2009: 45). The most effective teaching of reading takes place within the context of making meaning from texts. This helps children make sense of their knowledge, and provides a forum for testing it out. Hayes states that understanding requires: 'considerable re-inforcement and testing out in real contexts before a thorough grasp … has been accomplished' (2015: 181). Knowledge is one thing but understanding is something else.

Highly patterned and rhythmic texts can be great to read aloud and to play with sounds. Perkins (2015) says that they can help children to focus on rhyme, rhythm and alliteration that help reinforce syllabic pattern, phoneme/grapheme correspondences and enunciating the many different phonemes. Jez Alborough's *Where's my Teddy?* (1992) is a superb rhythmic tale which alliterates the 'eddy' consonants. Margaret Chamberlain and Kaye Umansky's *You Can Swim, Jim* (1998) is also a brilliant repetitive, patterned text that alliterates medial phonemes and must be read aloud for full effect. Both Perkins (2015) and Cremin (2009) also recommend Steve Webb's brilliant *Tanka Skunk* (2004), which forces the reader to get their mouth round the different sounds and invariably has had both myself and the various classes and children I have read it to laughing out loud.

Teaching word recognition creatively involves playing with words and playing with sounds. Songs, tongue-twisters, rhymes can all help children do this. Essentially, children need to explore and problem-solve with sounds and letters and this should translate into spelling, too. Perhaps, instead of children using suggested songs from a scheme, they could create their own with the teacher that is about their class and them or something they are doing. This is essential for motivation and for engaging the children to want to make meaning because the content is something in which they have an investment.

Children should be engaged with this in a multi-sensory way and within a positive reading environment. Ofsted's 2010 report *Reading by Six* highlighted that one of the key criteria for an effective phonics scheme is that it should draw on a multi-sensory approach. This is important because children tend to be more successful learners when they are active participants and when they use more of their senses to engage with learning, there are more opportunities for that learning to become embedded. I started this section by suggesting that effective word recognition teaching takes place within the context of strong texts and this is all about the reading environment provided for children. Joliffe et al. (2015) cite Rose's 2006 review of reading, drawing attention to the idea that children should have opportunities to learn in 'language-rich contexts' (2006: 32 and 2015: 104). One of these can and should be storytelling. Waugh et al. (2013) suggest that this process also involves recalling and retelling so that books become enjoyable and enticing and an experience that the children want to repeat again. With this motivation to make sense of the black marks on the page, to get more from the experience, children can crack the alphabetic code and find that a brave new world opens up to them.

The brave new world

Other facets to reading and creative ways to engage children and teachers

Reading encompasses many different facets. In recent years, seven assessment foci have been identified as core criteria for what makes an effective reader. These foci have been assessed through formal Standardised Assessment Tasks (SATs) and appear on many downloadable and published Assessment grids for reading. Table 2.1 states them.

As you will see, only one of these assessment foci relates to word recognition explicitly, the rest are mainly to do with language comprehension, indicating that these, sometimes more subtle, elements of reading are crucial to what it means to being able to fully read.

Table 2.1   Reading Assessment foci

1	Use a range of strategies, including accurate decoding of text, to read for meaning
2	Understand, describe, select or retrieve information, events or ideas from texts and use quotation and reference to text
3	Deduce, infer or interpret information, events or ideas from texts
4	Identify and comment on the structure and organisation of texts, including grammatical and presentational features at text level
5	Explain and comment on the writers' use of language, including grammatical and literary features at word and sentence level
6	Identify and comment on the writers' purposes and viewpoints, and the overall effect
7	Relate texts to their cultural and historical contexts and literary traditions

Nation and Angell (2006) make the point that comprehension does need to be taught. It is not something that happens automatically once word recognition is in place. The question is, how can this be taught in a way that does not become endless 'read the text and answer the questions' worksheets? One way to start is by using visualisation. The short case study below demonstrates this. As you read it, consider how the approach impacts on the children's understanding of the author's intent and figurative language.

Case study

Luke's Year 5 class were reading Nina Bawden's classic text *Carrie's War* as part of their topic on the Second World War. Luke began this unit of work by considering the impact of figurative language and, more specifically, the impact it has on the reader. He gave each child a copy of the first page of the text, which describes the setting, and whilst he read it he asked the children to pay attention to the images that formed in their minds. As he read it a second time, he gave the children the choice to read along with him but then to draw the images in their minds. Luke did this, too. The children then shared their images, why they had stuck in their minds and identified where they were in the text. A class discussion then took place about what made the images stick and why. Some children identified the image of trees having 'grown twisted and lumpy, like arthritic fingers' (1973: 1). They thought that the writer was trying to convey the tree being old because old people have arthritis and they thought that 'twisted and lumpy' meant not very friendly and a bit scary and strange.

Reflecting on the case study

- How did Luke's approach develop the children's understanding of why an author may use figurative language and why they may choose certain images?
- How was it creative? Was it an open activity? Do you think that Luke had a specific answer he was looking for?
- How could Luke have assessed the children's understanding?

Using strategies to engage children with comprehension such as visualisation can be much more motivating than traditional 'read the text and answer questions' type of activities. The open questions which Luke asked to stimulate discussion will have piqued the children's curiosity and imagination and may well have led to some different ideas that Luke could have been flexible enough to run with. As Cowley states:

> the creative teacher will light a fire within his or her children: making the whole process of learning seem worthwhile and exciting … what we need to do is inspire the children to want to find out about … things for themselves. (2005: 58)

Higher-order reading skills

There are many different ways to approach the many skills of language comprehension. In this section, I particularly want to focus on the skills of inference and deduction, explaining and discussing writers' use of language and relating texts to their historical, cultural or social traditions and the impact this has on understanding. Here, I will focus on fiction and will move onto particular non-fiction skills creatively later on in the chapter.

What is inference? Well, if we answer this question, we begin to understand why it is so challenging to teach. However, we understand that written text cannot be fully comprehended unless we make inferences. Tennant (2015) lists 33 different types of inferences. However, he then separates inference into during and after the reading event (coherence inferences and interrogative inferences). We may infer something from a text as we read it to make sense in the moment but then afterwards, as we take more time, we may make other inferences based on a bit more information. Inference then is filling in the gaps between the lines or between the words that are written. Getting behind what the writer is saying, finding the clues and piecing them together to make meaning, is a very creative enterprise. Thinking about teaching these skills creatively, we do need to see them as problem-solving activities or opportunities to crack the code and find the hidden messages.

The Bully (1995) is a challenging story by Jan Needle about, at surface level, a young boy, Simon Mason, newly arrived at a school that does not suit his own lack of wealth and status. He is essentially bullied by Anna Royle, the rich, beautiful and intelligent school darling and her friends. The story follows Anna's determination to ensure that Simon does not continue to attend her school and the way in which the different teachers deal with this or not. The story has many hidden agendas and subplots and is therefore great for teaching inference. A teacher used this text with her Year 4 class to explore some of the subplots. She began by showing the cover. The cover shows a scruffy-looking Simon in the foreground and a sultry but beautiful Anna in the background and is emblazoned with the title *The Bully*. Who is the bully? The teacher asked. Immediately, the girls responded with: 'It's the boy, girls don't bully' and 'The girl is too pretty to be a bully.' Wow. What assumptions had the children already made? Using open questions and prediction questions through chapter 1, the teacher demonstrated how the author led us to feel more and more sorry for Simon as the chapter unfolded. It ends with Simon on a heap on the floor, surrounded by Anna's gang with Anna later on pretending to be hurt as Deputy Head Miss Shaw comes round the corner. The teacher arranged a number of the children to form a tableau of the final scene and she played Miss Shaw coming round the corner. Did she believe Anna? What did she do?

The above example may sometimes be called 'shared reading', where, as Brien (2012) states, the teacher and children explore the text together in which focused learning objective(s) reading strategies are demonstrated, modelling occurs and there is significant interaction between teacher and children. Open questions are posed and explored and children should be fully active participants in the learning process. Shared reading is varied, dependent on the class, year group, genre, text and objective, but it should contain the above elements in some form or other.

If we deconstruct the approaches taken by the teacher, you will see a number of creative aspects of teaching. First, questioning. Notice how the questions are open. Whilst the opening 'Who is the bully?' could be seen as closed, there are a multitude of answers besides the two characters on the cover. It could be a teacher, parent or another child as well. The teacher was not looking for the right answer; she was looking for the children's thinking and why they gave the answer they did. This is far more interesting than just giving the right answer. A creative teacher is passionate and interested in what children have to say and their thinking and will want to find out more. This also translates into the prediction questions. Here we have an opportunity to assess understanding. Responses to prediction questions demonstrate an understanding of what is going on in the story and whether the children are solving some of the clue trail laid by the author about characters and plot. Again, open questions such as 'Why do you think that?' or 'What could happen next?' allow for understanding to be demonstrated. The questions we ask should always allow children to demonstrate their thinking.

Finally, notice the tableau at the end. This is creative because the teacher is taking a risk. She will be in-role at first but later give that up. She is being adventurous and the children are encouraged to step into a role and contribute. Through their contributions, they can show their understanding. They can venture alternative opinions and justify them based on knowledge and understanding gained. Children usually want to participate fully in their learning as they don't like being bored. As a result, their ability to learn increases. Boyd et al. (2015) discuss the importance of learning as more than just the transmission of knowledge and getting the right answer. They describe it as the: 'co-construction of knowledge, skills, values and dispositions through experience, practice or being taught' (ibid.: 8). Here, the learner and teacher interaction is crucial, their relationship is one of fellow travellers on the road to understanding, exploring the subject area together, not an 'I teach, you learn' mentality where the learner is passive in the process.

There are also important opportunities available for teaching those higher-order reading skills through guided reading. Medwell et al. (2014) pick up the co-construction philosophy as they describe it as a time to work with children to help them read and interpret the text. Guided reading takes place typically with a group of six children and involves the explicit teaching of reading skills and facilitates a focused assessment of children's reading capabilities. Research into guided reading demonstrates that often teachers do not fully understand its purpose (Challen, 2008), and it is often unsuccessful when the teacher dominates discussion (Skidmore et al., 2003) and there are no inferential strategies taught and children have no opportunity to read silently and engage in collaborative discussion (Fisher, 2008).

Figure 2.2 below gives an example of a plan for a guided reading session using the 1968 novel *The Iron Man* by Ted Hughes. The plan demonstrates the creative use of open questions, empathy through the dramatic technique of hot-seating (a child goes into role as a character and is questioned) and also focusing on the writer's use of figurative language for effect.

Relating texts to their historical, cultural or social traditions does have a significant impact on understanding. One of the main purposes of this is to

Date:	Grp/chn: (6)	Book: *The Iron Man* by Ted Hughes
Focus/objectives		

Focus/objectives

Focus on referring to the text to support opinions. To infer meaning using evidence and personal experiences and comment on language use – especially figurative language

NC2014 link

Discuss and evaluate how authors use language, including figurative language, considering the impact on the reader

Book introduction	**Resources**
Remind the children about chapter 1 'The Coming of the Iron Man', how he fell off the cliff and was all in pieces and then built himself up again. Talk partners – babble gabble what can you remember?	
Strategy check	
Ask the children for strategies when we are not sure of what a particular word means or even says – what clues can we look for?	Copies of chapter 2 (one each)
Independent reading	
As you read the chapter, focus on figurative language and have a think about why Ted Hughes uses certain images – focus particularly on p. 21: 'as if an iron skyscraper had collapsed', and p. 26: 'rolling it up like spaghetti and eating it'	Task cards
Focus on pp. 25–9, where Hogarth meets the Iron Man – how does Hogarth respond? Is it realistic? Do we get any hints that Hogarth might be afraid?	
Use talk partners to discuss	
Return to text	
Draw out figurative language responses	
Focus on the scene on pp. 25–9. How does Hogarth feel? Behave? What would you have done, and why?	
How do you think Hogarth feels about having caught the Iron Man in the farmers' trap? Was this his intention? (Ask for text evidence)	
Hot-seating – Hogarth	

Figure 2.2   Guided Reading Plan: Figurative Language

support children's understanding of the reasons behind the story and some of the text references. Some of the language in Needle's 1995 text *The Bully* is of its time. For example, Needle uses terms such as 'spastic' as an insult, something that would be unthinkable 20 years on. Victorian and early twentieth-century literature contains the 'crippled' child. Again, this is often the term used and the Victorian ideal of children being saved and healed through some utopia, often a garden, as in Oscar Wilde's 1888 story 'The Selfish Giant' and Frances Hodgson Burnett's 1910 [1911] work, *The Secret Garden*. These stories can also raise issues. For example, another text used in the earlier case study, Bawden's *Carrie's War* (1973), sets the scene through evacuation to the country at the time of the Second World War but also deals with other issues of the complexity of friendship, relationships and moving on. Another text by Needle, *My Mate Shofiq*, published in 1978, deals with issues of inclusion and racism and was a ground-breaking text at the time.

There are huge amounts of outstanding texts for all ages and interests that both transport the reader to a particular place and time and also raise pertinent issues and promote thought, discussion and empathy. One of the best ways to teach these is to provide opportunity to fully explore the texts. The implications for the teacher is that their subject knowledge has to be good. For example, it may pay to know a little about the Victorian ideal of children being healed through nature, or about the challenges of evacuation or about the prevailing world view in the 1970s. Understanding the social world within which the text was written is very important for promoting understanding. Cremin (2009) states that creative teachers provide opportunities for extended exploration of a text. She calls this: 'finding imaginative ways to journey inside a book' (ibid.: 65). The case study below shows how this could be done, as Henry, a Year 5 teacher, takes his class on a journey inside J.K. Rowling's 1999 text, *Harry Potter and the Prisoner of Azkaban*.

Case study

The children arrived that morning to a darkened classroom, desks in rows, eerie music playing and a row of scientific flasks containing steaming coloured liquids at the front of the class. As the new potions teacher, Professor Algernon Tanglewood, Henry appeared from the cupboard, cloaked, mortar-boarded and waving a wand. He handed each child a black cape to wear as their school uniform. Throughout the two weeks of exploration of the world of Hogwarts, each morning began this way. Henry had made some filmed news reports from 'Azkaban', getting updates from the prison and what was being done to step up security. The children explored the text and created new scenes based on possible subplots and understanding of characters. They interviewed other Hogwarts professors, and the Minister of Magic as one of their main roles that week was to present a report to Professor Dumbledore on how the prisoner had managed to escape and what recommendations they had to ensure damage limitation.

(Continued)

(Continued)

Reflecting on the case study

- Consider the importance of Henry's approach. How did it motivate, challenge and engage the learners in his class?
- Many of you will be thinking: I haven't got the time or the energy or the personality to pull off something like that. However, think about how you could take elements of this yourself so as to stimulate the children's interest and imagination.
- Make some inferences yourself as you reread the case study and have a think about the differing types of language comprehension learning that were facilitated and developed by Henry.

Throughout this chapter, I have emphasised the importance of the child, the reader, being an active participant in the learning process. Gardner says that, when the child is an active co-constructor of meaning, then there is 'the potential for a creative and liberating engagement with texts' (2010: 120). Cremin (2009) draws on the importance of the teacher in this process. The teacher must not just be an active participant, but also one who brings passion, excitement and commitment to the teaching of reading, thus inspiring their children to read and to learn, and providing imaginative experiences of text for their children.

Stop and think

How will you ensure that you and your class are co-constructors of knowledge? How will you light the fires of children's imagination and bring passion and excitement to reading for them?

Applying these approaches to a non-fiction context

There is a temptation to think that non-fiction texts are boring and tedious and what comes into a teacher's mind can often be 'How can I string out non-chronological reports for two weeks?' or 'Why do we have to do instructions again?' In fact, you may feel tempted to skip over this bit, or skim read it, or even scan the text for specific areas of interest. If you do, you will be using some important techniques for non-fiction reading that we should be teaching children: skimming and scanning. So, how can we do it creatively? Well, first, we need to challenge assumptions and extend our repertoire of non-fiction texts. Non-fiction texts can be fun, stimulating and interesting and can facilitate a problem-solving approach. When teaching Year 4, I developed a unit of work on non-chronological report-writing. Using some of my old school reports (not very glowing, I might add), we looked at some of the euphemistic language in it, e.g. 'presents challenging behaviour', and what it really meant. The children engaged in this fully and loved it. Once they had chosen a teacher in the school to write a report on, their task for the preceding week was to become a detective and find out information on that teacher's classroom performance: they would observe teaching and interview teaching assistants and children before writing. This exploration of language for effect was a wonderful tool for teaching inference. The following short case study builds on this and provides an example of a teacher using a variety of non-fiction texts and sources within the context of a topic on the Tudors and an understanding of historical interpretation. As you read it, notice how Maeve, the teacher, uses this context to develop the children's understanding of purpose, audience and authorial intent.

Case study

Maeve began her afternoon with this question: 'What was Henry VIII really like?' Around the room, she had copies of letters, diary entries, reports, history books, paintings, eye-witness accounts of Henry and life at his court. She asked the class to identify whether they thought he was a good or bad king, a good or bad husband and a good or bad man. She followed this with 'How do we know?' and 'Is the information we have reliable?' Children then, in pairs, had to engage with each source, consider who it was written by and why, explore the language and what they didn't say and compare the sources and then arrive at some conclusions about the opening question.

Reflecting on the case study

- How did Maeve's connecting of the historical and reading skills develop the children's understanding?
- How did this approach engage and stimulate the children's thinking?

David Wray (2006) presents some very clear strategies for non-fiction reading. He gives some very practical strategies that deal with the skills of prediction, modelling, using key words, questioning and visual representation of text. Waugh et al. (2014) take the National Curriculum objectives for teaching non-fiction and categorise the reading elements as: listening to and discussing information, retrieving and recording information and presenting information. All of these strategies and approaches can best be taught in a motivating context, as seen from the example above. Children learn more effectively when it make sense to them, when they are active in the process and when they are motivated, stimulated and encouraged to think.

Try this

Activity 1: Playing with sounds

Do you read aloud to your class? Do you get them to participate? Do you model alliteration, dissonant consonants, rhyming medial sounds? If not, why not? Make some opportunities to engage your class in text and play with sounds with them. Let them explore them.

Activity 2: Increasing your own understanding

To develop and enhance children's understanding of text, do your homework. Make sure that you know the cultural and social context within which the text was written where appropriate. This will help you teach inference more effectively and may well even enhance your enjoyment and excitement about the text.

Activity 3: Extended exploration

When next planning a unit of work, think about how you can facilitate children going deeper into a text. Give them time and space in your planning to get to grips with a whole text, not just extracts of it. Let them explore the worlds created and perhaps even live them. Remember Algernon Tanglewood?

Summary

Creative approaches to reading and enjoying texts are all about giving children ownership and making them an active part in the reading process as co-constructors of understanding. This is a recurring theme throughout the chapter. Through various contexts and a variety of texts, we have seen how considering the reading process as solving clues can be motivating for children. This problem-solving approach to reading is creative and stems from an ethos of there not being a single answer inside the teacher's head that the child must try and extract, but a multitude of interpretations which, if well-reasoned and justified, are equally valid. Cremin (2009) finishes her chapter on developing readers creatively by emphasising the importance of building communities of readers. She states that it is within these communities that imaginative ways into reading and creative ways of responding to text are facilitated. If we are to help children become great readers, rather than just great at reading, this must be an environment that creative teachers strive to create.

Further reading

Perkins, M. (2015) *Becoming a Teacher of Reading*. London: Sage.

This excellent text provides a very clear insight into what being a teacher of reading is all about. Perkins is brilliant on both subject knowledge and the pedagogy of teaching all aspects of reading, and presents a great mix of practical activities and reflective activities as well as considering pedagogy around how children learn to read.

Tennant, W. (2015) *Understanding Reading Comprehension*. London: Sage.

This is a wonderful text that explores reading comprehension in a very deep way. Whilst there are practical ideas, there is a much greater understanding presented by Tennant that facilitates application into a variety of contexts. His discussion of text selection as integral to comprehension development is superb.

Waugh, D. and Neaum, S. (2013) *Beyond Early Reading*. Northwich: Critical Publishing.

What happens when they can actually read? When they understand that the black marks on the page carry meaning? This excellent book provides very useful advice and support with teaching and engaging children with those many other facets of reading. It contains lots of very practical ideas, including engaging children through the power of electronic texts.

References

Alborough, J. (1992) *Where's my Teddy?* London: Walker Books.

Bawden, N. (1973) *Carrie's War*. London. Victor Gollancz.

Boyd, P., Hymer, B. and Lockney, K. (2015) *Learning Teaching*. Northwich: Critical Publishing.

Brien, J. (2012) *Teaching Primary English*. London: Sage.

Burnett, F.H. (1910 [1911]) *The Secret Garden*. London: Heinemann.

Challen, D. (2008) 'Small group literacy teaching: Pedagogy and control', Paper presented at the British Education Research Association Conference, Heriot-Watt University, Edinburgh, 3–6 September.

Chamberlain, M. and Umansky, K. (1998) *You can Swim, Jim*. London: Red Fox.

Cowley, S. (2005) *Letting the Buggers Be Creative*. London: Continuum.

Cremin, T. (2009) *Teaching English Creatively*. London: Routledge.

Cremin, T. Mottram, M., Bearne, E. and Goodwin, P. (2008) 'Exploring teachers' knowledge of children's literature', *Cambridge Journal of Education*, 38 (4): 449–64.

Department for Education (DfE) (2011) *Teachers' Standards*. London: DfE. Available at: www.gov.uk/government/uploads/system/uploads/attachment_data/file/301107/Teachers_Standards.pdf (accessed 28 October 2015).

Department for Education (DfE) (2013). *The National Curriculum for England, Key Stages 1 and 2*. London: Crown Copyright.

Dombey, H. (2009) *The Simple View of Reading*. Available at:www.ite.org.uk/ite_readings/simple_view_reading.pdf (accessed 4 May 2015).

Fisher, R. (2008) 'Teaching comprehension and critical literacy: Investigating guided reading in three primary classrooms', *Literacy*, 42 (1): 19–26.

Gardner, P. (2010) *Creative English, Creative Curriculum*. London: Routledge.

Gough, P. and Tunmer, W. (1986). Decoding, reading and reading disability. *Remnedial and Special Education*. 7, pp:6–10.

Hayes, D. (2015) *Foundations of Primary Teaching*, 5th edn. London: David Fulton.

Hughes, T. (1968). *The Iron Man*. London: Faber and Faber.

Johnston, R. and Watson, J. (2014) *Teaching Synthetic Phonics in Primary Schools*, 2nd edn. London: Sage.

Joliffe,W. Waugh, D. Carss, A. (2015). *Teaching Systematic, Synthetic Phonics in Primary Schools*. 2nd edn. London: Sage.

Medwell, J., Wray, D. Minns, H. Griffiths, V. and Coates, E. (2014) *Primary English: Teaching Theory and Practice*, 7th edn. London: Learning Matters.

Nation, K. and Angell, P. (2006) *Learning to Read and Learning to Comprehend*. *London Review of Education*, 4 (1): 77–87.

Needle, J. (1978). *My Mate Shofiq*. London. Lions Publishing.

Needle, J. (1995) *The Bully*. London: Penguin.

Ofsted (2010) *Reading by Six*. London. Available at: www.gov.uk/government/uploads/system/uploads/attachment_data/file/379093/Reading_20by_20six.pdf (accessed 28 October 2015).

Perkins, M. (2015) *Becoming a Teacher of Reading*. London: Sage.

Rose, J. (2006) *The Independent Review of the Teaching of Early Reading: Interim Report*. Available at: www.reall-languages.com/interimreport.doc (accessed 31 October 2014).

Skidmore, D., Perez-Parent, M. and Arnfield, S. (2003) 'The quality of teacher–pupil dialogue in guided reading', Paper presented at the British Education Research Association Conference, Heriot-Watt University, Edinburgh, 11–13 September.

Tennant, W. (2015) *Understanding Reading Comprehension*. London: Sage.

Waugh, D., Jolliffe, W. and Allott, K. (2014) *Primary English for Trainee Teachers*. London: Learning Matters.

Waugh, D., Neaum, S. and Waugh, R. (2013) *Children's Literature in Primary Schools*. London: Learning Matters.

Webb, S. (2004) *Tanka Skunk*. London: Red Fox.

Wilde, O. (1888). *The Selfish Giant*. In *The Happy Prince and Other Stories*. London: D. Nutt.

Wray, D. (2006) *Teaching Literacy across the Primary Curriculum*. Exeter: Learning Matters.

Creative approaches to teaching writing

3

Learning outcomes

By reading this chapter, you will have:

- Developed an understanding of the writing process
- Considered tools and techniques for teaching compositional and transcriptional elements of writing more creatively
- Developed an understanding of the purposes of whole-class and guided writing
- Considered the power and impact of working in-role and writing in-role

National Curriculum links

- The transcription and composition elements of all year group/age phase sections of the English subject section.
- Each year group/phase overview focuses a lot on transcription (especially pp. 18 and 25).
- Supplemented specifically for Lower Key Stage 2 (p. 33), where there is an added focus on developing competence and effectiveness and recognising the differences between written and spoken language. Upper Key Stage 2 summary (p. 45) states an understanding of

audience so that pupils can select vocabulary, grammar and sentence structures for a variety of purposes.

DfE (2013)

Chapter overview

This chapter considers a range of frameworks to explore the writing process. It focuses on composition and transcription and creative ways to engage children in those processes. It looks at creative approaches to shared and guided writing and how those techniques can develop children's attainment. The chapter also considers the use of teacher-in-role as a technique to stimulate writing, writing in-role and how to make writing purposeful and relevant for the learners. The chapter focuses on the role that careful scaffolding plays in delivering high expectations for children's writing and how to embed the teaching of grammar and spelling into the writing process so that it is meaningful. The premise for teaching grammar and spelling here is that it helps children become more intentional in their writing.

Introduction

There is no getting away from the fact that writing is hard. In writing, you only have the written word and are using only that one tool, your task is to communicate meaning effectively to an essentially unknown audience and for a specific purpose. There is no opportunity to support your words with gesture, facial expression or opportunity to seek clarification for understanding. The task is big and the risk is also big. Myers and Burnett (2004) share the many purposes that writing in daily life has: from the shopping list, the note on the calendar, to the challenging letter to a newspaper, the declaration of love and also the informative blog or social media post. If any of these miss the intended meaning, there could be chaos.

In the context of school, however, writing usually serves a different purpose. Writing is often how teachers ask children to display their understanding. Why? It provides evidence that learning has happened? It keeps the children busy? We've always done it that way? So, what implications does this use of writing have for children? I just want to ask the questions: Do children know what writing is for? Do children just see writing as something that is done because they are told to do it?

This chapter explores, first, a range of frameworks and models for teaching writing. These models will then be exemplified throughout the chapter. The next section explores teaching the writing process, focusing on two recognised key elements: composition and transcription. Within this, a number of key tools will be explored: shared and guided writing, teacher-in-role and writing-in-role. Through the exploration of these tools, creative approaches to teaching writing will be discussed and developed and the chapter closes by considering the importance of embedding spelling and grammar in context.

Frameworks for teaching writing

Writers and researchers agree that there are three main stages to the writing process and these are stages that all writing passes through at least once: composition, transcription and review. I have conceptualised this in a diagram, Figure 3.1. Interestingly, some writers such as Browne (1999) and Levine (1993) cited by Brownhill (2013) who provides developmental stages of writing, suggest a linear process, but I want to propose a spiral model as I believe the process of writing to be one of reviewing one piece and using that knowledge to bring to the start of the next composition.

Graves (1983) cited in Myers and Burnett (2004) advocates a process approach to writing as opposed to a product approach. But, this is more about the phases that writers pass through as opposed to the writing process itself. However, the process approach is important as it sets a marker on the ground as to what is valued in writing. To go back to an earlier question: What is writing for? Often, it can be about presentation, neatness, punctuation, what can be called the technical aspects of writing. I have lost count of the number of times I have heard children say, in response to being asked to review and edit their work, 'Yeah, but I've finished!' What should be valued about writing is the process. Graves (1983) emphasises skills, form, structure, vocabulary and redrafting, amongst others. Graves does discuss transcription but again values the editing process: recognising errors, recognising the impact of punctuation. Here, the emphasis is on the child understanding the purpose and process of writing, not about the sole goal of producing a beautifully neat piece of work. A focus on process requires children to think. We get children to think by applying creative approaches. Creative approaches encourage different possibilities, exploration, playing with language and, dare I say it, doing what the kings of screenwriting, novel writing and playwrights have been doing for several hundreds of years: breaking the rules. Some of these rules will no doubt

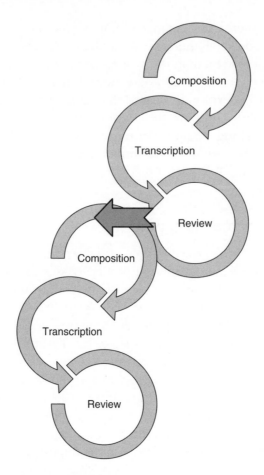

Figure 3.1   A Writing Process Model

come to mind as you read this chapter. I remember in one of my Year 5 (aged 9–10) classes, Charlie, having taken on board one of these rules from his Year 4 teacher, addressed me with: 'Excuse me Mr Copping, but you can't start a sentence with "because"'. For him, the word 'because' was a connective or conjunction and could therefore only be used to join two simple sentences. He had the misconception that connectives were not moveable. My response was to present Charlie with a range of classic and more contemporary literature and encourage him to test out his theory. Language must not constrain the writer, it is clay to be moulded and also a tool to be used and utilised to convey meaning, to be manipulated by the user for a range of purposes.

Research by Martello (1999), delivers a warning to teachers and to current pedagogies of teaching writing. This work builds on the emergent writing movement which places emphasis on what children already know about writing when they begin school. Martello's work indicates that upon entering school aged 4, children believed that they could write and could actually produce one recognisable word. Children in their Early Years will have seen writing for real purposes in the home (emails, texts, social media posts, lists, letters, cards) and for real people. Brien (2012) builds on this by reporting the confidence and freedom that a four-year-old girl displays as she explains the purpose, audience and composition of the text for a birthday card for a grandparent.

Why then do we see children struggling with writing so much later on in their school years? Sir Ken Robinson, in his 2006 talk 'Do Schools Kill Creativity?', suggests that children begin their school years very creative and confident learners but the performative nature of the English educational system has meant that children are being funnelled into a narrow definition of success and the drive to reach a certain 'grade' or 'score' has reduced teaching and learning to passing tests. Brien goes on to say:

> It's a great pity that our primary education system does not continue to emphasise the fun and freedom of writing. It seems all too often to focus on the aspects of writing that children find very difficult, particularly spelling and handwriting, while discarding the confidence and knowledge which children are able to bring to the first steps of becoming a writer. (2012: 80)

So, how do we get the balance right? How can we help children develop the understanding of writing which they bring with them and also help them become the best users and manipulators of language that they can be? There are many approaches and techniques to use: all are subject to the context of the particular classroom, teacher, children, purpose and genre. This means that teaching writing is a road fraught with stumbling blocks and challenges, some of which we will explore in the next section.

Teaching the writing process (composition and transcription)

Earlier in this chapter, I discussed the terms 'composition' (decisions about what needs to be written and how to do it) and 'transcription' (what that looks like in terms of sentence structure, grammar, spelling and punctuation). All writing, as Myers and Burnett (2004) suggest, involves these two aspects. The keys are how much time is spent on each, how they are structured together and how they are introduced and taught in a way that gets children to think for themselves and become manipulators of language for their own writing purposes.

Freire says that teaching children to write should be an 'artistic event' (1985: 79). Cremin (2009) responds to this by suggesting that, if children are to create, explore and investigate language, select, evaluate and manipulate ideas, then teachers must work in the same way. The challenge, of course, is how.

Liz Chamberlain (2011) emphasises the need for writing to be made relevant. She argues that this is when writing becomes powerful. Written tasks must have a meaning and a purpose as well as a clear audience.

Creating a writing classroom environment

A huge consideration in supporting children's writing is to create an environment which is conducive to exploration, enjoyment and fun and one that supports the writing process. We cannot realistically create the solitude of Roald Dahl's summer house where most of his writing was completed; the drawing room where Jane Austen produced *Pride and Prejudice*, or the oak-panelled library where Sir Walter Scott penned *Rob Roy*. But we can create a place where children can experiment with language, play with words and try things out without fear of 'getting it wrong'. When we consider a classroom environment, we must look beyond classroom layout and displays, we must think about the social environment created and also the cognitive one. The case study below considers the impact of a safe classroom environment on children's creative composition.

Case study: Part 1

Helen, a Year 3 teacher, was engaging her class in the adventure story genre. She had chosen to stimulate the class's thinking with a cartoon clip from *Scooby Doo*. The clip ended with a simulated conversation between Helen and the characters from the cartoon through the use of technology regarding a riddle to help solve the mystery from the cartoon clip. Helen engaged the class in solving the riddle and the result was finding a secret letter hidden in the classroom which, when found, the class discovered that it was in code. The writing task was to create a set of instructions for Scooby Doo and his companions to follow, moving from the coded letter to finding and apprehending the villain. Helen began the composing process by giving groups of four children the task of mind-mapping ideas to do with the mystery. This creative thinking technique encouraged a variety of possible solutions and included children of all abilities and attainment levels and therefore engaged the whole class effectively.

Craft (2005) suggests that possibility thinking such as this is the cornerstone of creative thinking. Helen regularly intervened in this process in order to highlight good ideas and good working practices. This focused on the processes and showed her the value of the ideas created. Waugh and Joliffe (2013) suggest that these approaches, often called 'mini-plenaries', whilst useful to assess progress and identify misconceptions, also create a positive working environment, focusing on what the children are doing well. Helen then asked the children in their groups to start to organise their ideas into some sort of logical progression, modelling the process and encouraging decision-making and clear rationale. Later, Helen asked the groups of children to explain their sequence and rationale to one another as groups so as to help cement their own thinking but also to allow others to input. Following this, Helen began to model and demonstrate some of the features of instructional writing, a reminder from work which they had previously done in Year 2, but this time within the context of an adventure/mystery.

Reflecting on the case study (part 1)

- What were the significant features of the classroom environment that enabled Helen's class to be successful?
- What was the significance of the possibility thinking approach?
- How did Helen scaffold children's learning?
- How did Helen's opening stimulus support the writing process?
- What will you take away to apply from this case study?

Towards the end of the case study, Helen moves on to demonstrating some of the key features of instructional writing within the adventure/mystery genre.

In this next section, we will explore a couple of 'tools of the trade', often called 'shared and guided writing', and how these tools can be used creatively and effectively to develop both composition and transcription skills.

Writing with the whole class – shared writing

Teachers writing with the whole class normally scribe children's ideas, sometimes reframing them to include genre specific language. Teachers will model the writing process themselves or support children's composition. However, questions still remain about why these are used and how. I am suggesting that creative approaches to shared writing are the most effective where teachers facilitate thinking and scaffold towards independent writing. Starbuck suggests that: 'creativity with a healthy dose of independent learning is the key to making learning more effective' (2006: 88). Starbuck is talking about engaging learners and making the link to higher attainment. So, how can we make writing with the class more creative? Firstly, we can think about the questions we ask children. Are they open-ended, and do they provoke thought and a variety of responses? Secondly, we can think about facilitating, rather than dictating. This would perhaps be the difference between filling up our learners with knowledge and supporting them to discover and make sense of the knowledge for themselves. In the first part of the case study, Helen did this through her framing of the session and the open-ended nature of the activity that encouraged a myriad of ideas.

Case study: Part 2

Helen began her demonstration by showing a variety of instructions for different purposes. She displayed instructions for putting furniture together, directions from the Internet for getting from her house to school, instructions for using a new computer and a recipe. Helen distributed these to small groups of children and asked them to identify the audience, purpose and any language or features that they might not expect to find typically in other text types such as stories. She also asked them to comment on the layout. Helen had created a working wall for her adventure/mysteries unit of work, which she would use as a tool to scaffold learning throughout. Her intention was that any work the class did in a shared way would go on the wall and this would also include key elements of the writing process. It would serve as a support for children throughout the unit as well as a visual assessment tool. The children annotated the instructions they had been given and Helen brought them to the front. She asked the children to discuss commonalities and they created their own checklist for effective instructional texts. This was then displayed with the examples on the working wall.

Reflecting on the case study (part 2)

- Identify the key elements of Helen's approach that facilitated the children's learning and could be deemed to be creative.
- Was Helen's approach more effective than simply telling the children what an effective instructional text looked like? If yes, why? If no, why not?

Guided writing with a small group

I believe that making the time and space to engage in guided writing activity with a small group of children is a powerful tool to develop both composition and transcription. Brien suggests that, whilst being a tool that teachers often find challenging, it does have the most 'power to ensure children's progress' (2012: 174). Within guided writing, the teacher is engaged in direct teaching with a small group of children for about 20 minutes. This focused work is targeted to meet the needs of that specific group of learners within the writing process during a unit of work and/or within developmental writing targets created by the class teacher. Children enjoy having this time with their teacher and it can be used effectively. In order to provide the most effective intervention, Gibson states that the teacher must have three key areas of in-depth knowledge:

a) writing development;
b) effective instructional frameworks; and
c) multiple, interacting causes of failure for individual students. (2008: 112)

Effective interventions cannot be through published schemes just picked up off the shelf: they must be taken as a platform to work from, thought through and adapted to meet the needs of the learners in your class. To do this, it is essential that teachers have an in-depth knowledge of the areas that Gibson shares. If not, there is a danger that guided writing will become a predictable technique that does not motivate, lacks purpose and does not bear the fruit that it could. In the third part of the case study, notice how Helen uses guided writing to support both composition and transcription elements of the children's writing.

Case study: Part 3

Having now identified some of the key features of an instructional text, the children are ready to start composing. They have their ideas in sequence, a framework and structure to help them frame their instructions, and now have to apply that knowledge to an adventure/mystery context and to a specific audience: Scooby Doo and his comrades. Helen has trained her class to work independently when required. She has clear routines for what children should do if they are stuck, in fact they have made posters which adorn the classroom walls, bearing slogans such as 'Remember the shared work' and 'Talk to a friend on your table'. All the resources they will need are easily accessible. The children are back in the groups they mind-mapped with and ready to draft some instructions. Helen has made it clear to the class that, at this drafting stage, she is not too worried about spelling and punctuation, but she is looking for instructional features and contextual features. Helen knows that her 'red' group will need some intervention and so she has planned a guided writing session to intervene at this drafting stage. Helen's plan for this guided session is shown in Figure 3.2.

Reflecting on the case study (part 3)

- Notice how Helen asks the children to create the success criteria for the guided writing session. What might the impact of that be?
- Whilst Helen is facilitating a highly structured session with a clear outcome, notice how Helen is still being very creative. Notice how the children are exploring the instruction genre and evaluating their work against criteria they have created. What might the impact of that be on their learning within Helen's unit of work?
- On Helen's planning pro forma, notice how assessment is included. Helen will add comments to this as the session progresses and involve children in that process. This includes an 'action needed' box. With the children's input, Helen will decide what action she, as a teacher, must take to develop the children's learning in her next lesson. What impact could this transparent approach to assessment have on the children's understanding of the learning process?

Date:	Grp/chn: (6)

Focus/objectives

- To apply knowledge of features of instructional writing to an adventure/mystery context
  National Curriculum: Lower Key Stage 2 (KS2) – plan, draft and write using oral rehearsal, organisational devices, write for purpose and audience

Success criteria

- Children to create these at the start of the session – based on objective and shared work

Structure and approaches	Resources
• Share objective and focus and ask children to share what they think successful writing would look like in this context. Record • Play 'commanding the troops'. This is where the teacher gives out cards with an action on it and children are chosen to ask/tell or command the rest of the group to do it. Teacher audio records the commands. Children then listen back and record on whiteboards. Address any misconceptions • Return to original organised mind-map and discuss concept of chronological order. As a group, edit and check order of events • In pairs, work together to orally rehearse and write two of the events as instructions. Check against 'commanding the troops' instructions	Activity cards Audio recorder Whiteboards and pens

Plenary

- Each pair shares their instructions in chronological order and performs with a command tone. Other pairs evaluate against instructions criteria. Discuss and edit to add adventure/mystery language – asking the question: 'Will you know what to do, Scooby Doo?'

Assessment and comments

Names	

Action needed

Figure 3.2   Guided Writing Plan: Instructional Texts

Guided writing should take place with different groups in the class. It would be helpful to teachers if children were all as good at all aspects of writing, both composition and transcription, in all genres and text types. This would make the organisation much easier. However, this is unfortunately not the case. Guided writing groups should ideally be formed during each unit of work and be based on an assessment of previous learning. Waugh and Joliffe (2013) state that guided work should provide differentiated support for groups. Children's writing needs will differ during each phase of the writing process and the guided writing groups should be created to reflect that. It is a very important supported step towards independent writing and can support planning, drafting, editing, revising and even presenting work.

Teacher in-role and writing in-role

The idea of using drama can fill some teachers with fear. Many are not comfortable with it as it can require a level of confidence which not all teachers feel they have. Some would feel the same way about the concept of creativity. However, these feelings can sometimes arise as a result of some misconceptions. In this section, I want to try and remove some of these misconceptions and through practical suggestions, explore the idea of working in-role and then of children writing in-role as a way of engaging and inspiring children to write but also of inspiring teachers to teach. Desailly (2015) suggests that using drama techniques is one of the key skills of a creative teacher. She argues that, amongst other things, drama can facilitate emotional engagement with the subject matter, allow children to demonstrate their learning in a different way, rehearse different opinions and make learning more memorable.

Teachers working in-role

Let's be clear, working in-role does not necessarily mean dressing up, delivering a monologue or reciting Shakespeare. It does mean coming to the subject matter in a slightly different way, where the teacher is part of the context they are setting. This is often called 'simulation'. Going back to our earlier case study, Helen was working in-role. Helen put herself into the Scooby Doo adventure/mystery simulation just by using technology to converse with the characters – no dressing up, no Oscar-winning performances. The result was that the children engaged with the learning and involved themselves through the seeking, finding and solving of a clue to help Scooby Doo and his comrades. This stimulated questions, thinking and ideas for the unit of work. In a different way, I did the same thing. In one of my Year 5 classes (aged 9–10), we were looking at an aspect of nineteenth-century local history and writing a diary from the perspective of a woman whose husband had sailed out to sea with his cargo of goods. I was in-role as the woman, dressed in a long skirt and wig, standing on a table in the middle of the classroom (the clifftop) speaking out my thoughts and fears for my husband, who may never come back. The children were asking me questions about what was going on for me and how I would cope. This, whilst appearing a bit more like 'drama', did the same job as Helen's approach: it stimulated questions, engaged the children in the atmosphere of what was happening and involved them in the simulation, ready to write in-role. The important message is not necessarily what is done but the reason for which it is done. Desailly states that: 'Even a seemingly simple technique such as hot-seating will be of little value unless the children understand how it can be used' (2012: 103). Children need to see the purpose of the drama or role play and how it is a support and scaffold for their learning.

'Hot-seating', mentioned above, is a dramatic technique, whereby a teacher or child is in-role, usually as a character from the text or topic being studied and they are in the 'hot-seat', being asked questions by the class to find out more about their lives, motivations and point of view.

Stop and think

How can you engage children by coming at a text or an idea from a slightly unconventional perspective? How can you show them that you are enthused about it? How can you make it real for them and get them into the story? Even if you lack confidence to do drama, why not try an approach like Helen's?

Writing in-role

Cremin (2009), drawing on some of her own research (2006), discovered that through writing in-role, children's work 'frequently demonstrates a higher than usual degree of empathy, a stronger and more sustained authorial stance and an emotively engaged voice' (2009: 99). So, what does this mean? It means writing as if they are another person, perhaps in another place or even – in the examples above – another time. Why is this important? Cremin (2006) observes that it improves the quality of writing. The extract

> Why did you have to go? You are always away. How can I take care of the little ones alone? I have no one to help since my mother died. I miss you so much, sitting by the fire at night we would talk about things, probably nothing really but the comfort of your voice warmed my heart. It was as if the fire was heating me up inside and not just the room. It felt right us together, the little ones asleep and it seemed we hadn't a care in the world. But now you are gone and it as if a part of me has gone cold inside.

Figure 3.3   Extract from Kieran: Writing in-role

in Figure 3.3 is from Kieran's writing in-role during the nineteenth-century local history example which I gave earlier.

Kieran has managed to get inside the character's thoughts and feelings and has understood the purpose of this diary – the character pouring out their heart onto the pages of a book.

Facilitating opportunities for writing in-role can almost be like opening doors for children. Children love stories. Children also love to role-play stories or certainly role-play characters and often use speech patterns or words and phrases from comics, books, characters, television shows, computer games and films. Giving them permission to do that at school through writing in-role can be exciting for them and help children see that writing at school can be fun and enjoyable and also expressive.

A word about transcription

Can you teach the transcription elements of the writing process creatively? Or is it just about gritting your teeth, getting on and learning those spellings and those grammar and punctuation rules? Horton and Bingle state that: 'to write effectively for a given purpose and audience, children need to have a conceptual understanding of grammar in preference to simply naming terms and features' (2014: 13). This suggests that a contextualised approach to teaching grammar and possibly spelling is preferable. Grammatical understanding helps writers write with authorial intent. It helps them make choices about language and structures that improve the quality of their work. Waugh et al. (2013) suggest a similar pedagogical approach to the teaching of spelling. They state that:

You may well have observed that spelling words correctly in a test on a Friday is no guarantee that they will be applied in a piece of writing on Monday. No matter how high the scores children achieve, unless they can apply their spelling knowledge to their own writing all the effort involved will have been in vain. (2013: 81)

The notion of context and application is crucial here. The idea of children making language choices and choices of linguistic devices is crucial to the concept of creativity. Children in this sense can take ownership of their work, explore language, play with words and linguistic devices to fit the purposes and audiences for which they are writing.

Try this

Activity 1: Working wall

When you are next planning a unit of work involving writing, plan to use a working wall. Give some display space to the process of writing, put up the work that the children do in shared work, put up examples of the writing process. Use it as a scaffolding tool for their writing and evaluate the results and responses.

Activity 2: Writing in-role

In your next unit of work, plan for the children to write in-role. Think about how you will engage the children and then let them write as a character.

What do you notice about the quality of their writing? Should it show a greater response to the purpose that you have set up? Discuss with the children how they felt when they were doing it.

Activity 3: Guided writing

In your next unit of work, plan and organise some guided writing. Use the example plan (Figure 3.2) if this helps to structure it. Think about the interventions which the children will need in your unit and plan engaging small group activities, where you facilitate the children's learning and development.

Analyse the success of these sessions in terms of:

a) The children's learning and development.
b) Your knowledge of the children's learning and development.
c) How the children responded to a more open-ended exploratory task.

Summary

A creative approach to teaching children to write starts with facilitating their engagement and thinking. Children must write for a purpose and for a specific audience so that they themselves can see that writing is more than just a task which they are being asked to do by the teacher and more than a means of recording their understanding. Writing is a creative process and should be introduced and developed as such. Tools such as whole class teaching should be utilised, where a teacher models and shares in the writing process, shows that they, too, are writers and that writing is a problem-solving process (Bereiter and Scardamalia, 1987) where language choices are made and linguistic devices are used with authorial intent. Small group intervention, such as guided writing should also be used to provide differentiated support, challenge thinking and explore concepts and language features in order to help children become more effective writers. These tools should be used alongside techniques such as writing in-role, where children can become people from other places, times and contexts, developing their language choices, purposes and understanding and increasing the quality of their writing through a deeper emotional attachment to the context.

Further reading

Desailly, J. (2012) *Creativity in the Primary Classroom*. London: Sage.

The text explores a number of the principles which I have shared in this chapter. Chapter 4 discusses establishing the ethos for a creative classroom and then chapter 6 explores key skills for the effective teacher including facilitation and questioning.

Gardner, P. (2010) *Creative English, Creative Curriculum: New Perspectives for Key Stage 2*. London: David Fulton.

This text provides a range of creative ideas, underpinned by strong pedagogical principles to support the notion of English as a creative process. It introduces and explores some engaging techniques to adapt and use to hook learners into English.

Horton, S. and Bingle, B. (2014) *Lessons in Teaching Grammar in Primary Schools*. London: Sage.

This text explores the notion of teaching grammar in context. As well as providing helpful subject knowledge, its pedagogical principles are well thought through and the resultant activities are engaging and purposeful.

References

Bereiter, C. and Scardamalia, M. (1987) *The Psychology of Written Communication*. Hillsdale, NJ: Lawrence Erlbaum.

Brien, J. (2012) *Teaching Primary English*. London: Sage.

Browne, A. (1999) *Teaching Writing at Key Stage 1 and Before*. Cheltenham: Stanley Thorne.

Brownhill, S. (2013) *Getting Children Writing*. London: Sage.

Chamberlain, L. (2011) 'Writing', in R. Cox (ed.), *Primary English Teaching*. London: Sage.

Craft, A. (2005) *Creativity in Schools: Tensions and Dilemmas*. London: Routledge.

Cremin, T. (2006) 'Creativity, uncertainty and discomfort: Teachers as writers', *Cambridge Journal of Education*, 36 (3): 415–33.

Cremin, T. (2009) *Teaching English Creatively*. London: Routledge.

Department for Education (DfE) (2013). *The National Curriculum for England, Key Stages 1 and 2*. London: Crown Copyright.

Desailly, J. (2015) *Creativity in the Primary Classroom*, 2nd edn. London: Sage.

Freire, P. (1985) 'Reading the world and reading the word: An interview with Paulo Freire', *Language Arts*, 62 (1): 15–21.

Gibson, S. (2008) 'Guided writing lessons: Second-grade students development of strategic behaviour', *Reading Horizons*, 48 (2): 111–32. Available at: http://scholarworks.wmich.edu/cgi/viewcontent.cgi?article=1080&context=reading_horizons (accessed 14 May 2015).

Graves, D.H. (1983) *Writing: Teachers and Children at Work*. Exeter: Heinemann.

Horton, S. and Bingle, B. (2014) *Lessons in Teaching Grammar in Primary Schools*. London: Learning Matters, Sage.

Levine, M. (1993) *Developmental Variation and Learning Disorders*, 2nd edn. Cambridge, MA: Educators Publishing Service.

Martello, J. (1999) 'In their own words: Children's perceptions of learning to write', *Australian Journal of Early Childhood*, 24 (3): 32–7.

Myers, J. and Burnett, C. (2004) *Teaching English 3–11*. London: Continuum.

Robinson, K. (2006) 'TED Talk: Ken Robinson: Do schools kill creativity?'. Available at: www.ted.com/talks/ken_robinson_says_schools_kill_creativity/transcript?language=en (accessed 14 April 2015).

Starbuck, D. (2006) *Creative Teaching: Getting it Right*. London: Continuum Books.

Waugh, D. and Joliffe, W. (2013) *English 5–11: A Guide for Teachers*. 2nd edn. London: David Fulton.

Waugh, D., Waugh, R. and Warner, C. (2013) *Teaching Grammar, Spelling and Punctuation in Primary Schools*. London: Learning Matters, Sage.

Speaking and listening scaffolds reading and writing

4

Learning outcomes

By reading this chapter, you will have:

- Considered a social constructivist approach to learning
- Considered the role of the teacher in creating a 'talking to learn' culture
- Looked at how talk, including exploratory talk, can act as a scaffold to support reading and writing
- Considered some talk techniques that can develop possibility thinking

National Curriculum links

Spoken language underpins the development of reading and writing. The quality and variety of language that pupils hear and speak are vital for developing their vocabulary and grammar and their understanding for reading and writing.

DfE (2013: 13)

Chapter overview

This chapter explores the role of talk in learning. Coming from a social constructivist approach, this chapter considers theoretical frameworks around the use of talk in learning and considers talk for writing approaches. The chapter also looks at the role that talk can play to promote creative thinking. It considers a range of dramatic techniques that develop creative and possibility thinking as well as helping children to engage with story and genres on a variety of levels. This chapter comes from the premise that if the children have nothing to say, then they will have nothing to write, and it presents a number of practical ideas, including looking at a classroom environment for purposeful talk, which can be utilised in the classroom.

Introduction

The National Curriculum 2013 states that teachers should be developing spoken language as a discipline in itself but also as integral to every other subject (DfE, 2013: 10). It goes on to say that 'spoken language underpins the development of reading and writing' (ibid.: 13). Previous iterations of the National Curriculum and other supplementary documents such as the *Primary National Strategy Framework for English and Mathematics* (2006) have made explicit learning outcomes for speaking and listening, setting year-by-year progressive targets for children to achieve in these areas. However, the danger here can be that speaking and listening are dislocated from other areas of English and can become just another set of goals for children to reach and for teachers to record. Waugh and Joliffe (2013) suggest that the various initiatives around speaking and listening have led to an inconsistency in understanding and have therefore contributed to a lack of teacher expertise in using talk to scaffold children's reading and writing development.

Then why is this concept of speaking and listening scaffolding reading and writing so important? Simply, for the majority of us, it is the way we learn and the way in which we construct new knowledge. Corden (2000) lists a number of psychologists and educationalists who have been pushing for this concept to be more prevalent in teacher pedagogy. He cites Bruner (1996), Wood (1988) through the latter's influential work *How Children Think and Learn* and Barnes (1992). These have all been influenced by the work of Vygotsky, who believed that discourse/talk/oracy played a vital role in the development of meaning-making. For Vygotsky, 'every function in the child's cultural development appears twice: first on the social level and later on the individual level' (1978: 57).

This chapter explores the concept in a practical way. It opens with a deeper look at Vygotsky's approach and the concept of scaffolding learning. The next section looks at establishing a classroom environment that enables talk for learning to thrive. This leads into looking at some techniques that can be utilised to develop creative thinking and also facilitate text exploration at a deeper level, including the use of drama to facilitate a deeper understanding of text and the author's intent. This acts as a springboard to the concept of talk to develop writing.

Vygotsky, ZPD and the concept of scaffolding learning

Russian psychologist Lev Vygotsky studied the link between language and thinking. He saw language as a tool to support us in our social lives as we interact with others but also as a tool for organising, developing and constructing knowledge. He believed that these two purposes were closely connected and suggested that learners therefore constructed new knowledge in social contexts. Through this connection, he developed the concept of the 'zone of proximal development' (ZPD), which he described as:

> The distance between the actual development level as determined by independent problem solving and the level of potential development as determined through problem solving under adult guidance or in collaboration with more capable peers. (1978: 86)

Figure 4.1 shows my reconceptualisation of this.

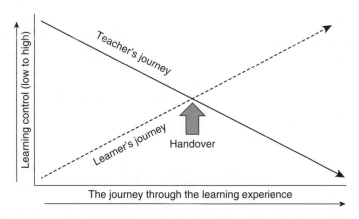

Figure 4.1 Reconceptualising Vygotsky's zone of proximal development

An alternative representation of Vygotsky's ZPD that seeks to illuminate what I see as two of the main ideas is presented in Figure 4.1. First, the concept of control in learning and teaching.

At the beginning of a typical learning activity, the teacher will be in control. In all likelihood, they will have set the learning intentions, devised the input they will make and set the activity. However, Vygotsky would say that throughout the learning process, a teacher's control lessens as learners begin to take more control over the learning experience. The key point here is the second idea I wish to pull out, which is the concept of 'handover'. Here is the point where the teacher's teaching and learning journey crosses with the learner's and they then move into taking more control as the teacher's control lessens.

So, does that process just happen?

Bruner (1985) suggests that the learner passes along this learning journey through developmental phases and that these phases are supported by learning experiences. These experiences, often designed by the teacher, are known as 'scaffolding'. The teacher would then vary the support, gradually removing it as the learner becomes more competent with the learning. This is shown on the left-hand side of Figure 4.2, which seeks to connect Vygotsky's ZPD with Bruner's notion of scaffolding.

This leaves us with the right-hand side of the figure after the teacher has handed over control of the learning to the learner. I would like to suggest that scaffolding continues. Whilst talk is vital in the left-hand side, I would argue that it is fundamental to the success of the right-hand side. The learner is now taking more control of the learning, but if the construction

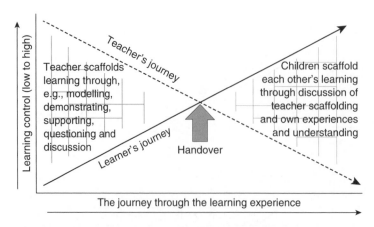

Figure 4.2   Connecting Vygotsky's zone of proximal development to Bruner's scaffolding

of new knowledge is a social practice, then scaffolding should occur here, too. Enter more learners. This scaffolding is between learners who are seeking to interpret material, bring their experiences to bear to make sense of what is being taught and hopefully take it further than what the teacher intended. The learner's goal should not be just to learn what the teacher intended but to explore other avenues on offer, develop alternative perspectives and deepen understanding of the whole area being taught. Here, learners discuss together in order to explore and make sense of what they are being asked to do.

Does this naturally happen then?

Mercer (2000) defines different types of talk. He suggests that there are three main types of talk that occur between learners.

Cumulative talk

This is where learners just comment on previous suggestions. Whilst studying for an MA, I was conducting some research into this area and, using a suitcase of objects, I asked groups of nine-year-old children to create a character with the objects. With one group of children, one child pulled out an object out, said what it was, then, in turn, children either responded with an affirmative comment or merely repeated what had been said. Not particularly effective for learning.

Disputational talk

This can be described where there is often argument between the parties involved. During the same study, discussion between another group centred around a ginger wig from the suitcase and the group spent five minutes disputing whether it could belong to a boy or girl. Not particularly effective for learning.

Exploratory talk

Here is where children seek to gain deeper understanding through asking questions such as: 'Why do you think that?' or 'What about …?' This deepens understanding and can help develop new perspectives. This type of talk does need to be facilitated. Alexander (2005) cited in Waugh and Joliffe (2013) discusses the concept of dialogic teaching to bring to the fore talk as a scaffolding tool and to support the development of exploratory talk. However, he states that it does take considerable time and effort. He suggests that dialogic teaching is collective (where children work together on tasks), and it is reciprocal (where teachers and children listen to each other and share ideas). Alexander states that it must be supportive (children are supported to discuss views freely). It is cumulative (children build on each other's ideas) and it is purposeful. This is where the role of the teacher is crucial in planning talk in the classroom with a specific learning purpose in mind.

However, dialogic teaching and exploratory talk for learning cannot take place unless an appropriate classroom environment is created to facilitate it.

Establishing a classroom environment that enables talk for learning to thrive

Discussion of the classroom environment can often mean shaping the physical space. For example, discussion can centre around displays, table layout, where the teacher teaches from, carpet space and accessibility of resources. Whilst these are all valid, and, indeed, very important considerations, I want to devote time here to considering some of the less tangible but equally important aspects of the classroom environment. The classroom environment has three main aspects: physical (as discussed above), social and cognitive, and it is the latter two that come to the fore in this section. Clearly, table layout and chair positioning are important here but they are of secondary importance to considering the social and cognitive environment that the teacher creates. Vickery calls this 'creating a culture of enquiry', which she defines as: 'a learning environment which is designed to develop children's curiosity, creativity and critical thought' (2014: 39). She goes on to say that this is encouraged through quality interactions both between children and between children and their teacher. Here, we have the central figure in this environment, the creator, the teacher. So, what can the teacher do to create a learning environment that promotes exploration, curiosity, creative and critical thought? Consider the case study below.

Case study

John is a Year 4 teacher in a primary school that believes that if children have nothing to say, then they have nothing to write. The school's Senior Management Team have invested heavily in training for staff in Pie Corbett and Julia Strong's *Talk for Writing* materials and are promoting children's and teachers' understanding of exploratory talk as a tool for scaffolding learning.

John plans the half-term's topic with his class. Together, they create mind maps that consider what the children already know, what they would like to know and then at the end of the half-term they examine what they have learned. The children feel that they are active participants in their learning and that the teaching team (John and his teaching assistant) are learning alongside them. John feels that this approach has greatly enhanced the engagement of the learners in his class. John starts most of his lessons with open questions and uses techniques such as talk partners to develop the children's interactions. He gives different children focused open questions to develop their responses. John actively encourages his class to question him and challenge the ideas he brings, present alternative perspectives and evaluate the variety of responses on offer.

Whilst initially nervous about this as he felt that it might mean that the children would lose respect for him, the reverse was true. Due to the ethos that John had created, the children saw that whilst there are right and wrong in some areas, for example 2 + 2 = 4 is not really up for debate, there are many areas where this is not the case and so the children are learning to hold opinions and justify them.

John has a 'class values' board on his wall which he and the children have created collaboratively. It includes the classics of 'Listen when someone is talking' and 'Always try our best' but it also contains values such as 'Exploration', 'Finding other ways of doing things' and 'Working together'. He has also developed some rules for talk which include questions which the children can ask each other to help clarify and extend interactions. Children don't put their hands up, they know that they talk to each other when a question is asked and John will listen in, support and then get them to talk to him. John has found this a great motivator for the children and at a recent parents' evening, he was pleased to hear that all of his class really loved being at school.

Reflecting on the case study

- In what ways has John facilitated an enquiring environment?
- What potential challenges can you see with this approach?
- How does this compare to your experience of a classroom environment?
- How do you think this approach is positive for learning?
- What further questions do you have for John?

This case study begins to explore the cognitive dimension of the classroom environment and how a teacher's pedagogy can develop exploratory talk for learning. But what about the social dimension? Pierce and Gilles (2008) refer to creating a classroom community through talk and how talk connects children socially. The social dimensions of a classroom are incredibly important to a child. Children, in my experience, want to know where they fit in the pecking order in the classroom. Where do they fit under the 'top dog'? Pierce and Gilles (2008) go on to discuss how class cohesion is created through talk using small group discussion and open questioning as a teaching technique, children get to know more about each other, talk in a safe environment and build friendships through this. Dörnyei supports this by stating that the: 'quality of teaching and learning is entirely different depending on whether the classroom is characterised by a climate of trust and support or by a competitive, cut-throat atmosphere' (2007: 720). But, again, the teacher is instrumental in creating this climate and supporting children to talk together and explore together through carefully planned activities and a talk for learning pedagogy that underpins them.

Stop and think

How will you ensure that your classroom climate is supportive so that children can talk and explore together in a purposeful way? The challenge is allowing yourself to have a classroom with some noise. Some noise can be a positive thing. It means that children are comfortable to discuss and work together. So, how can you promote a positive working noise whilst mitigating against a disruptive noise? How can you support those children who need quiet to concentrate and focus?

Drama, creative thinking and reading for meaning

First, a quick definition. The word 'drama' can conjure up a plethora of pictures in the mind. In this context, I am referring to a host of dramatic techniques such as freeze-framing, hot-seating and forum theatre which I will explore through a case study later in this section. These require no props, no acting training, no large hall space, just a willingness to explore the possibilities that a text can offer. Through this exploration comes creative thinking or 'possibility thinking' (Burnard et al., 2006), where children are encouraged to explore and offer alternatives, rather than seek a 'right' answer. I would argue that the classroom environment as categorised by

Dörnyei (2007) above is essential to developing possibility thinking and to getting the most beneficial learning from the use of dramatic techniques. One way to support this is if the teacher fully throws themselves into it, too. Cremin describes drama as 'the art form of social encounters' (2009: 26) and, as well as being a huge motivator for learning, it is hugely demanding, both intellectually and imaginatively. The case study below explores the power of dramatic techniques for understanding character and subplot in the fiction text, *The Bully* by Jan Needle (1995). This text, has already been introduced in Chapter 2 in the context of higher-order reading skills. Here, a Year 5 teacher uses drama to develop higher-order reading skills, using this wonderful text as a context for exploring character and motivation as well as for developing prediction skills.

Case study

Aisling's Year 5 class are getting involved with their school's anti-bullying week. They are helping the School Council and Senior Management Team to update the school's anti-bullying policy and, as part of this, they are reading *The Bully* by Jan Needle (1995). The main premise of the story is that Simon, a new boy to a fee-paying high school, is bullied by Anna (the school's Top Dog) and her friends and some of the teachers. The pivotal character is Louise Shaw (the Deputy Head), who swims against the tide of popular opinion in the story by trying to stop the bullying.

Aisling begins by showing the front cover image from the text and her intention is to challenge stereotypes as the cover shows both Anna and Simon. 'Who is the bully?' Aisling asks. The class are divided and a lively debate ensues. Aisling reads the first chapter. She asks them at each stage of the chapter what they think of Simon and encourages them to give evidence from the text. The text is divided into four sections, and the class are split into four groups and are given their section of text to 'freeze-frame'. Each group will act out their section of the story and when Aisling says 'freeze', the children will stop and Aisling will ask certain characters to unfreeze so that she can ask them about what is happening.

Grainger (2005) suggests that this approach is a helpful way for conveying meaning as so much more can be conveyed through action, rather than just words. The children perform their sections in order, and through Aisling's careful open questions, the children are able to explore other

(Continued)

(Continued)

possible subplots in the text. Are Anna's friends afraid of her? Is that why they are going along with bullying Simon? Why does Mr Kershaw's (the PE teacher) attitude to Simon change? Does he desire a relationship with Miss Shaw? Photos are taken for use on the working wall and two children are scribing ideas and questions onto the whiteboard for use later in the unit of work. The chapter ends with a tableau, which sees Simon sprawled out on the muddy field having been hit and Anna, feigning injury, saying that Simon had hit her. A melee of Anna's friends are gathered round and Miss Shaw arrives, confused at what she sees.

The children are asked to predict how the next chapter might start and why. After ideas are given, Aisling chooses the most popular, which is Simon and Anna being spoken to by Miss Shaw in her office. Aisling sets up a table and two chairs and assumes the role of Miss Shaw. This technique of teacher-in-role is immensely powerful. It means, as Cremin (2009) puts it, that the teacher is participating with the children from the same perspective. Two volunteers are chosen for the roles of Simon and Anna and the class gathers round the scene. However, Aisling is not finished here.

This activity is known as 'forum theatre'. The technique is used to explore other possibilities and alternative courses of action that the scene may take as children 'buzz' in to take over the roles. Aisling begins in the role of Miss Shaw and the children decide to both play the role very contritely. Instantly, someone shouts 'buzz' and another child comes to take the role of Anna, this time with more venom and indignation. 'Buzz' and someone comes in and takes the role of Miss Shaw, immediately giving in to Anna's demands and the scene continues. Meanwhile, the scenes are being recorded and notes are being made so that the power of this activity is not lost. This is a deep exploration of the text: exploring character development, motivation, relationships between the characters and character voice. The learning gained here will be immensely valuable, leading into writing a play-script for the next scene.

Reflecting on the case study

- Consider how Aisling's lesson develops possibility thinking.
- Consider the importance of the classroom environment, so that the children are used to working in this way, and also the importance of trust for the full potential of the learning to be realised.

- How important is the teacher's role in this case study? Why? What did Aisling do to ensure that learning occurred?
- How does Aisling's approach scaffold the children's learning?
- What will you take away to apply from this case study?

There are many other approaches that could be used, too many to be explored in this chapter. For example, any of the main or peripheral characters could be 'hot-seated'. This technique is used to understand a character's motivation more fully. A teacher or child is in the role of the character and they are asked questions related to the story. The learning is gained, monitored and assessed, not just through the character's responses, but also through the questions being asked. Both can demonstrate an understanding of the text.

Other techniques for creative thinking in the context of understanding text

Creative thinking techniques are myriad. Type 'creative thinking' into an Internet search engine and I can only imagine how many hits will be found. However, I want to introduce two in the context of this chapter; further chapters will add more information and practical application in specific contexts.

Six Thinking Hats

Edward de Bono's (2000) approach recognises that there are different types of thinking. He argues that the use of these helps generate more ideas as well as more innovative ideas. Originally used in the world of business, schools are now using this approach to help develop children's thinking, collaboration and effective discussion. Teachers also use de Bono's approach to help children explore situations thrown up by a text in a more holistic way. Sternberg (2003) suggests that de Bono's approach is to provoke ideas, stimulate possibilities and facilitate seeing things from different perspectives.

It is within this context that de Bono's hats can work so well. Children can take on the different coloured hats, which encourage them to think about what thinking is needed, how they feel about the situation, what new ideas are possible, what information they already know, what are the good points and what are the weaknesses. In the context of a text, there could, for example, be a problem to solve. For the three bears in their traditional tale concerning a young lady by the name of Goldilocks, it could be trying to prevent the problem of housebreaking, broken furniture and stolen porridge from happening again. For Simon, from our earlier case study, it could be the question of how will he talk to someone about being bullied without making the situation worse for himself? Both of these scenarios could be explored and discussed using de Bono's hats. Joyce et al. (2009) suggest that developing creative, independent thinkers who are enquiry-driven should be the goal of all teaching. This approach is one which does that. Through the use of discussion and open questions, learning takes place. This discussion also acts as a scaffold for further exploration of the tasks and any corresponding written work as the children will have developed a greater understanding of the text.

The Napoleon technique

The Napoleon technique appears on business blogs – *5 Best Creative Thinking Techniques to Help your Business Thrive* by Ruby Marketer (J. Bizdra) is a good one – and is essentially about looking at the problem from somebody else's perspective or asking: 'What would this person do if they were in this situation?' It is called the 'Napoleon technique' because often the enigmatic, talented, ruthless dictator, Napoleon Bonaparte, would be called upon to look at a situation from his perspective and see what he would do. For instance, in the earlier example of Goldilocks and the three bears, what would Daddy Bear do if he was Napoleon Bonaparte in order to help him deal with the situation? This technique once again promotes possibility thinking in that there is no right answer, in fact the opportunities here are endless. It promotes innovation, thinking differently and generating lots of ideas that will eventually help empathise with characters, look at alternative perspectives to bring to a text and also provide a very good scaffold for future writing. Of course, it doesn't have to be Napoleon Bonaparte, it could be, for example, Harry Potter that is used. These techniques and others will be further explored in later chapters and will be applied to a wider variety of contexts.

So far in this chapter, we have considered talk techniques that scaffold understanding of text and so the last section is what we are scaffolding towards, writing.

Talk to develop writing

Oral language development in preparation for writing is often seen superbly demonstrated in Early Years classrooms (3–5 years). Teachers facilitate this through a huge variety of opportunities. A shed in the outside area may be turned into a superhero house, for example. Children will work together with the teacher to design it, discuss what is needed to make it fit for a superhero and then discuss how they will make it. Here we have the beginnings of instructional texts. Children may work in the role-play area, wearing superhero capes and discuss 'Help' cards. Here the children will discuss what is needed to solve the problem and save the day. Children discuss their superpowers, building on each other's ideas (the beginnings of character portraits). Jones (2007) suggests that, through these activities, teachers can help children build up their vocabulary and sentence structure, navigate the challenges of social relationships in the classroom and sharpen up their comprehension skills. I had the privilege of observing such a setting when a young boy, Grieg, with some speech and language difficulty spoke in a sentence for the first time. What a landmark moment! Grieg had heard sentences spoken, and had worked out how to create his own orally. Now, he is ready to translate his skills to pencil and paper. Ciccone (2001) recognises this process and states that all of these activities support children to produce 'strong writing'.

Does talk still matter throughout the rest of a child's primary education? Surely, once they can write a sentence, then they can just get on with it? I would argue that opportunities for talk are fundamental. In *The Independent Review of the Teaching of Early Reading: Interim Report* (2006), Sir Jim Rose points out that at the roots of reading and writing are the fundamental skills of speaking and listening. As Brien states: 'Writing is difficult' (2012: 79). A teacher's job should therefore be to help children overcome those barriers to writing and one significant way to do this is by helping children overcome several key questions that they will undoubtedly ask:

- What shall I write?
- What should it look like?
- How do I start?

In fact, for any of us who write, and for myself writing this chapter, we have certainly asked the first and last questions. Also, as I write, I am constantly thinking about language and style.

Talk can help us overcome these difficulties. Take, for example, a lesson on discussion writing. The teacher may actually start the session by holding a debate, helping children discuss viewpoints and then enact the debate, noting down some of the key points raised, perhaps even recording the debate to refer to language and style later. This can provide essential content and therefore help children to know what to write. But how should it look? The teacher should be modelling style through the way they speak in order to introduce the formality of the debate, or perhaps use a model television debate to stimulate understanding of formal language and help introduce some of the key features such as emotive language, statistics and direct quotation.

Have children orally rehearsing these to help them know how to write it. How to start? Well, how did their mock debate start? Remind them, seek alternatives. These simple approaches, relying on the teacher's pedagogy of talk for writing, can and should help alleviate many of the key questions that children may ask. They scaffold understanding and provide the tools needed to undertake the difficult business of putting pencil to paper or finger to keyboard.

Try this

Activity 1: Scaffolding learning

When you are planning a lesson or a unit of work, think about how you are using talk to support thinking and learning. What talk techniques are you using to help towards your end product? Where is the point of handover? How are children being scaffolded from handover to finished piece?

Did this process result in a better quality of end product? Analyse how and why?

Activity 2: Questioning

How do you use talk yourself to scaffold learning? What type of questions do you ask? How do you elicit information from children? Do you end up playing 'Guess what's in my head?' Ask someone to observe one of your lessons, focusing on the questions you ask? Are they open questions? Do they allow children to present different alternatives? Do they encourage possibility thinking, where appropriate?

How do you feel as you ask more open questions? Does this support your assessment of children's thinking and learning more effectively?

Activity 3: Teacher in-role

In your next topic or English unit of work, have a go at using teacher in-role to help the children's understanding of the text you are using.

Perhaps try some hot-seating or, if you're feeling more adventurous, try some forum theatre. What alternative perspectives did the children venture?

How has this approach helped children open up more and share their ideas about the text or character?

Summary

Teachers need to have a deeper understanding of how children learn in order to be able to support them effectively. Many children do learn through the construction of new knowledge in social contexts and so in the classroom this needs to be taken into account. Through the use of questioning, dramatic techniques and facilitating possibility thinking, teachers can help prepare their children for writing. However, there must be careful planning as the techniques should be meaningful towards the end product and purposeful for learning. I have seen too much drama that is 'nice' and 'good fun' as opposed to being a tool to scaffold understanding. Talk for learning, such as exploratory talk, doesn't just happen, it does need to be taught and worked on so that the children can benefit as independent autonomous learners, confident writers and creative thinkers, and fully able to navigate the often stormy seas of social relationships in their classroom.

Further reading

Brownhill, S. (2013) *Getting Children Writing*. London: Sage.

This text has a lot of very practical ideas for teachers to scaffold the writing process. The book includes lesson ideas and plans and is also deeply rooted in a pedagogy of talk supporting writing.

Corbett, P. and Strong, J. (2011) *Talk for Writing Across the Primary Curriculum*. Maidenhead: Oxford University Press.

This text sets out the 'talk for writing' approach, which is very exciting and will help teachers understand that approach. The text takes the reader through various genres of texts and gives lots of ideas about how to implement them.

Lambirth, A. (2005) *Reflective Reader: Primary English*. Exeter: Learning Matters.

Chapter 5 is all about speaking and listening. For a more comprehensive look at social constructivism, Lambirth provides some really helpful readings.

References

Alexander, R. (2005) 'Culture, dialogue and learning: Notes on an emerging pedagogy', Paper presented at the Education, Culture and Cognition: Intervening for Growth, International Association for Cognitive Education and Psychology (IACEP), 10th International Conference, University of Durham, 10–14 July.

Barnes, D. (1992) *From Communication to Curriculum*, 2nd edn. Portsmouth, NH: Boynton/Cook-Heinemann.

Bizdra, J. (unknown) *5 Best Creative thinking techniques to help your business thrive*. Available at: www.rubymarketer.com/5-best-creative-thinking-techniques-to-help-your-business-thrive/ (accessed 10 June 2015).

Brien, J. (2012) *Teaching Primary English*. London: Sage.

Bruner, J. (1985) 'Vygotsky: A historical and conceptual perspective', in J. Wertsch (ed.), *Culture, Communication and Cognition: Vygotskian Perspectives*. Cambridge: Cambridge University Press.

Bruner, J. (1996) *The Culture of Education*. Cambridge, MA: Harvard University Press.

Burnard, P., Craft, A. Cremin, T., Duffy, B., Hanson, R., Keene, J., Haynes, L. and Burns, D. (2006) 'Documenting "possibility thinking": A journey of collaborative enquiry', *International Journal of Early Years Education*, 14 (3): 243–62.

Ciccone, E. (2001) 'A place for talk in a writer's workshop', *The Quarterly*, 23 (4): 25–7. Available at: www.nwp.org/cs/public/print/resource/239 (accessed 31 October 2014).

Corbett, P. and Strong, J. (2011) *Talk for Writing Across the Curriculum*. Maidenhead: McGraw-Hill.

Corden, R. (2000) *Literacy and Learning through Talk: Strategies for the Primary Classroom*. Buckingham: Open University Press.

Cremin, T. (2009) *Teaching English Creatively*. London: Routledge.

de Bono, E. (2000) *Six Thinking Hats*. London: Penguin Books.

Department for Education (DfE) (2013). *The National Curriculum for England, Key Stages 1 and 2*. London. Crown Copyright.

Department for Educations and Skills (DfES) (2006). *Primary Framework for Literacy and Mathematics*. London. Crown Copyright.

Dörnyei, Z. (2007) 'Creating a motivating classroom environment', in J. Cummins and C. Davison (eds), *International Handbook of English Language Teaching*, *Springer International Handbooks of Education*, Vol. 15. New York: Springer, pp. 719–31.

Grainger, T. (2005) 'Oral artistry: Storytelling and drama', in A. Wilson (ed.), *Creativity in Primary Education*. Exeter: Learning Matters.

Jones, M. (2007) 'Targeting talk', *Special Children*, January–February: 31–4. Available at: www.talkformeaning.co.uk/files/012.pdf (accessed 31 October 2014).

Joyce, B. Calhoun, E. Hopkins, D. (2009). *Models of Learning – Tools for Teaching*. Maidenhead. Oxford University Press.

Mercer, N. (2000) *Words and Minds: How we Use Language to Think Together*. London: Routledge.

Needle, J. (1995) *The Bully*. London: Penguin Books.

Pierce, K. and Gilles, C. (2008) 'From exploratory talk to critical conversations', in N. Mercer and S. Hodgkinson (eds), *Exploring Talk in Schools*. London: Sage.

Rose, J. (2006) *The Independent Review of the Teaching of Early Reading: Interim Report*. Available at: www.reall-languages.com/interimreport.doc (accessed 31 October 2014).

Sternberg, R. (ed.) (2003) *Handbook of Creativity*, 3rd edn. New York: Cambridge University Press.

Vickery, A. (2014) *Developing Active Learning in the Primary Classroom*. London: Sage.

Vygotsky, L. (1978) *Thought and Language*. Cambridge, MA: MIT Press.

Waugh, D. and Joliffe, W. (2013) *English 5–11: A Guide for Teachers*, 2nd edn. London: David Fulton.

Wood, D. (1988) *How Children Think and Learn*. Oxford: Blackwell.

Creative English

Early Years into Key Stage 1

With thanks to Kate Skellern, Stramongate School, Cumbria, UK

5

Learning outcomes

By reading this chapter, you will have:

- Developed your understanding of approaches to learning and teaching in Early Years Foundation Stage (EYFS)
- Developed your knowledge and understanding of the EYFS characteristics of effective learning and catering for these in practice
- Developed your understanding of how to support young children as learners
- Developed your understanding of creating a culture of enquiry

Links to Early Years Foundation Stage (EYFS) Framework

Sections 1.3 and 1.4 of this document (DfE, 2014) state that:

All areas of learning and development are important and inter-connected. Three areas are particularly crucial for igniting children's curiosity and enthusiasm for learning, and for building their capacity to learn, form relationships and thrive. These three areas, the prime areas, are:

- communication and language;
- physical development; and
- personal, social and emotional development.

Providers must also support children in four specific areas, through which the three prime areas are strengthened and applied.

One of these specific areas is literacy.

Section 1.5 states that:

> **Communication and language** development involves giving children opportunities to experience a rich language environment; to develop their confidence and skills in expressing themselves; and to speak and listen in a range of situations.

> **Literacy** development involves encouraging children to link sounds and letters and to begin to read and write. Children must be given access to a wide range of reading materials (books, poems, and other written materials) to ignite their interest.

DfE (2014: 8)

Chapter overview

This chapter will explore the importance of language and literacy development in the Early Years. Using a theme of castles, this chapter explores play as a tool to develop both language and literacy and the key role that storytelling plays. This chapter looks at children's understanding of story, the development of children's mark-making into writing and learning opportunities that prepare children for the more 'traditional' environments of the remainder of their primary career. The chapter includes planning for the Early Years, including child-led planning, the role of planning continuous provision and assessing progress. Incorporated into play will be the importance of the outdoor environment as a learning tool.

Introduction

In his much viewed TED talk, 'Do Schools Kill Creativity?' (2006), pioneer of creativity and chair of the National Advisory Committee on Creative and Cultural Education, Sir Ken Robinson comments that children enter school very creative, the problem is in keeping them creative. Wright supports this viewpoint as she states that: 'Early childhood is a time when children's thinking is still imaginative, flexible and linked to fantasy and children' (2010: 10). In fact, it was only last week when, as I was working with a small group of young children on a gardening project in a school, Leo, refusing to wear gloves to pick up leaves, said that he would use his skin. He then paused, thought and then commented that under his skin was a dog's skin and he could change into a dog at any point. This child, having just entered Key Stage 1, struggled to engage with the more conventional aspects of school and was working towards being integrated into his class but in this couple of lines, demonstrated more creative and imaginative thinking than I had seen anywhere else.

The statutory framework for EYFS, as quoted above, implores the Early Years practitioner to 'ignite children's curiosity and enthusiasm for learning' (DfE, 2014: 10). One of the challenges is to do that whilst dealing with curriculum coverage, cognitive concept, knowledge and skill development and harnessing the creative powers that my dog-skinned friend demonstrated in the garden.

Whilst the statutory guidance for EYFS separates out the Early Learning Goals (ELGs) into three areas and seven goals, as Figure 5.1 exemplifies, the document states that they are all interconnected. So, although this chapter focuses primarily on development in language and literacy, there will be significant links to the other ELGs and consequently to prime areas of learning. Alongside this, and heavily influential in the Early Years, are what are called 'Characteristics of Effective Learning'. These are playing and exploring, active learning and creating and thinking critically. These characteristics connect with prime areas of learning: personal, social and emotional development, communication and language and physical development. They also connect with specific areas of learning: literacy, mathematics, understanding of the world and expressive arts and design. Children's progress and achievement in these characteristics are reported on by teachers and underpin all learning and teaching in EYFS.

Desailly (2012) states that, primarily, children need to learn to be good learners, and it is my aim through this chapter to look at learning in a more

Prime area of learning ⇨	Communication and language development	Physical development	Personal, social and emotional development
Related Early Learning Goals (ELGs) ⇨	listening and attention	Moving and handling	Self-confidence and awareness
	Understanding	Health and self-care	Managing feelings and behaviour
	Speaking		

Figure 5.1 EYFS prime areas of learning and related Early Learning Goals (ELGs).

holistic way and how excellent foundation stage practice can and should provide a great basis for children, not only in their development of language and literacy, but also as learners, ready to take on what the rest of school throws at them.

Literacy through play and storytelling

As a teacher educator, I regularly receive emails from students and am told about concerns regarding spending time in foundation stage. Most of those concerns centre round the idea of play: 'How will I see what I need, if all they do is play?' 'But I can't see anything about planning, if all they do is play?' are two of the favourites. However, this all comes from a misconception about how children learn and a misconception about play and what it is. Howard and Alderson (2011), in their update of Mary Sheridan's work of 1977 on the importance of play, define play as involving: 'eager engagement in pleasurable physical or mental effort to obtain emotional satisfaction' (2011: 5). Play is not frivolous or too much fun, which, for any of you who have witnessed children at play, will know. Children at play can be seriously exploring, problem-solving, negotiating, creating, visualising and devising, to create something that matters to them. Is that not what learning in school should encompass and be about?

The National Literacy Trust (NLT) states that play lays the foundation for literacy. In its *Talk to Your Baby* newsletter, the NLT suggests that play helps babies and young children develop language, they hear it and they practice it. Being from the south, my children pre-school would speak with a southern accent, saying 'barth' and 'glars' and 'carstle'. Why? They heard us using the language and picked it up. Then, on going to school in Lancashire, were soon disabused of that and the short vowel sounds, 'bath', 'glass', 'castle', were utilised like their peers.

So, how does this work in practice? What is play in a school context, and how does it relate to literacy? Below, is a short case study that exemplifies the importance of play in children's literacy development.

Case study

The playhouse in the outdoor area connected to Kim's Foundation Stage Classroom had been transformed into Grandma's cottage. There was a rocking chair outside the door, a coat hanging on the peg, a knocker attached to the door and a bed and table inside. Previously, Kim had been outside with the children, listening for long and short sounds in the environment and practising making loud and soft sounds with environmental objects. A group now went outside with Kim to explore the 'cottage'. Kim observed this conversation:

Kieran: I wonder who lives here today?

Dominic: *(Whilst banging the door to within an inch of its life)* Nobody is there.

Katie: I will go and look in the window.

Kieran: What can you see?

Katie: *(Screams)* There's a wolf in there! It's big and has big teeth!

           (Lots of running, screaming, shouting, and a bit more running)

Dominic: Did he eat Grandma?

Kim: Why do you think a wolf would eat Grandma, Dominic?

Dominic: 'Cos that's what wolves do.

Reflecting on the case study

- What knowledge and understanding was being demonstrated by the children?
- Look back at Table 5.1, which ELGs were being demonstrated through this small piece of a play?
- What literacy development was being demonstrated?

In response to this case study, you may bring up the environment as the stimulant for this literacy development and I would probably agree to an extent. But how did Dominic know one key element of traditional tales? – that wolves are bad and eat people. This knowledge and understanding of story comes through the storytelling skill or reading skills of adults in that child's life. Children need to experience story in order to develop those literacy skills. Reading is much more than gaining phonic knowledge, it is also about an understanding and appreciation of story. Palmer and Bayley (2008) describe how storytelling increases vocabulary and sentence structure and, if you take the next step and invite children to storytell, confidence in language use is develop. As a younger teacher, I would sneer at the seeming lack of learning value in children sharing their 'news', but, actually, with more experience, I realise that every opportunity is a development opportunity and so children telling their stories is a powerful tool for them to develop their own use of language, which helps with writing.

Six top tips for storytelling in your classroom

- *Magic Mirror:* Send a mirror home with the children – wrap it up in bubble wrap for health and safety reasons. What does the mirror see in your house? Tell the story of the magic mirror the next day.
- *Use props:* Puppets, hats, wigs, jackets, bags, anything that helps bring the story alive. Dress up the children, dress up yourself.
- *What's different today?* Before the children arrive, set up some toys (I used garden gnomes) around the classroom doing things or in places they shouldn't be. How did they get there? What are they doing?
- *What's in the box?* Leave a clue as to what is in the box today. A map? An old key? A book? A photo? Tell the story? Who? What? Where? When? Why?
- *Develop the use of different voices:* Engage children by giving them different characters and different voices in your story. Can you develop movement for them? This will make your storytelling more memorable and children will copy it.
- *Modelling:* Use correct grammar and interesting language. Don't dumb it down as children are more attuned to language than you may think.

These are just a few of my own ideas but there are many more for developing language through storytelling in Pie Corbett's brilliant book, *The Bumper Book of Storytelling into Writing at Key Stage 1* (2006).

Developing early writing

Spoken language development is a natural process, as long as children have plenty of experience of quality language interactions. However, the acquisition of reading and writing skills involves, as Palmer and Bayley put it: 'the patterning of complex intellectual behaviour, employing a range of visual, auditory and cognitive skills, ... learning to write ... is even more complex – and requires in addition quite taxing physical co-ordination of hand and eye movements' (2008: 65). These skills need careful teaching. They can be, and should be, done creatively. So, what does that mean? In exploring creativity in earlier chapters, the notion of exploration, process and environment are crucial and they can be applied here. Children can explore written communication through mark-making. To the reader, used to conventional black squiggles that represent sounds, they mean nothing, but ask the child to interpret those marks for you and a careful meaning is brought to life. Whitehead (2010) states that mark-making is highly dynamic, not only does it represent meaning to the child, but it is also usually shaped by what they can do with the tool they are making the marks with and how they bodily explore the space. Their mark may be a series of concentric circles and mean: 'I am watching *Octonauts*'. Bruce and Spratt (2011) state that children's drawings emerge into writing. Early forms of letters start to appear in the drawings and they start to take over as children develop.

Children also tend to know what writing is for. They see adults communicating through writing, so, providing environments for children to have a go is really important, for them it will be quite natural and they will want to have a go. There may be a postbox with a table and postcards next to it. Your 'superhero' role-play area may have paper to write the missions on. It could be a travel agent with holiday forms to fill in. It could be a restaurant with menus to write. As Browne states: 'By using writing in role play children come to recognise the uses of writing and the many types of writing that exist. They are given the opportunity to experiment with writing in a relaxed environment' (2009: 103).

Through these opportunities, children are focusing on literacy, communication and language, and all three of the characteristics of an effective learner which demonstrates their interconnectedness.

Using phonics creatively to support writing

For some, the teaching of phonics has become the antithesis of creativity. I have seen some schools using a scheme slavishly as if the strict adherence to 20 minutes of phonics each day, as the scheme suggests, will develop their children into great readers and writers. For some, it might, but, actually, phonics teaching can be intensely creative. Children can explore sounds (see the case study of Kim's exploration of long and short sounds earlier in this chapter). Children can have fun with writing and the process of understanding the mechanics of reading and writing can be great fun. Glazzard and Stokoe (2013) suggest that children should be provided with a wide range of activities to practise gross motor skills. Children could use fingers in shaving foam to trace shapes, or they could use sand or water. They could use ribbons, broad brushes on big paper, chalk on the playground. Once these are mastered, then fine motor skills can be developed.

Bruce and Spratt (2011) state that a child's name is usually the first fixed word they will write and know. Their name is part of their identity and it is therefore important to them and so, as children develop through their understanding of phoneme/grapheme correspondences from initial sounds, to digraphs and adjacent consonants, they will display some significant writing characteristics. Some of these may be repeated patterns, repeated letters from their own name, a mix of drawings and letters, a mix of upper- and lower-case letters and inconsistent formations. These are important stages for children to go through. Offering plenty of opportunities for this in the foundation stage classroom is vital for children's development. The adult should be scaffolding through modelling implement-holding, letter formation and the connections between phonemes and graphemes. Glazzard and Stokoe (2013) go on to say that children's achievements at this stage should be celebrated. Typically, as Glazzard and Stokoe describe it, children should be supported through writing words and labels (perhaps for a display, a class museum, their name for the class photo; they may label classroom resources and things which they have made). This would then lead to captions, followed by sentences. Children need to build their writing development in bite-size chunks and all too often some of these stages are missed out. Teachers are very good at the early work but then launch straight into sentences, and this overwhelms children and leaves them feeling that they can't do it, which leads to dissatisfaction and a lack of desire to write. Children need positive experiences.

The spectre of 'real work'

In the school playground, I do hear parents of children approaching Year 1 comment to their young charges that they'd better watch out, they'll have to do really hard work in Year 1, sitting at tables all day doing real work. I hope that these parents are not part of a marketing team for the school, or education for that matter, because what better way is there to turn a child off learning than to instil fear? Some people thrive under pressure, I don't. When I am a bit nervous or fearful, I do not do my best work and I know that it is the same for a lot of children. This is why I see many senior managers in schools employing their most outstanding staff to their foundation stages and working hard to ensure that the excellent practice in terms of developing children as learners carries on throughout the school. Foundation Stage should build strong foundations. Everything I have written in this chapter so far should point to the concept of the foundation stage teacher creating a culture of enquiry, exploration, enjoyment, freedom, fun and learning to be learners. This is the essence of creativity. In fact, creativity shines through the characteristics of an effective learner. I would also argue that real work is children developing as learners and being active participants in their own learning.

Children as active learners

Did you have any say in what you learned at school? Probably not. Did you contribute to the classroom design? I doubt it. Did you contribute to the teacher's planning? I don't think so. Did you know what the point of learning what you were learning was? Perhaps it's just me, but I didn't.

Why not?

I have been into many wonderful foundation stage classes with fabulous role-play areas, amazing displays, organised learning stations: writing areas, maths areas, travel agents, shop – small world play set out beautifully. I have wanted to stay and play because it is all so inviting and so beautiful. However, I wonder what input the children had into it? Vickery (2014) states that active learning and enquiry-based learning put the child at the centre of making decisions about what they will learn. She draws on the work of Pardoe (2009), who recommends that the teacher discusses the learning and environment with the children, the things that help or hinder and as a result the children and teacher together create the environment and are responsible for its success. The case study below shows this in action and the impact it has on learning for these very sophisticated discussions for four-year-olds.

Case study: Part 1

Claire wanted to spend the first day with her new reception class discussing what they would be learning: the topic they would be doing for this first half-term and how the classroom could work to make the best learning environment for the children. She had left out some books, some pencils, paper, chalks on tables and some small world play. The role-play area was empty. It wasn't very inviting and Claire did worry about what the parents would think while

(Continued)

(Continued)

they brought in their children. As the children busied themselves, chatting, negotiating, exploring, wandering, finding their way around their new territory, Claire did the register and invited the children to come and sit on the carpet. She had noticed that Dylan and Tom had brought some paper with them. Claire enquired as to the purpose of the paper and Dylan showed the drawing. He explained that during the holidays he had been to visit a castle. He said that he had seen some real knights and they were fighting on horseback. This created a great flurry of excitement and it transpired that other children had also been to castles and one wanted to visit a castle. 'Shall we all learn some more about castles?' Claire asked the class and Miryam replied: 'Dylan could teach us.' Dylan rose up about 10 feet taller, beaming. As the excited chatter subsided, Claire turned to a wall covered in white paper and wrote the word 'Castles' in the middle. She asked the children to talk to each other about what they wanted to learn and having summarised and interpreted what the children said, Claire arrived at the drawing shown in Figure 5.2.

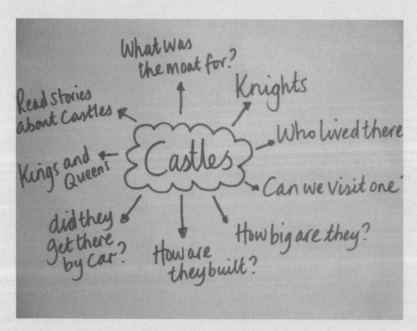

Figure 5.2   Initial planning sheet with children for a castles topic

Claire then asked the children to draw what they wanted the classroom to look like if they would be learning about castles. Rani wanted Claire to be dressed as a princess all day, every day, and wanted a big dragon to live in a big egg in the corner. These were two rather more notable headlines. Other ideas were: 'We could build a castle in the corner the role-play area,' 'We could dress up as knights,' 'We could make up stories about knights and dragons and princesses,' 'We could draw knights and princesses and make up names for them.' This gave Claire an idea for an interactive register. Once the castle is made, Children could use their knights or princesses to self-register by putting them in the castle.

Reflecting on the case study (part 1)

- How did Claire create a community of enquiry?
- How did Claire ensure that the children were active in their own learning? What could some of the limitations of this be?
- How do you respond to the risk that Claire took by choosing this approach?

John Hattie (2012) highlights the importance of the teacher being a role model for the children. He suggests that the teacher should illustrate how they are learning, too, not always about the content perhaps but certainly about the children and their responses to learning. Claire embodies that approach. The result: enthusiastic learners. Wright (2006) builds on this by suggesting that children are much more likely to learn if they are engaged and motivated and I would add to this, if they see their learning as purposeful.

Planning learning opportunities

Figure 5.3 is not Claire's half-termly plan – it is a starting point. Claire has to demonstrate that concepts, knowledge, skills and understanding are being taught, and that ELGs, characteristics of an effective learner developed as well as prime and specific areas of learning are being met. Claire also has to make space for phonics. As well as taught input, Claire has to ensure purposeful continuous provision that facilitates the development and practice of children's gross and fine motor skills and social and emotional skills. Figure 5.3 shows how Claire started to break down some of the ideas which the children came up with and mapped them onto a weekly plan. I must stress that the plan is not finished, so, for the purposes

Foundation Stage Weekly Plan				
Theme: Castles		Learning experiences		
Early Learning Goals (ELGs)	*Learning objectives*	*Taught input*	*Continuous provision*	*Assessment*
Listening and attention Understanding Speaking	Listen to stories, accurately anticipate key events and respond to what they hear with relevant comments, questions or actions Answer 'how' and 'why' questions in response to stories	Tell the story of the Peanut Butter Princess. Introduce some key characters from traditional tales. Use voices and props. Have children acting some characters	*Role-play area:* Castle to role-play the story. Dressing up as knights and princesses *Workshop*: Make dragon masks, knights' helmets and armour. Painting them (Scissors, paint, design, drawing) *Writing area:* Sand tray to practise writing letter shapes. Write to the dragon with ideas to help catch the prince. Post in 'dragon postbox'	Observe skills of negotiation, managing behaviour, retelling elements of story, voices, etc. Photograph
Moving and handling Health and self-care				
Self-confidence self-awareness				
Managing feelings and behaviour				
Making relationships				
Literacy	Use their phonic knowledge to write graphemes in ways which match their spoken sounds	Phonics: Exploring initial sounds s,a,t,p,i,n. Hearing, saying, reading, starting to write the graphemes		
Numeracy	Count reliably with numbers from 1 to 20	Counting the stairs to the top of the castle (20 steps) 1s and 2s		

Figure 5.3   An extract from one of Claire's developing weekly plans

of this chapter, the gaps are intentional, but it does show how Claire used the children's ideas, and then began to map them against the Early Learning Goals and included some of the more specific elements of the EYFS statutory guidance: literacy and mathematics to develop the children's learning.

Case study: Part 2 – How the theme developed

Claire, with some help from the children and other willing volunteers, transformed her role-play area into a castle for the children to role-play the story or create their own story. Knights and princesses outfits were acquired and the children spent some time making a very large paper maché egg for the dragon to hatch from. Each day, Claire added a few more cracks to the egg and the children had to predict when the dragon would hatch. The children took photos of each other in knights and princess outfits or dragon masks to create self-registering pictures and these went into the castle when they arrived. The workshop became an armoury, transforming card into breastplates and helmets as quickly as more card could be acquired.

In the coming term, Claire has a trip planned to a castle and a visit from a medieval re-enactor. The children's phonics knowledge is developing and Claire is planning some writing of captions for the role-play area and the display of their castle visit. They will use some of the pictures taken in the role-play area for a speech bubble competition.

Where have all these ideas come from?

Before the children leave on a Friday, Claire has a review session with the class. Every child has the opportunity to share their favourite aspect of the week (ELGs: listening, attention speaking, self-confidence and making relationships) and what they think they have learned that week. Next, ideas for the following week are discussed – what they would like to learn and do more of. Claire and her teaching assistant review these ideas and skeleton-plan the following week for Claire to write up and flesh out.

Reflecting on the case study (part 2)

- From the start, Claire has fully involved the whole class in their own learning. She has created a culture of enquiry, made the learning purposeful and interesting. She has adopted a variety of multi-sensory approaches and has generally been very inclusive. Some may argue that she is the teacher and should dictate the learning: what do you think?
- It would appear from this case study, that the loudest shouters get what they want. Did all the children want to look at castles? What about if there are children who hate it? What do you do then?

(Continued)

(Continued)

What do you think? How do you ensure that all the children are being encouraged to learn and develop through your approaches to learning and teaching?

- You may say, 'Well, it's alright for Claire, she is experienced, she can plan week to week, but I have to hand in a termly overview. This approach is too risky for me, I need more experience and confidence to work in this way.' So, what can you take from Claire's approach. Can a beginning teacher take risks? What do you think?

Claire did take some risks as a teacher, but actually there is a big risk in getting children involved in their own learning. Essentially, you, the teacher, are giving up some control and that is not easy, especially as teaching is measured on results. However, whatever you do should have an impact on learning. Looking at Claire's experience, her approach had a huge impact. The children were discussing and working together and interacting with resources, adults and experiences. Mujis and Reynolds state that children who have these kinds of experiences of learning 'have been found to be able to transfer their knowledge to other situations' (2011: 160). This type of learning also builds confidence. Hart et al. (2004) say that confidence must be in place before engagement. We know, ourselves, that if we feel confident with a topic, an environment, a type of learning, then we are more likely to engage.

One thing is clear: Claire knows exactly what she believes about learning and teaching in the Early Years and she knows that it works. Claire believes in collaborative learning, children as active participants and the importance of excitement and engagement in learning. Claire knows that it makes her work and that of the children more enjoyable. Do you?

Stop and think

Have you ever paused for thought amidst the cut and thrust of the classroom and reminded yourself about why you came into teaching? What do you believe about learning and teaching, and how does this impact on the way you work? If you haven't thought about it, stop now and remind yourself.

Try this

Activity 1: Outdoor space

Do you have an opportunity to develop any outside space near your classroom? I was at a wonderful inner-city school last year that was built in the grounds of a former monastery. Children walk through a small wood and come out into a picturesque red-bricked-walled garden, which the school governors have turned into a series of outdoor classrooms. The learning that Kim (case study – part 1) created from a playhouse outside was brilliant. Try something and notice the impact on learning.

Activity 2: Maximise opportunities for writing

Whether it is writing their name on a label, mark-making on a chalkboard, whiteboard or playground; whether children are writing captions for displays or speech bubbles for characters; whether children are writing letters to the head teacher, local MP or an author – get the children writing for a purpose. Make sure that there are a variety of opportunities for the children to engage and that their efforts are praised and valued.

Activity 3: Collaborative planning with the children

Take a risk and ask the children what areas they are interested in. This could spark a really good range of ideas and a meaningful and relevant topic on which to hang all their learning. For Claire's class (case study – part 2), it was castles; for your class, it might be something very different that you can use to engage and motivate children whilst meeting statutory requirements. Use one of your display areas as a collaborative planning wall. Add to it so that the children can see how their ideas are being developed and parents can see what the children are learning.

Summary

Throughout this chapter, I have focused on two key ideas: creating a culture of enquiry and involving children in their own learning. These are essential foundations for children becoming enthused about learning as they move through school. They help develop confidence in learning, too. As children feel safe in their environment because they have been involved in its creation, they are more able to take risks and play with language, have a go at writing, suggest an answer, engage in story through the use of props and voices and develop some resilience. Crick (2006) suggests that it is the teacher who creates this through modelling the ethos that is desired. Our case studies have put forward two very inspiring teachers who understand this and the results are there to be seen. It could be said that creativity and statutory requirements are incompatible but these two case studies have shown the opposite: being creative is about an approach to learning and teaching, how you teach, not necessarily what you teach.

Further reading

Glazzard, J. and Stokoe, J. (2013) *Teaching Systematic Synthetic Phonics and Early English*. Northwich: Critical Publishing.

This great text, as well as developing understanding of the rudiments of how to teach phonics, is also very good on early reading and writing and how these two areas can be developed. Case studies on creative approaches are very helpful.

Vickery, A. (2014) *Developing Active Learning in the Primary Classroom*. London: Sage.

If you want to understand more about collaborative learning and creating a culture of enquiry, then Anitra Vickery's book is brilliant. I use it a lot. As well as her chapter on a culture of enquiry, her chapter on developing questioning is very informative.

Wright, S. (2010) *Understanding Creativity and Early Childhood*. London: Sage.

This very accessible text gives a great overview of how young children learn and develop. Susan Wright focuses on the child voice and how children communicate. Her chapters on drawing as communication are quite superb.

References

Browne, A. (2009) *Developing Language and Literacy 3–8*, 3rd edn. London: Sage.

Bruce, T. and Spratt, J. (2011) *Essentials of Literacy from 0–7*, 2nd edn. London: Sage.

Corbett, P. (2006). *The Bumper Book of Storytelling into Writing at Key Stage 1*. London: Clown Publishing.

Crick, R. (2006) *Learning Power in Action: A Guide for Teachers*. London: Paul Chapman.

Department for Education (DfE) (2014) *Statutory Framework for the Early Years Foundation Stage: Setting the Standards for Learning, Development and Care for Children from Birth to Five*. London: DfE.

Desailly, J. (2012) *Creativity in the Primary Classroom*. London: Sage.

Glazzard, J. and Stokoe, J. (2013) *Teaching Systematic Synthetic Phonics and Early English*. Northwich: Critical Publishing.

Hart, S., Dixon, A., Drummond, M. and McIntyre, D. (2004) *Learning without Limits*. Maidenhead: McGraw-Hill.

Hattie, J. (2012) *Visible Learning for Teachers: Maximising Impact on Learning*. Abingdon: Routledge.

Howard, J. and Alderson, D. (2011) *Play in Early Childhood: From Birth to Six Years*. London: Routledge.

Mujis, D. and Reynolds, D. (2011) *Effective Teaching: Evidence and Practice*. 3rd edn. London: Sage.

National Literacy Trust (NLT) (unknown) *Talk to Your Baby*. Available at: www.literacytrust.org.uk/talk_to_your_baby/news/2332_10_reasons_why_play_is_important (accessed 3 January 2016).

Palmer, S. and Bayley, R. (2008) *Foundations of Literacy*. 2nd edn. London: Continuum.

Pardoe, D. (2009) *Towards Successful Learning: Furthering the Development of Successful Learning and Teaching in Schools*. 2nd edn. London: Network Continuum.

Robinson, K. (2006) 'TED Talk: Ken Robinson: Do schools kill creativity?'. Available at: www.ted.com/talks/ken_robinson_says_schools_kill_creativity?language=en (accessed 3 January 2016).

Vickery, A. (2014) *Developing Active Learning in the Primary Classroom*. London: Sage.

Whitehead, M. (2010) *Language and Literacy in the Early Years 0–7*, 4th edn. London: Sage.

Wright, D. (2006) *Classroom Karma: Positive Teaching, Positive Behaviour, Positive Learning*. Abingdon: Routledge.

Wright, S. (2010) *Understanding Creativity and Early Childhood*. London: Sage.

Reading into writing

Key Stage 1 Fiction

6

Learning outcomes

By reading this chapter, you will have:

- Developed an understanding of how reading provides a context for writing in Key Stage 1
- Developed an understanding of ways in which to engage children creatively in responding to a text
- Developed an understanding of some of the principles and processes involved in teaching writing
- Developed some ideas as to how you could use *Amazing Grace* and apply them to other texts

---

National Curriculum links

Key Stage 1 Reading comprehension

Pupils should be taught to:

develop pleasure in reading, motivation to read, vocabulary and understanding by:

- listening to, discussing and expressing views about a wide range of contemporary and classic poetry, stories and non-fiction at a level beyond that at which they can read independently
- discussing the sequence of events in books and how items of information are related
- becoming increasingly familiar with and retelling a wider range of stories, fairy stories and traditional tales

Key Stage 1 Writing (Composition)

Pupils should be taught to:

- develop positive attitudes towards and stamina for writing by:

  - writing narratives about personal experiences and those of others (real and fictional)
  - writing about real events

- consider what they are going to write before beginning by:

  - planning or saying out loud what they are going to write about
  - writing down ideas and/or key words, including new vocabulary

- make simple additions, revisions and corrections to their own writing by:

  - evaluating their writing with the teacher and other pupils

Key Stage 1 Writing (Transcription)

Pupils should learn how to use:

- sentences with different forms: statement, question, exclamation, command
- expanded noun phrases to describe and specify [for example, the blue butterfly]
- the present and past tenses correctly and consistently including the progressive form
- subordination (using when, if, that, or because) and co-ordination (using or, and, or but)

DfE (2013)

Chapter overview

Drawing particularly on the creative use of the classroom environment, creating innovative learning contexts and teacher in-role, this chapter explores the key concepts, ideas and learning that children in Key Stage 1 need to develop in fiction. The chapter draws on the 2013 National Curriculum and exemplifies ideas in context from the 'Creative approaches to …' chapters. The chapter will also consider an approach to integrated planning and present a case study using as a stimulus *Amazing Grace* and other *Grace* books by Mary Hoffman and Caroline Binch. As part of the planning process in this case study, formative assessment and record-keeping will be addressed. This will provide some questions and reflective activity for students/teachers to explore. A list of recommended texts will be given at the end of this chapter, with ideas of ways in which they can be used to promote creativity.

My aim in this chapter is that whilst exploring Hoffman and Binch's wonderful text *Amazing Grace*, you will be able to transfer the approaches and ideas across to other texts that you may prefer to use or feel more drawn to. In Appendix 6.1 at the end of this chapter, you will find a table with other great texts and ways in which you may wish to take ideas from this chapter forward. This is, of course, by no means exhaustive.

Setting the context

Hoffman introduces us to Grace. Grace lives with her mum, her nana and her cat, and her father lives in South Africa with his new wife. Grace loves stories, pantomimes, acting and playing, and the wonderful illustrations by Binch bring this playful aspect of her character to life. *Amazing Grace*, the first book in the series, and one which I will be focusing on in this chapter, shows how Grace battles to win the part of Peter Pan in the school play, despite being a girl and despite being black. The story shows how Grace, having been put down by her classmates, is helped by her family to believe in herself and her talents. The school play is wonderful and, of course, its star is Grace as Peter Pan. It is a wonderful, heart-warming story, which is all about resilience, triumph and believing in yourself.

So, what learning opportunities does *Amazing Grace* provide? Using what Robin J. Fogarty would term a 'webbed model' (1991), Figure 6.1 is a possible starting point for an integrated plan. Fogarty suggests that the webbed model is all about using a theme to then overlay different subjects. Here, I am using a text to then overlay different learning opportunities.

Again, this is by no means exhaustive but gives some ideas to start thinking.

Figure 6.1   Amazing Grace starting points, a webbed approach

Responding to the text

Gabrielle Cliff Hodges (2010) suggests that, due to other curriculum imperatives, teachers no longer have either the time or the space to develop and support children's reading for pleasure. She goes on to say that: 'under pressure to raise standards, there has been a strong emphasis on meeting objectives and managing the curriculum, but reasons for reading in the first place seem to have been neglected' (ibid.: 60). I want to argue that these do not have to be mutually exclusive. You can facilitate reading for pleasure whilst meeting objectives. In fact, at least one of the National Curriculum objectives at the start of this chapter demands it. I believe that one of the main ways to do this is by encouraging children to respond to the text in creative ways. After all, what is primary education for? Robin Alexander, in the recommendations of the *Cambridge Primary Review* (2010), suggests that it is to excite children's imagination. He states that: 'to experience the delights-and the pains-of imagining, and of entering into the imaginative world of others, is to become a more rounded person' (ibid.: 199).

One of the main ways in which to encourage children to respond to a text and to excite their imagination is through the questions we ask. However, too many questions, as Edwards and Mercer (1987) warn, can be counterproductive in inducing the kind of talk that builds knowledge and promotes inquiry and exploration. Too often a feature of the English educational culture is what Edwards and Mercer call the I-R-F pattern of classroom discourse. This is Initiation (the teacher asks a question), then a Response, followed by Feedback from the teacher usually affirming or correcting the answer given. Gardner (2010) builds on this, suggesting that this type of discourse promotes monosyllabic answers. Far better is a model of discourse that promotes further responses, and not just a teacher–pupil discourse but a pupil–pupil one.

A type of questioning that could help this, apart from the notion of open questions, is 'Socratic questioning'. This type of question probes assumptions, clarifies concepts and questions viewpoints. I first encountered this type of questioning through changingminds.org which trains therapists and counsellors. It is the type of questioning that demands deeper thought. Using this alongside open questioning also allows for possibility thinking and creative responses to the text.

Stop and think

How would you characterise the discourse of your classroom?
How much talk do you do? How much talk do the children engage in?

Whilst reading the text, think about the kind of questions that children may wish to ask the author. Also, what about some of the characters? What would the children like to ask the characters about what they are feeling? thinking? Does that change at different points during the story? Why are we asking these questions? These questions allow children to bring themselves to the story, they can interact with the characters and the characters stop being abstract and two-dimensional and start becoming real people with thoughts, feelings, worries and problems, just like them. This excites them, this makes them want to read and want to engage, and the more children are engaged then, usually, the more learning will take place.

Classroom environment

The importance of the classroom environment is an significant feature in many of the chapters in this book. A questioning environment promotes thinking and learning. Effective questioning often arises out of the environment you create. By the term 'environment' I am not discussing wall display, where your resources are placed or even to an extent how the tables and chairs are laid out. I am referring to the cognitive environment. The cognitive environment relates to how children are encouraged to engage with tasks and to think and respond. It directly relates to the questions you ask and the activities you ask the children to engage in, and usually is more related to a facilitator teaching approach, rather than teacher instruction.

Children often need to be given permission to think, particularly where they have been in classrooms in which the answer to the question is where the teacher plays 'Guess what's in my head'. Goouch, in Lambirth says that the 'environment you construct in your classroom will be influenced by your educational goals' (2005: 31) What do you, as a teacher, desire? Is it children who think or children who are conditioned to get the answers you want? The environment you create will reflect this. A creative classroom environment is one that values the process of learning as being as or more important than the product. This is not to deride the notion of a product but to suggest that the majority of learning will take place during the process of creating the product.

One main way of supporting and scaffolding the process of learning is by creating a working wall. The working wall is a display that is ongoing throughout the unit of work. It provides a capturing of all the learning undertaken towards the end product, thus valuing the process and demonstrating to children how the work they are doing contributes to it. Primary National Strategy (2006) advice states that: 'Working walls make use of a visible display outcomes, modelled examples and success criteria. This approach enables children to know what they are learning and how this learning process develops over a period of time' (2006: 4).

Back to *Amazing Grace*

Desiring enquiring learners, learners who you want to give ideas and possibilities, might lead you to certain teaching approaches. One of those may be working in-role. This has been explored in more detail in Chapter 4, but this teaching technique serves to bring the characters and situations to life.

In terms of responding to the text, you as teacher might be in role as Grace's teacher, asking the children who should be Peter Pan. An interesting dramatic technique to use is 'Conscience Alley'. The teacher chooses a child to be the character who needs to make a decision. Two lines of children stand to form either side of an alley. On each side will be children with different views on what decision to make and then, after walking through the alley, a decision is made. In this context, Grace's teacher could walk down the alley, deciding on who to choose to be Peter and why. You could be Grace's mum or nana, concerned about Grace and the things she has been told by her friends. How would you approach the situations? Perhaps you could be Grace, displaying different thoughts and feelings and asking advice on what to do. All of these require the children to respond to you and to the text. They talk about the issues raised. Waugh et al. suggest that:

> fiction for young children can have a two-fold effect, it alerts children to the inner life of others, and, chosen carefully, enriches children's language in ways that enable them to build understandings of others and develop the language to talk about internal states within themselves and others. (2013: 113)

Children can talk together in character, thinking how they should respond to situations in character, exploring the text and looking for clues as to what the characters are like and then inferring how they would respond.

Other techniques to facilitate possibility thinking through responding to text

The Napoleon technique

This technique was first introduced in Chapter 4 but is also really interesting in this context. Higgins (1994) offers many different creative thinking techniques. One of these is called the 'Napoleon technique'. This technique allows you to act as if you were somebody else. The idea of the technique is to solve problems as if you were Napoleon Bonaparte. Justyna Byzdra puts it like this: 'You face a problem from somebody else's perspective, thinking outside the box and envisioning the solution being surrounded by the super characteristics of the hero you choose' (2010: 1). How would, for example, Harry Potter respond to the problems that Grace is having? How would he solve it? How would Thor respond? Creating some form of opportunity for children to think differently about situations, to bring themselves to bear on imagined scenarios, is how readers make sense of text.

As Gamble states: 'The imaginative landscape is furnished from the vicarious experience of bringing readers, through the pages of a book, into contact with experiences they will never encounter in real life' (2013: 40).

Forum theatre

Forum theatre, introduced in Chapter 4, is a very powerful dramatic technique that allows the audience to take control of the production, rather than the actors. In fact, the audience can become the actors. This form of theatre was originated by Augusto Boal, who used theatre for political purposes, best known for the 'Theatre of the Oppressed'. The idea is that members of the audience can shout 'Stop!' at any time and take on the role of someone on stage and take the scene in a new direction or respond to the situation differently. This would first need modelling for the children. In the context of *Amazing Grace*, the scene could be where the teacher is choosing parts for the play and Grace is being told by other children why she can't be Peter Pan – any other child not in the scene could come and take the part of a child, maybe even Grace or the teacher, and respond in a different way. This is all about imagining 'what would happen if?' – which takes us back to questioning and creative thinking.

So much learning and understanding: how can you assess it?

'Assessment' is not a dirty word. In fact, it is fundamental to successful teaching and learning. Children must make progress, they must learn and the only way to know how to move them on is to assess them. The key to assessment is knowing what you are looking for. In the above piece of learning – children responding to a teacher in-role and then dialoguing together in character – you might be looking for children to discuss their views about a story. You might be asking them to discuss how different parts of the story are related and understanding the sequence and structure of the story. These objectives all came from the National Curriculum links at the start of this chapter. Why not audio-record discussion: ask the children to note their key ideas on whiteboards, you could observe their discussion and probe deeper through clarification questioning. You could photograph the children and use speech bubbles to then record their ideas and thinking. Your analysis of this should then inform where you take which children next: who needs more consolidation and who needs to be moved on.

Moving into writing

Figure 6.2 provides a possible plan for working with *Amazing Grace*. I want to stress that it is an idea and the concepts and ideas in it may not work for you or your class, so I urge you not to take it as it is and use it. Feel free to use it as a starting point. Also, it is not separated into days but into stages and therefore acts as a plan for a unit of work, not for a specific time frame.

Objectives *(From KS1 English NC)*	Outcome
Express views about contemporary stories	To write an issues-raising story using the structure of *Amazing Grace*
Discuss the sequence of events in books	
Writing narratives about personal events	**Stimulus text**
Plan and evaluate writing	*Amazing Grace* by Mary Hoffman and Caroline Binch
Know how to use: sentences with different forms – statement, question, exclamation, command	
• expanded noun phrases to describe and specify [for example, the blue butterfly] • subordination (using when, if, that, or because) and co-ordination (using or, and, or but)	
Shared Learning and Teaching Stages	**Independent Work Stages**
Read and respond to the text Discussion of the issues raised in the story. Teacher in-role and children in-role, exploring characters and how characters respond to situations. Use creative thinking techniques such as forum theatre and the Napoleon technique to explore possibilities towards structure and content for story	Paired work – dialogue in character, use of whiteboards/post its/speech/thought bubbles to record main thoughts. Put work onto the working wall. Key language also recorded and added to the working wall. Create a checklist of what successful writing looks like in this genre
Ideas and planning Children explore the structure of the story, pinpointing key moments and turning them into a story graph to show the narrative journey of the story	Children create their own story plan in pairs through story-boarding and role-play. Another option is to create a photo-story as a scaffold to their writing and to act as a plan. Add examples to the working wall
Drafting and editing Modelled writing and shared writing, scaffolded support through working wall. Explicit teaching of grammatic structures of the text type and the transcriptional elements of writing (spelling tricky words, sentence structure)	Writing partners support the drafting process. Guided work supports sentence structure and spelling work. Oral rehearsal and editing, using the genre checklist. Model the editing process and writing partners support each other

Figure 6.2 Possible plan for working with Amazing Grace

Children creating ideas, planning and drafting

Having interacted with the text *Amazing Grace* in ways that promote a variety of possibilities and bring themselves to the text, the children may well have an overflow of ideas, but teaching writing is not just about letting them flow. In my early days as a teacher, I would be giving a choice of titles and asking children to write a story. This is not teaching writing. Chamberlain (2011) states that teachers must be aware of their role in

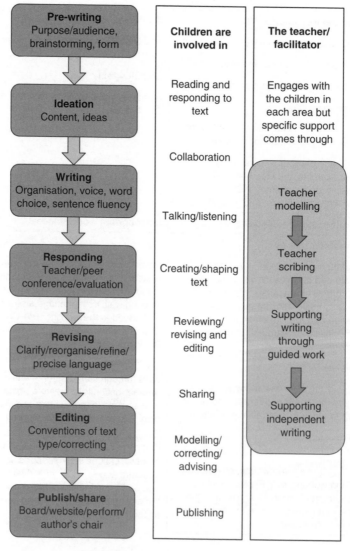

Figure 6.3   Writing process model

supporting young writers, and that role is not to sit back and watch children write and then mark it when it is done. Chamberlain cites the work of Bearne, who encourages teachers to write in the presence of their classes, to act as a 'reflective guide as well as a demonstrator of techniques' (2002: 30). It also provides the teacher with a shared understanding of the creative process and models for children what the writing process is and what they should be going through.

Figure 6.3 provides a writing process built on the work of Janette Hughes (publication date unknown) at the University of Ontario and also from Teresa Cremin (2009). It demonstrates both what children will be involved in and the integral collaborative support of the teacher, but also gives specific ways in which the teacher's knowledge and understanding of both writing and how to teach it are fundamental.

Please do not think that the writing process is formulaic. If the steps that I have advocated above are followed, then all will be well. Brownhill (2013) serves us a warning, drawing on the work of Flower and Hayes (1981) and Bereiter and Scardamalia (1982). They contend that these stages, or for that matter any stages, in a writing process are: 'fluid and overlapping, implying that the writing process is recursive and somewhat messy, depending on what is being written' (Bereiter, 2013: 23).

In the context of the staged plan in Figure 6.2, the first job is to get children engaging with the structure of the story. The easy way to do this would be to tell them what it is and give them a worksheet identifying the main stages so that they can fill it in. However, with that option, there is very little learning. The only possible advantage to this would be that it is quick and straightforward. However, as Chamberlain states: 'writing is also messy and untidy and sometimes it can be slow but … children need to engage with writing in meaningful ways' (2011: 49). The case study below considers an innovative way in which to engage children with the structure of a story in a manner which fosters learning and understanding of how a story builds up.

Case study

Megan is working with her Year 2 (aged 6-7) class using the story *The Peanut Butter Princess* by M K. Grassi. Megan has shared the story with the children, they have responded to the main characters through

(Continued)

(Continued)

'Role on the Wall', where Megan has put pictures of the characters up on the working wall and the children have used sticky notes to add their ideas about them from the text and their own thoughts and feelings. The children have engaged in a freeze-framing activity, where the story has been split into four sections and the children have worked in groups to portray each stage. Megan has told the actors to freeze at certain points, so she can discuss things with some of the characters to examine their feelings, motivations and viewpoints as to why things are happening the way they are. All of the new information gained is on the working wall. At the end of the story is a half an hour gap that the author, Grassi has left for the reader to only imagine what has happened. Megan has set up a scenario, where the children are helping the author fill the gap in with their ideas. Now Megan needs the children to examine the structure of the story and its contours to determine what kind of feel the half hour gap should have. Should it be exciting, calming, a bit of both? Megan decides to create a story graph. She asks the children to decide on what the key events of the story are through looking back at the text and the whole class coming up with their list. She then invites the class to rate the event on an excitement scale of zero to ten. On her graph, she places the events along the bottom axis and her 0-10 scale up the side. The children then plot the graph together to help gain an understanding of what level of excitement is needed. In so doing the children have also identified the key events themselves and this has helped them gain an understanding of what a story plan would look like for this traditional tale.

Reflecting on the case study

- Even though Megan's aim was not about planning the whole story, consider how identifying the key events and mapping the contour of the story supports an understanding of story structure.
- Consider how Megan promoted learning and thinking rather than just telling children the answer
- Consider the ideas Megan uses to engage children in the text. How did the use of the freeze-framing and 'role on the wall' contribute to the children's understanding of the traditional tale genre and support them towards their end product of filling in the half hour gap.

> • Consider the authentic context and purpose for writing. Megan
> has set up a scenario to help the author. She will then send the
> children's work off to him. How could this impact on the children's
> engagement.

Children learn better when they are exploring and discovering. In the context of *Amazing Grace*, children could identify the key things that happen and look at the purpose of the story. Through activities such as storyboarding, children can piece the story together and then work together to turn that into some general stages, thus creating a plan. It may take more time but the learning will be deeper.

It is important that children understand the different elements of stories as they will need this for writing their own. Browne (2009) suggests some useful questions that children could use to produce a plan. In fact children could use these as tools to explore the story of *Amazing Grace*. They provide a simple analytic tool that children can then mirror with their own ideas.

These are:

- What is my story about?
- Who will be in it?
- Where and when will it be set?
- What is the first event?
- What is the problem?
- What happens to solve the problem?
- How will my story begin?
- How will my story end? (Browne, 2009: 120–1)

Drafting

One of the challenges we face as teachers when planning for writing is to be brave enough to give the drafting process enough time. I am not necessarily talking here about time to write, time to put pencil to paper or finger to keys. Brien (2012) reminds us that writing takes a long time, a great deal of movement, often procrastination and sulking. Do we factor in time for this? Thinking and talking, as Brien (2013) reminds, are crucial to the drafting process and often denied to children as they are metaphorically chained to their desks, having to stare at paper, willing the right words to come in the right order, without fault or blemish. As an adult, I write a bit, I get up, I move, I have a drink, I do a bit more, I stop, think, go back. Brien (2013) also states that *'the teaching of writing should be focused on leading children towards adopting adult models of the writing process.* (2013: 85). Children need an environment within which to write that allows them to do these things. They need space to create, to think, to talk, share, make mistakes, go back, re-write in the knowledge that this process is positive and good.

Children also need to be able to draft their work without fear of having all their spelling, grammar and punctuation checked and underlined. These are often called transcriptional elements of writing or secretarial aspects. I am not for one minute saying we should ignore these things, but perhaps focusing on them at this point in the process could be counter-productive. As a teacher, at the drafting stage, I am looking for ideas, content, adventurous vocabulary and concepts. If I am then marking this work in terms of spelling, grammar and punctuation I am not marking against my objectives and also demoralising the child. Transcriptional elements should be taught and engaged with more explicitly at the editing and revising stage of the process within a context.

Assessment

Looking at Figure 6.3, part of the writing stage is responding through teacher–pupil conference. Assessment is crucial at this stage. Part of giving time for the drafting is giving time to discuss children's drafts with them, editing with them, through guided group work, paired or individual work. Again, Brien is helpful here. She reminds us that: 'editing is not the same as marking. It is part of the process of writing rather than a response to a product' (2013: 95). A discussion between teacher and child models the questioning and reflection on a text required to make it more fit for purpose. It also helps clarification and is an opportunity for the child to act on immediate feedback, discuss their own thoughts with the teacher and lets the teacher gain more assessment information as to the child's understanding of the genre, process and specific objectives for which the teacher has planned.

Reviewing, revising and transcription

By the end of Key Stage 1, children need to be able to use sentences with different forms: statement, question, exclamation, command. Also, children need to be able to expand noun phrases to describe and specify (for example, the blue butterfly). Children should also be looking at different sentence structures: subordination (using when, if, that, or because) and co-ordination (using or, and, or but). Teaching grammar, punctuation and spelling is often seen as boring and needing to be done by rote, but it can actually be taught creatively and should be taught in the context of the writing process that is being worked through. Cremin states that: 'focusing on language features of texts ....can be tedious and ineffective if children are not actively engaged in exploring issues related to the text's meaning' (2009: 89).

So, now that we have some first drafts written for our *Amazing Grace* unit of study, what techniques can be used to engage children in the reviewing process that are creative? How can we ensure that the process of learning is the focus and that the end product is not the be all and end all but that we have accuracy and authorial intent? As Horton and Bingle remind us, we should be 'fostering a curiosity about language, words and clauses explored within a meaningful context' (2014: 15). In this context, children can use the text as a basis for exploring different sentence types. Children can play language games such as giving clues, where they have a noun, add more information to turn it into a noun phrase and then make it more specific, until no more clues are left. Children can explore different sentence types, set each other sentence type challenges, play 'what sentence am I?' games that explore why writers use different sentence types and the effect they may have. Children in Year 1 and Year 2 can have control over their writing and have some authorial intent. Modelled writing is crucial here, too, because, as teachers, we should be modelling these sentence types and the reasons for using them. Make sure that opportunities are provided for children to read their work and discuss their work with peers and teachers so that oral feedback can be discussed and acted upon straight away.

Try this

Activity 1: Napoleon technique

When you are next planning a unit of work which involves a story with a problem to solve, set the children the challenge to try and solve it using the characteristics of a superhero or character such as Harry Potter, or even Napoleon Bonaparte. Note the responses and how creative they may be.

(Continued)

(Continued)

Activity 2: Dialogic feedback for assessment

When planning your next unit of work which involves writing, leave plenty of time for the drafting process. Allow children to talk, to move, not always to be on task. Bear in mind that they may need time to think and process. Also, plan your time to be giving oral feedback to children for them to act on. Discuss their work with them and note those discussions.

Activity 3: Explore grammar in context

Within either of the units above, or another one if you wish, plan to focus on the transcriptional elements of writing after the drafting and in that context. Use guided writing (see Chapter 3) to support this. Also, plan some activities where children can explore text and investigate sentence structures, rather than just being told what they are.

Summary

The text *Amazing Grace* provides a useful context within which to explore reading into writing at Key Stage 1. Children need time and opportunity to read and respond to a text in a variety of ways. In this chapter, a few have been presented. The dramatic techniques of forum theatre, conscience alley and freeze-framing provide opportunities for children to explore the text creatively. Using the principle of possibility thinking, discussed in Chapter 1, these techniques give permission for children to think, present their own ideas and contribute to the imaginative journey on which they will take their own story. There is no convergent 'correct' answer that the teacher is looking for, but the desire is that possibilities are created and can be taken forward. Children explore and enquire. This approach to responding to a text, alongside creative thinking ideas such as the 'Napoleon technique', motivate children to want to read, to want to learn and the knock-on effect is that deeper learning will take place. These provide a firm foundation for writing at Key Stage 1.

Children writing a whole story at Key Stage 1 need a model, but also permission to bring their own experience to bear. As a text, *Amazing Grace* provides the model because it can be easily translated into a more general structure to which children add their own thoughts. Children should be involved in planning, too. Providing a writing frame for them is helpful, but more helpful for learning would be for children to create that writing frame themselves, or in pairs, as it will help them understand the structure on which they can map their own ideas. Drafting ideas needs time and opportunity to talk, discuss, edit, respond and share, and the feedback given should focus on those things. It is at the redrafting and editing stage that attention should be given to the grammatical features, punctuation and sentence structures.

Appendix 6.1 Other good texts for Key Stage 1 and creative opportunities

This list is by no means exhaustive.

Text and author	Creative opportunities
Grace and Family by Mary Hoffman and Caroline Binch	Exploring family, travel, other cultures, opportunity for postcards, email
The Hurricane Tree by Libby Purves and Priscilla Lamont	Opportunities for prediction, explore the main character and tracking thoughts, feelings. Good text for a model structure
The Highway Rat by Julia Donaldson and Axel Scheffler	Poetry, exploring a journey structure. Napoleon technique – the problem of the rat
The Garden by Dyan Sheldon and Gary Blythe	Possibility thinking around historical enquiry. Outdoor learning, problem-solving
Rhinos Don't Eat Pancakes by Anna Kemp and Sara Ogilvie	Possibility thinking. Imagine your house if a rhino moved in!
The Three Little Wolves and the Big Bad Pig by Eugene Trivizas and Helen Oxenbury	Play around with the characters in another fairy tale. Imagine, the bear and the three Goldilockses?
The Paper Bag Princess by Robert Munsch, illustrated by Michael Martchenko	Problem-solving and opportunities to create inventions to rescue the prince
The Lion and the Unicorn by Shirley Hughes	This heart-warming story of evacuation provides plenty of cross-curricular work as well as problem-solving and drama
Badger's Parting Gifts by Susan Varley	A story that deals with bereavement. Lots of opportunity for possibility thinking about how to remember people
What's Cooking Jamela? by Niki Daly	Jamela has a problem to solve. Help?
The Worst Princess by Anna Kemp and Sara Ogilvie	What makes the perfect princess? This book provides opportunity for creativity and debate

Further reading

Cremin, T. (2009) 'Developing drama creatively', in *Teaching English Creatively*. Oxford: Routledge.

This chapter helps get into the reasons for doing drama with children and the benefits it can bring to developing their reading and writing skills. For more information on specific techniques, go to: dramaresource.com

Gamble, N. (2013) *Exploring Children's Literature*, 3rd edn. London: Sage.

This wonderful text by Nikki Gamble emphasises reading for pleasure. It is full of ways to develop your own reading as well as children's and it provides lots of practical ways to engage in texts of all genres. The book also provides a rich source of children's literature to develop your own libraries.

Waugh, D. Warner, C. and Waugh, D. (2013) *Teaching Grammar, Punctuation and Spelling in Primary Schools*. London: Learning Matters, Sage.

This book gets to the heart of teaching these transcriptional elements of writing in context. As well as being very readable, highly practical and useful as a pedagogical tool, it also provides some insightful subject knowledge for an area that many teachers find challenging.

References

Alexander, R. (2010) *Children, their World, their Education: Final Report and Recommendations of the Cambridge Primary Review*. London: Routledge.

Bearne, E. (2002) *Making Progress in Writing*. London: Routledge Falmer.

Bereiter, C. (2013) 'Principled practical knowledge: Not a bridge but a ladder', *Journal of the Learning Sciences* (ahead-of-print): 1–14. London: Taylor & Francis.

Bereiter, C. and Scardamalia, M. (1982) 'From conversation to composition: The role of instruction in the development process', in R. Glaser (ed.), *Advances in Instructional Psychology*, Vol. 2. Hillsadle, NJ: Erlbaum.

Brien, J. (2012) *Teaching Primary English*. London: Sage.

Browne, A. (2009) *Developing Language and Literacy 3–8*. 3rd edn. London: Sage.

Brownhill, S. (2013) *Getting Children Writing*. London: Sage.

Byzdra, J. (2010) '5 Best creative thinking techniques to help your business thrive'. Available at: http://EzineArticles.com/3918221 (accessed 10 May 2015).

Chamberlain, L. (2011) 'Writing', in R. Cox (ed.), *Primary English Teaching*. London: Sage and United Kingdom Literacy Association (UKLA).

Cliff Hodges, G. (2010) 'Reasons for reading: Why literature matters', *Literacy: The Journal of the United Kingdom Literacy Association*, 44 (2): 60–8.

Cremin, T. (2009) *Teaching English Creatively*. Oxford: Routledge.

Department for Education (DfE) (2013). *The National Curriculum for England, Key Stages 1 and 2*. London: Crown Copyright.

Edwards, D. and Mercer, N. (1987) *Common Knowledge: The Development of Common Understanding in the Classroom*. London: Routledge.

Flower, L.S. and Hayes, J.R. (1981) 'A cognitive process theory of writing', *College Composition and Communication*, 32 (4): 365–87.

Fogarty, R.J. (1991) 'Ten ways to integrate the curriculum'. Available at: www.ascd. com/ASCD/pdf/journals/ed_lead/el_199110_fogarty.pdf (accessed 4 May 2015).

Gamble, N. (2013) *Exploring Children's Literature: Reading with Pleasure and Purpose*, 3rd edn. London: Sage.

Gardner, P. (2010) *Creative English: Creative Curriculum*. London: David Fulton.

Goouch, K. (2005) 'Places and spaces for literacy', in A. Lambirth (ed.), *Planning Creative Literacy Lessons*. London: David Fulton.

Higgins, J. (1994) *101 Great Problem-Solving Techniques*. Winter Park, FL: New Management Publishing Company.

Hoffman, M. and Binch, C. (2007) *Amazing Grace*. London: Francis Lincoln Children's Books.

Horton, S. and Bingle, B. (2014) *Lessons in Teaching Grammar in Primary Schools*. London: Sage.

Hughes, J. (unknown) 'The writing process'. Available at: http://faculty.uoit.ca/ hughes/Writing/TheWritingProcess.gif (accessed 4 May 2015).

Lambirth, A. (2005) *Reflective Reader: Primary English*. Exeter: Learning Matters.

Primary National Strategy (2006) *The Learning Environment as a Tool for Learning*. London. Department for Education and Skills (DfES).

Waugh, D., Neaum, S., and Waugh, R. (2013) *Children's Literature in Primary Schools*. London: Sage.

Reading into writing

Key Stage 2 Fiction

7

Learning outcomes

By reading this chapter, you will have:

- Considered the importance of creative approaches to transcription and composition
- Considered the importance of assessing the process of writing as well as the product
- Seen the importance of the role of talk in the writing process
- Seen how the use of film and multi-modal literacy can engage learners and develop literacy knowledge, skills and understanding

National Curriculum links

From Lower and Upper Key Stage 2 Reading

Pupils should be taught to understand what they read, in books they can read independently, by:

- checking that the text makes sense to them, discussing their understanding and explaining the meaning of words in context
- asking questions to improve their understanding of a text

- drawing inferences such as inferring characters' feelings, thoughts and motives from their actions, and justifying inferences with evidence
- predicting what might happen from details stated and implied
- identifying main ideas drawn from more than one paragraph and summarising these
- identifying how language, structure, and presentation contribute to meaning

In addition, from Lower and Upper Key Stage 2 Writing

Pupils should be taught to plan their writing by:

- identifying the audience for and purpose of the writing, selecting the appropriate form and using other similar writing as models for their own
- noting and developing initial ideas, drawing on reading and research where necessary
- in writing narratives, considering how authors have developed characters and settings in what pupils have read, listened to or seen performed

draft and write by:

- electing appropriate grammar and vocabulary, understanding how such choices can change and enhance meaning
- in narratives, describing settings, characters and atmosphere and integrating dialogue to convey character and advance the action
- using a wide range of devices to build cohesion within and across paragraphs

evaluate and edit by:

- assessing the effectiveness of their own and others' writing
- proposing changes to vocabulary, grammar and punctuation to enhance effects and clarify meaning
- ensuring the consistent and correct use of tense throughout a piece of writing

DfE (2013)

Chapter overview

This chapter draws on the 2013 National Curriculum and exemplifies ideas in context from the 'Creative approaches to ...' chapters. It also builds on approaches put forward in the previous chapter. This chapter will focus on moving through some of the higher-level demands of the National Curriculum at Key Stage 2 and consider creative approaches to achieve them. It will also focus on the importance of language use, embedding more sophisticated grammatical structures and how guided work can facilitate that effectively. The chapter will consider specific techniques such as de Bono's *Six Thinking Hats* (first introduced in Chapter 4) and how considering different perspectives develops the writer's viewpoint. The chapter will also consider an approach to integrated planning and present two case studies, using as a stimulus *How to Train your Dragon* by Cressida Cowell (2003) as a modern text for Lower Key Stage 2 and *The Hobbit* by J.R.R. Tolkien (1937) for Upper Key Stage 2. As part of the planning process in this case study, formative assessment and record-keeping will be addressed. This will provide some questions and reflective activity for students and teachers to explore. There will also be consideration of digital literacy and how film can be a vehicle for promoting higher-order reading skills. A list of recommended texts will be given at the end of this chapter, with ideas on how to use them (Appendix 7.1).

Being creative with Cressida Cowell

My aim for this section is that whilst exploring Cressida Cowell's expressive, captivating and hilarious text, *How to Train your Dragon*, you will be able to transfer the approaches and ideas across to other texts which you may prefer to use or feel more drawn to. At the end of this chapter, you will find a table (Appendix 7.1) with other great texts and ways in which you may wish to take ideas from this chapter forward. This is, of course, by no means exhaustive.

Figure 7.1. below provides possible 'planning stages' for how you can approach working with this text and/or any others. The cautionary note is that it is for Class X, so if you wish to use it, please adapt it for the learning needs of your own class and your own ways of working.

Creating a new chapter for a text does a number of things. It allows creativity within parameters, which is important. If children are purely left to their own devices, they will usually default to ideas they already know and which are familiar to them, but give them parameters within which to work and more innovative ideas become necessary. With set materials to work with, you are forced to think about using them differently. It also means that children pick up on the author's intent and it allows them to become part of it as they become the author and have to get into the author's mind,

Objectives (*From Lower KS2 English NC*)	Outcome
Predicting what might happen from details stated and implied	To create an additional chapter for the book that adds an adventure for one of the main characters
Identifying main ideas drawn from more than one paragraph and summarising these	**Stimulus text**
Identifying how language, structure, and presentation contribute to meaning	*How to Train your Dragon* by Cressida Cowell
Composing and rehearsing sentences orally	
Organising paragraphs around a theme	
In narratives, describing settings, characters and atmosphere and integrating dialogue to convey character and advance the action	
Evaluate and edit by:	
• assessing the effectiveness of their own and others' writing and suggesting improvements • proposing changes to grammar and vocabulary to improve consistency • proof-read for spelling and punctuation errors	
Shared Learning and Teaching Stages	**Independent Work Stages**
Read and respond to the text Explore the story, the issues for the characters. How the characters respond and the setting. Look at audience and purpose and explore the language used for dialogue and also narration. Explore form and style	Respond to the characters by rating them in terms of 'brave' or 'cowardly', 'quiet' or 'noisy', etc. on a Likert scale. Give evidence. Add your own criteria. Explore dialogue through drama activities and how you might replicate voices using the written word. Explore setting, create guides for the Isle of Berk?
Ideas and planning Possibility-think where a new chapter might be needed and why. Explore different directions and alternatives. Create new characters if appropriate	Explore scenarios: What would happen if …? Mind-mapping different scenarios and ideas. Create different story structures to work from. Imagine possible new characters and tribes? What is likely? What would fit?
Drafting and editing Explore a variety of sentence structures and devices for authorial intent. Look at the use of simile and metaphor to add complexity. Convey	Use writing partners to work together to create the chapter and use copies of the text as a model for style. Explore different sentence structures and also types of sentences. Consider the impact of paragraphing and cliffhangers. In guided work, focus on maintaining authorial intent

Figure 7.1   Possible plan for working with *How to Train your Dragon*

looking for clues in the text to help them see what the author is trying to achieve. It also provides a sense of purpose and a real audience. Why not publish the additional chapter and have a display of several copies of the text in the school entrance or the library for children to read. Or why not create your own 'The Bits Cressida Cowell Didn't Write' book as a new text for the library or class reader. Perhaps send the new chapters to the author herself, with a suggestion to publish.

Responding to texts: exploring character

One of the ways I have suggested responding to the text within the context of this book is by exploring the characters. There are a number of ways to do this. However, one that I have found most effective is by rating the characters using a Likert scale. I originally came across this idea through First Steps, and a copy of their *Writing Resource Book* can be found on the Department of Education Western Australia website (DoE WA, 2013). A version that I have developed called 'Character Rating Scale' can be seen in (Figure 7.2). This allows children to respond to what they think and to

Character name:						
	Strongly agree	Agree	Don't know	Agree	Strongly agree	
Strong						**Weak**
Evidence (from any source)						
Loud						**Quiet**
Evidence (from any source)						
Confident						**Unsure**
Evidence (from any source)						
Peaceful						**Likes conflict**
Evidence (from any source)						
Adventurous						**Boring**
Evidence (from any source)						
Evidence (from any source)						
Evidence (from any source)						

Figure 7.2   Character rating scale

Note: The last two criteria boxes are left blank for you to add your own

reason with others and provide evidence, which may come from the text, a film version or even some role-play that others in the class have put together. It means that children explore and enquire and look at the character's attributes, beyond what they look like.

Creative approaches and improving writing performance

Using all of the creative ideas in Figure 7.1 will not automatically improve writing performance. Children do not learn writing conventions by osmosis and do need some direct input and teaching of those conventions. Graham et al. (2004) discuss the importance of teaching genre-specific strategies to help learners with some of the key features of writing conventions. Their paper focuses on older children and students, but the principles, I believe, are the same. Children will not automatically make connections, we as teachers must do that for them. Wyse et al. cite a study by Andrews et al. (2004) that stated that: 'pupils need to learn to control language as one part of learning to write' (Wyse et al., 2013: 259). This is supported by the work of Myhill et al. (2012), whose findings included that where grammar teaching was set within meaningful contexts, and connections made between what the grammatical convention is and what it is for did lead to a greater quality of writing. Myhill et al. (2013) add that where grammar input is completely linked to the demands of the writing being facilitated, is where it is most effective. Therefore, input is important as are how and where it takes place.

Creative approaches to transcription

Appendix 2 to the National Curriculum for Year 3 demands this:

> Expressing time, place and cause using **conjunctions** [for example, *when, before, after, while, so, because*], **adverbs** [for example, *then, next, soon, therefore*], or **prepositions** [for example, *before, after, during, in, because of*]. (National Curriculum for English, DfE, 2013 Appendix 2: 66)

First, children need to understand why this is important. The main reason is that it gives more information and helps set context for the reader. Children can understand this through a creative technique called 'problem-solving'. Starko (2010) suggests that this is great for applying and extending content knowledge. Therefore, once the concepts of conjunctions, adverbs and prepositions have been taught through input around purpose (I like to call these 'writing tools for the writer's toolbox'), we can then extend thinking. So, perhaps have some pictures of objects or actual objects from the text *How to Train your Dragon* and the children have to create some possibilities around where it was found, when it was found and why it was found. This allows them to explore conjunctions, adverbs and prepositions. Perhaps step up the challenge by asking the children to see how many different places they can put these words in their sentences so that they still make sense. Then read the various sentences to each other and derive some generalisations about the use of these language devices. Waugh et al. remind us that: 'Teaching grammar can involve investigation, problem-solving and language play as part of developing children's awareness and interest in how language works' (2013: 19).

Appendix 2 to the National Curriculum for Year 4 demands this:

> Noun phrases expanded by the addition of modifying adjectives, nouns and preposition phrases (e.g. the teacher expanded to: the strict maths teacher with curly hair). (National Curriculum for English, DfE, 2013, Appendix 2: 67)

Let's look again at why expanding noun phrases is important for improving writing. The author would use this to give more information about a specific character and tell us more about them and perhaps leave us wondering why that detail is important. In the above example from the National Curriculum, I am wondering what is significant about the curly hair. Why has the writer included that detail? An example of how this could be taught, applied and developed is given in the case study below.

Case study

Andrew and his Year 4 class had been reading *Bill's New Frock* by Anne Fine. This is a wonderful story that explores gender issues and friendship on a number of levels, as well as prejudice and conflict resolution. Andrew had asked his class to explore some of the key scenes through freeze-framing and then predict a following chapter through the use of forum theatre. After that, Andrew planned a story with his class, one that raised an issue that was pertinent to the children. It had to be set somewhere familiar to them. One of the key aspects of the writing that

(Continued)

(Continued)

Andrew was working on with his class was not giving too much away but giving clues for the reader to make them want to read on and find out more about the characters and create pictures of them in their heads. Andrew's focus on this particular day was expanded noun phrases. He started by explaining that they were going to play a game called 'Guess what's in my head'. He displayed a noun phrase, 'the father'. 'What's in my head?' said Andrew. The children didn't say much because there was not much to go on. Andrew then displayed a slightly expanded version, 'The tired father'. 'What's in my head?' Andrew asked. This time, the class asked questions around why the father was tired? Did he have a job? A new baby? Worked very hard? Was he ill?

Just by expanding the noun phrase, a number of messages could be conveyed. Finally, Andrew expanded it further 'The angry father with cold eyes'. The children's responses swung from compassion to thinking that he was the villain. Andrew went on to explain the power of language to create pictures and also to change the reader's mind with a couple of words. He then set the class the challenge of doing the same as he had done, in small groups using cards on which were initial noun phrases.

Reflecting on the case study

- Consider how Andrew's approach cemented the children's understanding of the purpose and effect of expanding noun phrases.
- Consider how Andrew handed the learning over to the children so that they could uncover it for themselves. What impact did this have?
- Consider how this approach developed the children's understanding of authorial intent.

Exploring film literacy: *How to Train your Dragon*

With the DreamWorks film version of *How to Train your Dragon* (2010) and *How to Train your Dragon 2* (2014), it is important to discuss the role of film in developing children's literacy knowledge, skills and understanding. Wileman (1993), cited by Stokes (2014), defines visual literacy as 'the ability to "read", interpret, and understand information presented in pictorial or graphic images. In other words, being able to read the pictures and what they convey to the reader. The British Film Industry's document *Reframing Literacy*, states that: 'Literacy is not just about the written word' (2007: 4). This is, of course, a recognition of the digital culture of the twenty-first century, with multimodality being a crucial way in which children see and process information. *Reframing Literacy* goes on to add:

> Long before they learn to read, they can readily answer questions about films like 'can you tell what is going to happen next?' and 'how can you tell?'. These questions develop their ability to infer and predict: essential skills in the reading of any kind of text. (2007: 10)

So, children coming to this unit of work on *How to Train your Dragon* may have seen both films and also interacted with the website (at: www.how totrainyourdragon.co.uk/) where they may already have interacted with the Isle of Berk and the characters, and understood a lot of what is going on in the stories. However, the films are quite different to the books, so care is needed. Often, films can be used as a stimulus for writing, but Bearne and Wolstencraft (2007) suggest other uses. They suggest using frames to pace the narrative and select key moments. This helps to plan the story. Using Interactive Whiteboard Technology, it is possible to do screen grabs for key sections of the story. Bearne and Wolstencraft go on to state that this technique can help children see how to increase narrative tension.

Using film is a helpful tool for understanding narrative structure, plot development and character development, and it can be helpful for children to see how film-makers represent characters, manipulate plot and why sometimes the book is so different from the film. Using film also allows children to engage with narrative structure in a way which means that they are not hampered by the black squiggles we call 'words'.

Waugh et al. remind us that, whatever mode of language they explore:

> All children need to know that reading, writing, speaking and listening are powerful ... They need to experience the pleasure that having a voice brings, and the opportunities that it offers ... Meaning has to be at the heart of all teaching of literacy. (2013: 21)

Into Upper Key Stage 2

Chapter 6 focused more on the aspect of responding to text in writing fiction and the earlier part of this chapter gave more space to transcription, so the remaining part of this chapter will focus on creative and effective ways of composing, drafting text and editing. The context for this is a plan

Objectives (*From Upper KS2 English NC*)	Outcome
Discuss and evaluate how authors use language, including figurative language, considering the impact on the reader In writing narratives, considering how authors have developed characters and settings in what pupils have read, listened to or seen performed Draft and write by: • selecting appropriate grammar and vocabulary, understanding how such choices can change and enhance meaning • describing settings, characters and atmosphere and integrating dialogue to convey character and advance the action • using relative clauses beginning with who, which, where, when, whose, that or with an implied (i.e. omitted) relative pronoun	Creating a multi-modal text (graphic novel) version of *The Hobbit* as a class for a younger reader **Stimulus text** *The Hobbit* by J.R.R. Tolkien
Shared Learning and Teaching Stages	**Independent Work Stages**
Read and respond to the text (Text has been/is being read over the half-term), alongside watching extracts from all three films. Children explore the notions of a fantasy world, the characters, setting, fantasy genre expectations, language, tone and style	Using the map from the book, create electronic fact-files (almost social media profiles) on each place. Focus on the structure as a journey and plot narrative structure, perhaps using freeze-framing and screen-grab from film scenes to help with the graphic novel structure. Divide story up into six parts, one per group
Ideas and planning Using screen grabs from film, model the use of dialogue to convey character and advance action. Use models from text for the language style and also the way in which Tolkien does the above. Focus on narration: show graphic novel style, model use of relative clauses	Children use screen grabs to add speech and thought bubbles, using effective dialogue that advances the action in the story and conveys motivation. Discuss scene setting and narration to add at the side of each picture. Narration sections, plan content
Drafting and editing Model style and use graphic novel examples to provide support Once drafted, check against style and model how to edit and check for story cohesion. Whole class edit	Children compose narration, checking against Tolkien style. Continue to compose speech, ensuring character is represented and also action is furthered using dialogue. Use oral rehearsal and oral editing in pairs to ensure desired authorial effect is created. Whole class edit for cohesion and consistency

Figure 7.3 Possible plan for working with *The Hobbit*

for using *The Hobbit* by J.R.R. Tolkien, alongside Peter Jackson's *Hobbit* trilogy of films from 2012, 2013 and 2014, respectively. As with Chapter 6 and the earlier part of this chapter, my aim is that you will be able to transfer the approaches and ideas across to other texts which you may prefer to use or feel more drawn to.

Figure 7.3 provides, once again, possible 'planning stages' for how you could approach working with this text and/or any others.

Composing text in creative ways

You will notice from figure 7.3 that the outcome here is to produce a multi-modal text in the form of a graphic novel version of *The Hobbit*. Annmaree O'Brien presents some helpful advice through her blogs and web resources to support the process here. She does stress that the ways in which children need to think about literacy is different and, actually, the process is very complex but does provide a lot of motivation and reward. One of the main reasons for multi-modal texts is that there can be a much stronger focus on the quality of language used without the worry of writing masses of quantity. A blank page is a highly daunting and sometimes demoralising prospect for an adult, let alone a child. So, a graphic novel, for example, as I have suggested in Figure 7.3, allows focus on not having to write the whole story but instead for focus on the quality of dialogue and key information for narration. At Upper Key Stage 2, where the curriculum demands character and plot development through dialogue, this acts as a perfect tool. Asking children to develop this in groups is also important. Bearne and Wolstencroft state that:

> A group of children composing on screen can readily amend work, so that composition benefits from collaborative support and the facilities of a computer. All of this experience forges strong examples of how an individual can gain satisfaction from crafting a piece of writing until it does the job the author intended it to do. (2007: 3)

In terms of creative approaches, we are talking here about the process of writing. In earlier chapters, I stated how important the process of learning is and that children should see the value of that. So, although the end product of a class graphic novel is the outcome, the main learning takes place through the process. In Chapter 6, I exemplified the writing process, focusing not only on the generic process but also on what children are engaging in and how the teacher is supporting them. The compositional process itself can be broken down into stages and these stages, Cremin (2009) reminds us, are very much like how creative thinking might be conceptualised. The process involves planning, where ideas are brought forward and captured. There is then a phase of translating and into drafting, where those ideas are translated into the appropriate genre features and shaped into text, and then evaluating or reviewing where the piece may be subject to alteration. This process, Cremin (ibid.) suggests, is very much a problem-solving one. The ideas need to be moulded, shaped, often remoulded and reshaped, so it is a dynamic process, very much like creative thinking where the challenge is identified, suggestions and ideas offered and then translated into the most workable solutions. In the context of the plan for *The Hobbit*, we see the idea of creating a graphic novel being very much about problem-solving. Which screen grabs best depict the structure of the story? How will the dialogue further the action? How can we demonstrate which characters have which characteristics through how they speak? Composing a text should be just that: exploring, trying out a range of divergent ideas, working with them, discussing them, putting them against the benchmark of the genre expectations and selecting the most effective ideas for the job, the job being what you are intending as the author.

The role of talk in the compositional process

This section builds on concepts and ideas introduced in Chapter 4. Bereiter and Scardamalia (1987) suggest that talking together at this point in the writing process helps reflection on and refinement of their thinking. They also suggest that it helps writers develop a metalanguage to talk about writing. Children can support one another and the whole business of writing becomes less risky. Aidan Chambers (1995) reminds us that most of us do not know what we are thinking until we hear what we say. This is very truthful and an important fact to keep in mind for the composing process. The very act of speaking out what is in our heads, brings those words into being and gives those thoughts shape, investing them with the power to be a means of communication.

Stop and think

Do you allow children to discuss their writing and compose together, talking out their thoughts? Or, do they have work alone and in silence? What might the impact be on the writing climate in your classroom if you did the former?

Scaffolding

The use of talk is an essential piece of scaffolding in the writing process, but I think that it is important to consider other tools to scaffold writing for children. There is a myth that suggests that creativity is unstructured and placing any structure is robbing children of their opportunity to go and be creative. Craft et al. (2001) in discussing learner-centred creativity suggest that offering patterns for children to use is helpful. However, they do also say that one standardised model which all must conform to is where the scaffolding becomes a straitjacket. It is important to consider what barriers to learning we, as teachers, put up to mitigate against children learning. It might be a blank sheet of paper, the organisation of how learning will take place, resources or lack of, support or lack of, level of challenge of activity. Therefore, supporting children through some of these challenges is important. In the plan for *The Hobbit* in Figure 7.3, the outcome of writing a graphic novel means that pictures can already provide the scaffold, but the children explore and create those themselves. Whatever scaffolding is provided, children should be part of the process of creating it. Talk is also essential at every stage.

Assessing the process of composition

If the learning takes place during the process, then assessment should take place during the process. We could, of course, take each group's section of the graphic novel in once finished and mark it against the key objectives. If we were worried that not everyone was contributing in the group, then we should make sure that everyone did a page of the graphic novel, so we could take it in, mark it and put a tick in our mark-book. This assessment means only that we have ticked off that the children have completed the task, and not necessarily that they have learned what we intended. Therefore, we must assess the learning, not the doing. How do we then do that in this context? Black and Wiliam (1998), cited by Medwell (2011), first of all stated that assessment must be about improving learning. They then suggested five key factors:

- Provision of effective feedback to pupils
- The active involvement of pupils in their own learning
- Adjust teaching to take into account the results of assessment
- A recognition of the profound influence assessment has on the motivation and self-esteem of pupils ...
- The need for pupils to assess themselves and understand how to improve. (Medwell, 2011: 104)

In the context of the plan for *The Hobbit*, it is important to start assessing understanding when the children are in the planning and drafting stage. Guided work (introduced in Chapter 3) is a good tool here, especially as the children are working in groups. Be transparent with the children about what you are looking for so that they can help each other and help them to articulate when they are meeting the objective. The types of questions you will use here are very important. Medwell (2011) suggests some useful question types, for example 'looking back questions' such as 'Why have you got Bilbo saying that?' and 'looking forward questions' such as 'How will you show that this action is coming through what Thorin and Gloin (the dwarves) are saying here?' She also advocates the use of 'thinking out loud' questions such as 'How can you work out what key event is needed next?' Also, use every opportunity to discuss children's work with them. Every learning and teaching opportunity should be an opportunity to find out what the children are learning. Here, Key Stage 2 teachers can learn a lot from Foundation Stage Practitioners, who spend every opportunity making notes to create a child's learning and development journey based on what children are learning. The focus here is on moving the children on in their development and understanding whilst collecting their key moments of success.

Stop and think

What do you do whilst your class is working? Do you patrol the classroom like a tiger pacing their cage? Or do you work with groups? Discuss learning with the children? Get involved in how they are responding to the task?

Now what?

A wonderful reflective model from Rolfe et al. (2001) starts with three questions: 'What?' 'So what?' 'Now what?' This is a very useful approach to take to the process of learning, teaching and assessment. The teaching and activity is the 'what'. The assessment is the 'so what … does this mean in terms of learning and attainment'. But, there has to be a 'now what'. What will I do as a result of the new information I have?

What do I do if I discover that not all groups are ready to move on to the drafting phase? What happens if one of my groups manages the dialogue to indicate action within five minutes? What happens if other groups just don't get it?

You will only know this and be able to plan alternative approaches such as additional guided work or more cognitively challenging extension activities if you are working with them, discussing, giving feedback, using mini-plenaries to provide 'What A Good One Looks Like' (WAGOLL) or provide whatever is needed to enhance the children's learning.

A further word on film literacy

Looking at Figure 7.3, the use of the *Hobbit* films is integral to the unit of work through using screen grabs. However, as mentioned earlier in the chapter, using film can be helpful for developing children's understanding of narrative structure and authorial intent. One such activity is called 'zone of relevance'. It is widely used but the case study below explores how it can be effective for developing understanding of the atmosphere which a film-maker is trying to create. Alongside it, the activity can be used to compare the author's original version.

Case study

Milena is working with her Year 6 class on the classic Frances Hodgson Burnett story, *The Secret Garden* (1910 [1911]). Alongside this they are watching the film version, created in 1993, written by Caroline Thompson and directed by Agnieszka Holland. The children are working in groups and as they watch an extract from *The Secret Garden*, they are sorting describing words into the categories of: 'very relevant', 'quite relevant', 'partially relevant' and 'not relevant'. They also have other cards to add their own words. After watching the extract, the children discuss with each other and then place their cards on the zone of relevance board, shown in Figure 7.4.

These are then displayed for the children to come back to later on. Milena then reads the same extract from Burnett's novel. The children use a further zone of relevance board with the same words. After some discussion, the words are placed on the board. The children are then encouraged to compare their responses from the book and the film and they are found to be quite different. This prompts Milena to start a discussion with the children about what the film-maker was trying to achieve and how they have interpreted Burnett's words on the page.

(Continued)

(Continued)

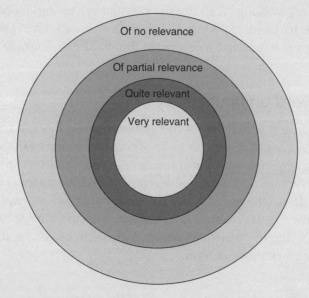

Figure 7.4   Zone of relevance board

Milena follows this up by considering the nature of interpretation before the children embark on using texts to inspire their own mini-films.

Reflecting on the case study

- Consider how the zone of relevance activity supported children's response to text and scaffolded their understanding of authorial intent.
- Consider how the comparison between the book and the film encouraged children to see different interpretations of the written word.

Try this

Activity 1: Zone of relevance

Give the children a variety of words on cards and, as they read a text, read a graphic novel, or watch a film extract, get them to decide which words are 'very relevant', etc. to describe the scene. Explore the notion of authorial intent. Try the activity for a number of scenes. How do the positions of the words on the zone of relevance board change?

Activity 2: Creating a multi-modal text

Multi-modal texts are simply texts that combine words, pictures, media, graphics, music. Have a go at planning a unit of work where the outcome is a multi-modal text. Children may create a graphic novel, as in Figure 7.3, a video story or photo story. Take note of the learning that children engage in during the creation process.

Activity 3: Assess work at the composing phase

When you are next doing some composition work with the children, make sure that you use the time when they are composing to discuss their work with them. Make notes on their progress against the outcomes. You may discover more than you thought. Assess the process and it makes the assessment of the product less time-consuming and more meaningful.

Summary

J.R.R. Tolkien's text, *The Hobbit*, provides a wonderful opportunity to explore children composing text in a variety of ways. Here, I have chosen to look at graphic novels using screen grabs from the film version to act as a scaffold and support. This allows children's learning to focus on the quality of the language they are using, rather than the quantity. The use of talk and group work as a scaffold removes some of the risk from the writing process and, also, along with the structure given by screen grabs, the risky business of the blank page. All the support is in place for the children just to focus on the quality of language needed as the National Curriculum objectives for Upper Key Stage 2 dictate, in terms of dialogue to demonstrate character development and also signpost action. During this process, we, as teachers, should be active in discussing children's work with them, asking them the type of questions that Medwell (2011) suggests earlier in the chapter. This assessment of the process of learning is crucial as it provides information on what children have actually learned and understood, not just on what they have completed. Finally, exploring literacy as not just the words on the page but the images, music, colour and scenery perspectives from the film can also help children see how the written word can be interpreted for different reasons and how directors, as well as authors, can manipulate language for their own intent and purposes.

Appendix 7.1 Other good texts for Key Stage 2 and creative opportunities

This is by no means exhaustive.

Text and author	Creative opportunities
Lower Key Stage 2	
Double Act by Jacqueline Wilson	Divergent thinking opportunities for how these identical twins can carry on when it all gets a bit tricky
The Vicar of Nibbleswicke by Roald Dahl	Find a cure for the Reverend Lee's back-to-front dyslexia
The War of Jenkins' Ear by Michael Morpurgo	Lots of problems to solve in many different contexts for all the main characters
Gangsta Granny by David Walliams	What new adventures can Ben and his Granny get up to?
You're a Bad Man, Mr Gum by Andy Stanton	Lots of 'what would happen if …' opportunities in this story
Upper Key Stage 2	
The Wish List by Eoin Colfer	Help Meg complete her tasks? Create innovative ways for her to win through
The Last Wolf by Michael Morpurgo	What happens if Grandpa's attempt to explore his family tree doesn't go to plan?
The Thieves of Ostia by Caroline Lawrence	Help the four friends solve the mystery of the Thieves of Ostia
Eragon by Christopher Paolini	Create some new adventures for Eragon. What would happen if …?
Harry Potter and the Half-Blood Prince by J.K. Rowling	Help Harry complete the death-defying tasks. Can you create a way that he can succeed?
Dragon Rider by Cornelia Funke	Change the adventure for Firedrake the dragon. What possibilities can you create?
The Invention of Hugo Cabret by Brian Selznick	Create some dialogue and narrations for the wonderful illustrations
Warhorse by Michael Morpurgo	How can Albert ever find Joey again? Help?
The Machine Gunners by Robert Westall	Chas McGill finds himself in a bit of trouble. What should he do?
I am David by Anne Holm	How will David get all the way across Europe? What adventures could he have?

Text and author	Creative opportunities
Mortal Engines by Philip Reeve	Create something for Tom Natsworthy to help face the most terrifying weapon ever
Noughts and Crosses by Malorie Blackman	Help Callum and Sephy find a way to be together, despite significant cultural differences and much hostility

Further reading

Bearne, E. and Wolstencroft, H. (2007) *Visual Approaches to Teaching Writing*. London: Paul Chapman, Sage.

This really helpful text provides lots of ideas for creating and working with multi-modal texts. Packed with practical examples as well as theoretical perspectives, it supports multi-modal work in fiction, non-fiction and poetry.

Brien, J. (2012) 'Assessment and targeting in English', in *Teaching Primary English*. London: Sage.

This excellent chapter from Jackie Brien gets to grips with the fact that assessment is integral to teaching, not just an add-on. There is clear consideration of assessing the writing process, not just the end product, which is very helpful.

Waugh, D., Neaum, S. and Waugh, R. (2013) *Children's Literacy in Primary Schools*. London: Learning Matters, Sage.

This very interesting book is a real motivator to use quality literature with children. The writers' journey through a variety of genres, providing research foci, case studies and practical ideas for using a whole range of fiction. It starts with younger children and goes all the way through to classic fiction, fantasy fiction and everyday fiction.

References

Andrews, R., Torgerson, C., Beverton, S., Locke, T., Low, G., Robinson, A. and Zhu, D. (2004) 'The effect of grammar teaching (syntax) in English on 5-to-16-year-olds' accuracy and quality in written composition', *Research Evidence in Education Library*. Available at: http://eppi.ioe.ac.uk/cms/ (accessed 16 May 2015).

Bearne, E. and Wolstencroft, H. (2007) *Visual Approaches to Teaching Writing*. London: Paul Chapman, Sage.

Bereiter, C. and Scardamalia, M. (1987) *The Psychology of Written Communication*. Hillsdale, NJ: Lawrence Erlbaum.

Black, P. and Wiliam, D. (1998) *Inside the Black Box: Raising Standards through Classroom Assessment*. London: (National Foundation for Educational Research) NFER Nelson.

British Film Institute (BFI) (2007) *Reframing Literacy*. Available at: www.bfi.org.uk/sites/bfi.org.uk/files/downloads/bfi-education-reframing-literacy-2013-04.pdf (accessed 16 May 2015).

Burnett, F.H. (1910 [1911]) *The Secret Garden*. London: Heinemann.

Chambers, A. (1995) *Tell Me: Children, Reading, and Talk*. London: Stenhouse Publishers.

Cowell, C. (2003) *How to Train your Dragon*. London: Hodder Children's Books.

Craft, A., Jeffrey, B. and Liebling, M. (2001) *Creativity in Education*. London: Continuum.

Cremin, T. (2009) *Teaching English Creatively*. Oxford: Routledge.

Department for Education (DfE) (2013). *The National Curriculum for England, Key Stages 1 and 2*. London. Crown Copyright.

Department of Education (Western Australia) (DoE WA) (2013) *Writing Resource Book: Addressing Current Literacy Challenges*. Government of Western Australia. Available at: http://det.wa.edu.au/stepsresources/detcms/education/stepsre-sources/first-steps-literacy/writing-resource-book.en?oid=com.arsdigita.cms.contenttypes.FileStorageItem-id-13760408 (accessed 2 June 2015).

Graham, S., Harris, K. and Mason, L. (2004) 'Improving the writing performance, knowledge, and self-efficacy of struggling young writers: The effects of self-regulated strategy development', *Contemporary Educational Psychology*, 30 (2): 207–41.

Medwell, J. (2011) 'An introduction to assessing English', in R. Cox (ed.), *Primary English Teaching*. London: Sage and United Kingdom Literacy Association (UKLA).

Myhill, D., Jones, S., Lines, H. and Watson, A. (2012) 'Re-thinking grammar: The impact of embedded grammar teaching on students' writing and students' metalinguistic understanding', *Research Papers in Education*, 27 (2): 139–66.

Myhill, D., Jones, S., Watson, A. and Lines, H. (2013) 'Playful explicitness with grammar: A pedagogy for writing', *Literacy*, 47 (2): 103–11.

O'Brien, A. (2011–15) 'Creating multimodal texts', Blog. Available at: http://creatingmultimodaltexts.com/ (accessed 10 June 2015).

Pullman, P. (1995) *The Northern Lights*. London: Scholastic.

Rolfe, G., Freshwater, D. and Jasper, M. (2001) *Critical Reflection in Nursing and the Helping Professions: A User's Guide*. Basingstoke: Palgrave Macmillan.

Starko, A. (2010) *Creativity in the Classroom*, 4th edn. Oxford: Routledge.

Stokes, S. (2014) 'Visual literacy in teaching and learning: A literature perspective'. Available at: www.k12photoed.org/wpcontent/uploads/2014/03/Visual_Literacy_stokes.pdf (accessed 10 June 2015).

Tolkien, J.R.R. (1937) *The Hobbit*. London: George, Allen and Unwin.

Waugh, D., Warner, C. and Waugh, R. (2013) *Teaching Grammar, Punctuation and Spelling in Primary Schools*. London: Learning Matters, Sage.

Wileman, R.E. (1993) *Visual Communicating*. Englewood Cliffs, NJ: Educational Technology Publications.

Wyse, D., Jones, R., Bradford, H. and Wolpert, M. (2013) *Teaching English, Language and Literacy*, 3rd edn. Oxford: Routledge.

8

Reading into writing

Key Stage 1 Non-fiction

Learning outcomes

By reading this chapter, you will have:

- Developed an understanding of effective learning and teaching of non-fiction texts
- Developed an understanding of how using non-fiction connects with learning in other subjects
- Developed an understanding of how digital literacy can enhance and develop learning in this area
- Developed an understanding of the contribution of guided writing to developing children's understanding of form

---

National Curriculum links

From Key Stage 1 Year 1

Pupils should be taught to:

develop pleasure in reading, motivation to read, vocabulary and understanding by:

- listening to and discussing a wide range of poems, stories and non-fiction at a level beyond that at which they can read independently
- being encouraged to link what they read or hear read to their own experiences

Listening to and discussing information books and other non-fiction establishes the foundations for their learning in other subjects. Pupils should be shown some of the processes for finding out information.

Pupils should be taught to:
  write sentences by:

- saying out loud what they are going to write about
- composing a sentence orally before writing it
- re-reading what they have written to check that it makes sense
- discuss what they have written with the teacher or other pupils

In addition, from Key Stage 1 Year 2

develop pleasure in reading, motivation to read, vocabulary and understanding by:

- being introduced to non-fiction books that are structured in different ways

  make simple additions, revisions and corrections to their own writing by:

- evaluating their writing with the teacher and other pupils
- re-reading to check that their writing makes sense and that verbs to indicate time are used correctly and consistently, including verbs in the continuous form

  learn how to use:

- sentences with different forms: statement, question, exclamation, command

DfE (2013)

Chapter overview

This chapter explores the key concepts, ideas and learning that children in Key Stage 1 need to develop within non-fiction. The chapter draws on the 2013 National Curriculum and exemplifies ideas in context from the 'Creative approaches to …' chapters, specifically with regard to reading skills, scaffolding the writing process and creative ways to present non-fiction texts that make them relevant, meaningful and purposeful for the children to engage in. The focus will also be on the writer's knowledge for non-fiction genres but will have reports as its focus case study. The chapter will also return to key techniques such as shared and guided writing and how they can be used in the transcription process to develop understanding and usage of the text type. As part of the planning process in this case study, formative assessment and record-keeping will be addressed. A list of recommended alternative texts will be given in Appendix 8.1 at the end of this chapter, with ideas on how to use them.

Introduction

Often, student teachers, when sharing with me what units of study they have to plan for English on placement, will contort their faces as they give the title of a non-fiction unit. 'How will I do instructions for two weeks?' or 'Why did they give me non-chronological reports to do, they are so boring?' I will also often be asked how it is possible to be creative with non-fiction. The fact is that non-fiction provides possibly the most relevant collection of texts to study and the most important for children to understand as it is one they will meet throughout their lives. Children will meet instructions, they may read reports, persuasive letters, take part in discussion and have to justify opinion as they move through their various stages in life. One of the first things for children – and for student teachers – to know and understand is that non-fiction has various forms. Table 8.1 gives an overview of these forms, what their purpose is and some key points.

Table 8.1 Non-fiction forms, purpose and key points

Form	Purpose	Key points
Recount	To retell an event in a way that engages the reader	Chronological order Opening paragraph to hook the reader Past tense Connectives that signal time

(Continued)

Table 8.1   (Continued)

Form	Purpose	Key points
Instructions	To tell the reader how to do something in a clear way	List of what is needed and steps in chronological order
		Diagrams
		Connectives to organise steps (temporal connectives)
		Use of imperatives
		Subject specific vocabulary
Non-chronological report	To tell the reader about a topic describing the main features in a way that engages the reader	Information organised logically using headings, subheadings
		Present tense and third person
		Formal tone
explanation	To aid understanding of a process or why something occurred	Logical steps that provide cohesive explanation
		Diagrams often used to illustrate steps
		Formal tone, present tense, connectives that link points
		Specific vocabulary
persuasion	To promote a product or a particular viewpoint to influence the reader to buy in to your viewpoint or product	Logical sequence
		Points that build to a main viewpoint
		Emotive language
		Opinions presented as fact
		Other language features such as statistics, quotations
discussion	To present an issue in a balanced way giving for and against	Opening context
		Paragraphs that outline key aspects of the argument in terms of for and against
		Ends with a summary conclusion
		Connectives that order viewpoints and help introduce other viewpoints

Non-fiction reading at Key Stage 1: Creative approaches

What skills do children need in order to be able to read non-fiction and are they any different to those needed for fiction and poetry? Lewis and Wray's (1997) study on children's approaches to non-fiction affirmed that the skills were very different and, more importantly, that children needed to know and understand the differences in how they should approach fiction and non-fiction. They suggested that reading for non-fiction should be taught with care, otherwise children will approach them as they would fiction because they come across these much more frequently. Lewis and Wray (ibid.) suggest four key skills children need to have and these are cited by Brien:

- Frame questions before reading
- Know how to locate the necessary information as quickly as possible

- Know how to distinguish between fact, opinion and persuasion
- Know how to discover the authority of the writer. (2012: 47)

How can we teach these creatively and in a way that children will be engaged? One of the key points is to use material that children are interested in? Perhaps you are exploring the influence of historic characters on Great Britain in your topic work and you decide to use some of Terry Deary's *Horrible Histories* texts for children to explore. The first thing is not even to open the books but to think about two crucial questions. These are suggested by Wray:

- What do I already know about this topic?
- What do I want to know about it? (2006: 30)

Wray goes on to suggest that children's understanding is built on schemas (structures of knowledge that already exist) in their minds. For us, as experienced and expert readers, the title and cover illustration automatically ignite our schemas and information that we already have stored is sent to our minds ready for us to come to the text. Less expert readers or less experienced readers will need support to activate their schemas in order to be able to access the text more effectively. This requires what Desailly (2012) suggests are two key skills of the creative teacher: facilitation and questioning. Facilitation, in this context, is supporting the reader to explore the *Horrible Histories* text and these two skills often go hand in hand as questioning the reader could support them to use headings, subheadings and cartoons to lead them to the information needed. Why this approach? Children will be engaged because it is what they want to find out and they have a reason for looking at the text. This, of course, as Desailly states: 'establishes a questioning and enquiring culture in the classroom' (2012: 97).

Children also need to be taught how to find information as quickly as possible. Some key aspects of non-fiction texts that help this are headings, subheadings, diagrams, contents pages and indexes. Helping children to use these text features effectively and know to turn to them is crucial. Drawing on how these tools are used on web-based non-fiction texts is also important. Encouraging children to set each other challenges using these tools is a good way to get them experimenting: 'On which page would you find …?' Perhaps even creating a simple board game for children to explore these tools: throw the dice and where they land is a challenge that is then checked. Desailly (2012) states the importance of giving children more autonomy over their learning by giving them more choices as to how to do a task, and the above gives a perfect example.

However, dealing with fact, opinion and the authority of the writer is quite a challenge at Key Stage 1. Soalt (2005), cited in Cremin (2009), suggests that linking it to fiction is helpful so that children can understand that facts are not neutral. For example, a non-fiction text on the Second World War could be linked to Shirley Hughes's (1998) emotive text about evacuation called *The Lion and the Unicorn*. Children could ask questions about each text and see how the other text corroborates information, or if alternatives are provided. This would allow children to see which authors could be relied upon and what the purpose of each text is. Hughes's priority is to create an emotive and evocative story, whereas the non-fiction is to convey the facts and use evidence to support this.

Reading into writing

Reading is often a precursor to writing in a unit of work and, alongside, talk acts as a clear scaffold for producing a piece of text. The case study below explores this idea, using non-chronological reports with a Year 1 class after a class trip to a museum.

Case study: Part 1

Melissa and her Year 1 class are spending a half-term looking at a local history topic: exploring their city, how it has changed over time and who some of the main characters were in making those changes happen. Melissa has decided that her class will create a documentary about the city to be published on the school website. They will also produce some local guidebooks to be displayed in the school's foyer and then use the text to accompany the documentary online. Melissa is aware that this will be very challenging but prior to the half-term holiday, she broached it with the children for them to share in the planning. They were very excited and have come back with lots of questions and areas of enquiry to explore. Whilst a number of the children did go and explore some of the city's historic sites and museums during the holiday, not all did, so Melissa began her unit with a trip to one of the city's historic houses that is also a museum. The children had the opportunity to go behind the scenes in the historic house, learn about and carry out some of the servants' duties and find out more about who lived there and the contribution the owner and his family made to the city.

Now back in class, the children work together to remember all the things that they have experienced. They use photographs from the trip to help them. Melissa asks them to group their experiences into sections as she prepares them for the idea of a non-chronological report. The children struggle with this as they want to see things in time order. So, Melissa realises that she needs to model it first and suggests a couple of headings: 'What Servants Did' and 'The House's Owners', and the children put sentences and photos into these headings. Together, the children create some more headings such as: 'How to Get There' and 'Things in the House'. In groups, the children write sentences and captions for the photos and organise them into these sections onto large sheets of paper. The final sheets are stuck to the wall to help when writing.

The next day, Melissa provides a variety of non-chronological reports for the children to look at. Initially, the children just look at the texts and explore them – Melissa is keen for them to make connections themselves initially, rather than have analytical tasks to do at this stage. Many of the children comment about headings, like the ones on their posters and how the texts are organised with pictures, like their photos. They start comparing the books and draw out similarities without any intervention from Melissa. The children have begun their understanding of a non-chronological report. They have made a start to the content from their class trip, they have been introduced to purpose and structure from their exploration of text and now they are ready to start creating and shaping text.

Reflecting on the case study (part 1)

- Think about how Melissa has involved the children in the planning and motivated them to be engaged in this project. Notice Melissa's intended outcomes for her unit of work and how she does not shy away from challenge and high expectations.
- Think about the shared experience at the start of the unit of work. Why is this so important?
- How does Melissa scaffold the children's understanding of what a non-chronological report is?
- Why does Melissa let the children just explore the texts to start with? Why not give them some focused tasks and things to find?

The case study above, of course, does not mention the usual cut and thrust of the Year 1 classroom, the challenges, the children for whom there are barriers to learning, the children who for whatever reason do not engage and I have not made mention of all the scaffolding that Melissa made available to the children: word banks, a teaching assistant, sentence openers and the guided work that Melissa and her teaching assistant did as part of this case study. I do hope that it presented a structure and sequence of steps to support effective learning and teaching. I also hope that you can see how a shared experience provided a purposeful context for reading, which in turn provided a strong foundation for writing. It is also important to remember that talk is central at every stage of the process, as talk helps construct learning.

Writing non-fiction

This section will focus on reports following on from the case study but I will draw out key principles that can be applied across other forms of non-fiction writing.

One of the key challenges when writing in a particular non-fiction form is making it true to the form. With the above example, a non-chronological report could easily become a recount if not taught carefully. Children need to understand the audience and purpose of their writing before embarking on it. In the case of reports, the author, as Corbett and Strong state: 'needs to be an expert in the subject otherwise the information will be meagre' (2011: 91). Facilitating children to be experts is very important in terms of creativity, too. Children should want to write. In my experience, children are collectors of information and love to share what they have found out. My youngest daughter enjoys telling me the various statistics of all the Pokemon characters she has found out about and how good at fighting they are. Children I have taught loved to come in with the latest book about sealife, world records and dinosaurs and share with me what they have discovered, delighted to find that they know something I don't. This is the excitement of literacy, exploring the world, finding out about it and telling others. The challenge for teachers is making sure that their non-fiction units of work do the same, blurring the lines between what happens at school and what happens outside. The danger – and the problem lots of teachers face – is where children just copy information. This danger is, of course, much easier to succumb to with the copy-and-paste function on computers. Wray (2006), citing earlier work by Wray and Lewis (1992), states that children know why they shouldn't just copy from information books. He uses the example of eight-year-old Anna, who 'claimed that "you learn a lot more if you write it in your own words". Yet when faced with the activity of finding out from books, most children at some stage resort to copying' (Lewis, 2006: 28). The problem here is the task – information retrieval activities are most common: 'Can you find out about …' as opposed to the more creative task of representing the information in a different way. Whilst being about the activity, it is also about the environment and ethos of the teacher. Craft et al. (2001) state that creativity can be fostered by mental play. Asking children to mentally play with information, mix it up and reformulate it in a different way asks children to manipulate language and structure and develop and extend ideas. It also has the added bonus of helping the teacher assess whether the child really does understand the information. They go on to say, citing the NACCCE report: 'All our futures' that 'creativity can be stimulated by an environment full of ideas, experiences, interesting materials and resources, and in a relaxing atmosphere where unique ideas are encouraged' (NACCCE, 1999: 102, in Craft et al., 2001: 25).

Stop and think

How will you ensure that when reading and writing non-fiction, the tasks you set encourage children to be creative with information and reconstruct it, rather than opting for information retrieval activities that don't necessarily promote understanding?

Writing across the curriculum

The case study of Melissa's non-chronological reports utilises the concept of writing across the curriculum. Writing is a complex business and should transcend subject boundaries, so in the case study earlier in this chapter I have stayed away from subject labels. Melissa's aim was to develop literacy skills through her topic. However, as Brien makes clear: 'care must be taken to ensure that it doesn't overwhelm the lesson or take focus away from the main learning objective' (2012: 89). In this sense, and in Melissa's example, the writing she wanted from the children was not just about obtaining evidence that they had learned about local history from the school trip, but it was also about enhancing learning, writing as learning as opposed to writing as evidence of learning.

Case study: Part 2

Before composing the text, Melissa wanted the children to talk about what they should write first. In order to do this, she arranged for the children, in groups, to create a variety of presentations about one of the headings created. These presentations would be shared with another class in the school. This provided a clear purpose and motivation for what they would do. It also meant that the children had to find out more and reformulate it in a different way. One group used some photos to create a PowerPoint presentation and described everything in the photos using present tense and third person, so no 'we did this' and 'we saw this'. Language prompts and scaffolds were provided. They were then asked questions by the other class to help hone their knowledge and provide other avenues for enquiry to become more of an expert.

Melissa now wants the children to start understanding the language use in a non-chronological report. Her main focus here is to avoid this becoming a recount and already she had assessed during the presentations which children would require support in writing in the present tense and use of third person. Some of the children presented their work as if they were recounting the school trip. Melissa returned the children's attention to the large sheets of paper in sections already created and reacquainted the children with the use of headings. She then started writing a sentence herself – she wrote in two ways: 'We cleaned the silver like the servants did' and then 'The servants used to clean the silver.' They discussed the differences. In pairs, children explored different sentences, like the ones Melissa had modelled, printed on cards and sorted them into 'report' and 'not report' categories, according to which ones they felt were appropriate for a report and which were not. The children then discussed some of the differences and decided on some checklist criteria such as 'Don't use we or I'. Melissa then asked the children to work in writing partners to write effective non-chronological report sentences about some of the photos. The more able children were asked to find more information and extend some of those sentences using 'and' and 'because'. Melissa had chosen a group of six children, identified from the presentations and supported by her ongoing formative assessment during the above work, to support with some guided writing.

Reflecting on the case study (part 2)

- Why did Melissa use this approach of presenting orally to another class before writing? What did it give the children in terms of learning and development? How did it scaffold their learning?
- Notice how Melissa used modelled writing to draw the children's attention to appropriate language features of a non-chronological report. Why did she then ask the children to explore different sentence cards? How did it scaffold their learning?
- Why didn't Melissa just give the children a non-chronological report checklist?
- Notice how Melissa used formative assessment during the case study to identify those children needing support. Notice how she used key parts of whole class teaching to do this. How can you make assessment a key part of your teaching?

The importance of guided writing

Guided writing has already been introduced in Chapter 3. I have deliberately returned to it here and in other chapters as it is important to see the different contexts and purposes for which this useful tool can be utilised. Lan et al. (2011) state the imperative need for teaching writing skills, otherwise motivation decreases in children. One specific tool with which to do this is guided writing. Guided writing is typically a 20-minute session, where the teacher works with a small group of children specifically developing writing skills and processes. It can take place anywhere in the writing process: ideation, composition, transcription, editing, revising and publishing. It should also be planned to address the needs of the children in terms of their writing development within the genre or writing form being studied. This can take many forms. Lee (1994), for example, shows how using pictures in guided writing can facilitate the writing process and develop writing proficiency. However, as Silva (1990) points out, the role of the teacher is crucial in supporting children to get started and develop ideas. It is important, nevertheless, that any strategy such as guided writing does not become formulaic and something to use because we are supposed to. Formulaic approaches decrease motivation and demonstrate a lack of purpose. The teacher must be intentional about tools such as guided writing. The most important point of guided writing is that children learn about what writing is, how it works and how to make sense of all of it.

Gibson states that: 'learning about writing can be accelerated when teachers are able to build students' abilities to notice and interact with specific features of the construction of text' (2008: 112).

In our case study, Melissa identified a group of children whom she knew she needed to work with in order to provide an intervention for them at the composition into transcription stage of the writing process. These children needed more support in terms of understanding what a non-chronological report is for and therefore how the language use (in this case, tense and person) is crucial. Melissa needs to do exactly what Gibson above says is needed in order to accelerate their progress.

Figure 8.1 below shows Melissa's plan for her guided writing session.

As the plan demonstrates, a guided writing intervention can just be a further scaffolded version of the independent task. The main scaffolding tool is the teacher who supports the children's understanding through careful questioning and small steps to learning using lots of reinforcement.

Guided writing and creativity

At first sight, this might not seem terribly creative, however it is not necessarily the activity that needs to be creative, it should be more about how the teacher facilitates creativity through their ethos and approach. Essentially, creativity, as Desailly points out, means: 'spending less time in transmission mode, telling children information, and more time in facilitating enquiry, investigation and children drawing their own conclusions.' (2012: 70).

You will notice in the guided plan that Melissa plans for the children to be discussing, exploring and investigating language, developing learning from each other, facilitated by the teacher. The interactions that Melissa will have with the children will be about her asking questions, being open-minded about their responses and allowing them to take a little longer. That is why the plan is not packed with lots of activity. Melissa recognises that learning and understanding take time.

Non-fiction and digital literacy

The case study of Melissa's local history and non-chronological reports unit of work also draws on digital skills and the development of children's digital literacy. One of the outcomes is for the children to use their non-chronological reporting skills to create a documentary about their city, the historical buildings and the characters that have shaped its past. In

Date:	Grp/chn: (6) RA, PC, KM, IT, DV, AC (Year 1)

Focus/objectives

(Assessment Focus 2: Produce texts which are appropriate to task, reader and purpose)

- Purpose established, e.g. main features of report utilised
- Some appropriate features of non-chronological report used – present tense and third person
- Some attempts to adopt appropriate style – formal tone

Success criteria

- Children can use present tense and third person in their writing
- Children understand the purpose of the non-chronological report

Structure and approaches	Resources
(1) Using the sentence cards from shared work, discuss in pairs some of the differences, highlighting some of the key words such as 'we' and the verbs (2) Paired work: independently highlight key words (3) Discuss why these words are important in the sentence (4) Using a photo from the school trip, orally rehearse a sentence that would be suitable for a recount and teacher scribe – dealing with any misconceptions (5) Paired work using photos: establish content, and children orally rehearse and write sentences – reinforce checklist from shared work	Enlarged sentence cards Mini-whiteboards Pens Photos from trip

Plenary

Play 'sentence in or out'. Share some sentences on cards and decide if they are 'in' the non-chronological report form or 'out'. Discuss reasons

Assessment and comments

RA	
PC	
KM	
IT	
DV	
AC	
Action needed	

Figure 8.1   Guided Writing Plan: Non-chronological report

terms of creativity, Savage and Barnett state that: 'As a teacher you want to introduce them to the approaches and tools that are going to empower them to express themselves and convey their capabilities, knowledge and understanding in the most enabling form available' (2015: 70). They go on to cite the work of Payton and Hague, who state that creativity is a key facet of digital literacy, in that children are facilitated to 'create outputs and represent knowledge in different formats and modes' (Payton and Hague, 2010: 6, in Savage and Barnett, 2015: 70).

The National Curriculum for computing at Key Stage 1 states:

> Use technology purposefully to create, organise, store, manipulate and retrieve digital content. (DfE, 2013: 189)

Within digital literacy comes the term multimodal texts and multimodal literacy. This idea has been introduced in the previous chapter in the context of film literacy, but here it used in a very different context and age group. This term refers to documents which have a variety of modes of content. For example, in the case study considered in this chapter, creating a documentary will contain video material with an accompanying text. It is important to state here that creating digital text after doing lots of writing on paper is not necessarily the best use of time. It can feel like 'copying-up' work, which is not the best use of technology. One of the advantages of writing on screen is that editing can be done quickly and easily and changes can be tracked for assessment purposes. Savage and Barnett (2015) exhort the value of Web 2.0 technology that can be used on tablet or desktop and laptop computers. They suggest that one of the values of this technology is the ease of publishing it to an audience and this gives children a much more immediate sense of audience and writing for a real purpose. With creating content for the documentary, publishing it to the school's website is quick and easy. Children can orally rehearse their documentary and use devices such as digital flip cameras to record and then publish. Children can also use simple Movie Maker technology to edit and add a soundtrack and captions for a more accomplished effect.

The use of class blogs and wikis also adds significant purpose to writing. Children can in addition contribute to a wiki, set up by the class teacher. This brings in the added bonus of collaborative learning and the co-construction of knowledge that involves, as Miyake states: 'making things visible, shareable, reflectable and modifiable by the participating learners' (2007: 249). Children could contribute to an electronic non-chronological report, adding their own sections via a wiki. They can work together to agree correct tense and person and, in so doing, are learning all sorts of collaborative skills, negotiation and cementing understanding, as Richardson (2009) states. Children are working together, supporting each other's learning, challenging each other and teaching each other.

Try this

Activity 1: Purpose, context and audience

When planning your unit of work on non-fiction, make sure that you plan a motivating context for the children. Ensure that you utilise a shared experience and give it some relevance by making the purpose of the writing clear and make sure children are clear on who they are writing for.

Activity 2: Guided intervention to support text-specific language

In your shared learning and teaching, use formative assessment to identify children who need support. Use a guided intervention (perhaps using the plan in Figure 8.1 as a framework) to help children with the specific language features of a non-fiction text. Make sure that your approach is one of facilitation, rather than of transmission.

Activity 3: Creating digital texts

When planning a unit of work for non-fiction, think about how you could utilise technology to create a multimodal text. Think about how to use a class blog or wiki to get children collaborating together and think about how you can use technology to compose, revise and publish text. Try using photo or video material to complement what is being done.

Summary

I have chosen to use non-chronological reports as the focus of this chapter but the key principles can be applied across all forms of non-fiction. It is important to start with a shared experience. This may be providing something tangible for the children to write instructions for, as well as a class trip. The key point is that there is a context and purpose for the writing. Children must be clear on the purpose of their writing and it must have an audience in mind. Motivating and engaging children in working with non-fiction usually means that they have to see the point of doing it – a real purpose – not just because the teacher says so. Children should also be exploring the text and its key features for themselves. The teacher should be facilitating understanding, rather than being in transmission mode. This is one of the key tenets of creative approaches to learning and teaching:

children explore, discover and learn, guided by the teacher. With technology rapidly growing and improving and many sources of information available online, it is important that teachers use it to support learning. Children at Key Stage 1 will be using online texts out of school, so it is important that teachers are using these in school. Children should be seeing the learning benefits of working digitally and have their worlds opened up to the plethora of learning resources available.

Appendix 8.1 Text resources

There are a myriad of non-fiction resources available for Key Stage 1. The following is a tiny selection which is available.

BBC's cbbc website, has a huge variety of opportunities for children to explore, including *Newsround*. Available at: www.bbc.co.uk/cbbc/ (accessed 4th June 2015).

School History also presents some great resources and opportunities. Available at: www.schoolhistory.co.uk/ (accessed 4th June 2015).

In terms of texts, I will just mention a few key series:

- *Heinemann Groundbreakers* series: This is perfect for looking at historical characters who influenced Great Britain over time. This provides a clear opportunity to reframe text and mentally play with it to demonstrate understanding.
- *Heinemann Living in History* series: This is a great non-chronological report series which facilitates ease of comprehension.
- *Eyewitness Guides*: These are high-quality non-chronological reports, which use photographs rather than stylised artwork to add additional information.
- Terry Deary's *Horrible Histories* series: These provide a fun and accessible approach to history which do give children unique information. Deary also has a *Horrible Science* series.

Further reading

Barnes, J. (2011) *Cross-Curricular Learning 3–14*, 2nd edn. London: Sage.

This text supports the pedagogy of cross-curricular learning and teaching. It gets underneath the process and practice and supports the development of a clear philosophy. It also gives practical guidance.

Savage, M. and Barnett, A. (2015) *Digital Literacy for Primary Teachers.* Northwich: Critical Publishing.

This highly practical text gives lots of ideas and learning opportunities for working with technology. It presents very clear implications for learning and teaching and lots of great examples from existing practitioners.

Wray, D. (2006) *Teaching Literacy across the Primary Curriculum.* Exeter: Learning Matters.

This great text outlines systematic approaches to teaching non-fiction reading and writing. It provides detailed activities and ideas and great practical examples. Wray also provides an excellent research base.

References

Brien, J. (2012) *Teaching Primary English.* London: Sage.

Corbett, P. and Strong, J. (2011) *Talk for Writing across the Curriculum.* Maidenhead: Open University Press.

Craft, A., Jeffrey, B. and Liebling, M. (eds) (2001) *Creativity in Education.* London: Continuum.

Cremin, T. (2009) *Teaching English Creatively.* London: Routledge.

Department for Education (DfE) (2013). *The National Curriculum for England, Key Stages 1 and 2.* London. Crown Copyright.

Desailly, J. (2012) *Creativity in the Primary Classroom.* London: Sage.

Gibson, S. (2008) 'Guided writing lessons: Second-grade students' development of strategic behaviour', *Reading Horizons,* 48 (2): 111–32.

Hughes, S. (1998) *The Lion and the Unicorn.* London: Random House Children's Books.

Lan, Y., Hung, C. and Hsu, H. (2011) 'Effects of guided writing strategies on students' writing attitudes based on media richness theory', *Turkish Online Journal of Educational Technology* (*TOJET*), 10 (4): 148–64.

Lee, L. (1994) 'L2 writing: Using pictures as a guided writing environment', Paper presented at the Rocky Mountain Modern Language Association Conference Proceedings, State University of New York, Plattsburgh, 13 May.

Lewis, M. (2006) *Phonics Practice: Research and policy.* London: Sage (UKLA).

Lewis, M. and Wray, D. (1997) *Extending Literacy: Children Reading and Writing Non-fiction.* London: Routledge.

Miyake, N. (2007) 'Computer-supported collaborative learning', in R. Andrews and C. Haythornthwaite (eds), *The Sage Handbook of e-Learning Research.* Los Angeles, CA, and London: Sage.

National Advisory Committee on Creative and Cultural Education (NACCCE) (1999) *All our Futures: Creativity, Culture and Education.* London: NACCCE.

Payton, S. and Hague, C. (2010) *Digital Literacy in Practice: Case Studies of Primary and Secondary Classrooms,* Futurelab. Available at: www2.futurelab. org.uk/resources/documents/projects_reports/digital_literacy_case_studies.pdf (accessed 18 July 2015).

Richardson, W. (2009) *Blogs, Wikis, Podcasts and Other Powerful Web Tools for Classrooms*, 2nd edn. Thousand Oaks, CA: Corwin Press.

Savage, M. and Barnett, A. (2015) *Digital Literacy for Primary Teachers*. Northwich: Critical Publishing.

Silva, T. (1990) 'Second language composition instruction: Development, issues, and directions in ESL', in B. Kroll (ed.), *Second Language Writing*. New York: Cambridge University Press.

Soalt, J. (2005) 'Bringing together fictional and informational texts to improve comprehension', *The Reading Teacher*, 58 (7): 680–3.

Wray, D. (2006) *Teaching Literacy across the Primary Curriculum*. Exeter: Learning Matters.

Wray, D. and Lewis, M. (1992) 'Primary children's use of information books', *Reading*, 26 (3): 19–24.

9

Reading into writing

Key Stage 2 Non-fiction

Learning outcomes

By reading this chapter, you will have:

- Developed an understanding of effective learning and teaching of non-fiction texts
- Developed an understanding of how using non-fiction connects with learning in other subjects
- Developed an understanding of how real and relevant contexts powerfully assist learning in non-fiction writing
- Developed an understanding of the role that talk plays in the writing process

National Curriculum links

From lower Key Stage 2

Pupils should be taught to:

develop positive attitudes to reading and understanding of what they read by:

- listening to and discussing a wide range of fiction, poetry, plays, non-fiction and reference books or textbooks
- reading books that are structured in different ways and reading for a range of purposes
- retrieve and record information from non-fiction

Children should understand the conventions of different types of writing:

In using non-fiction, pupils should know what information they need to look for before they begin and be clear about the task. They should be shown how to use contents pages and indexes to locate information.

In writing non-narrative material, use simple organisational devices [for example, headings and subheadings]

In addition, from Upper Key Stage 2

Pupils should be taught to:

- distinguish between statements of fact and opinion
- retrieve, record and present information from non-fiction
- explain and discuss their understanding of what they have read, including through formal presentations and debates, maintaining a focus on the topic and using notes where necessary
- provide reasoned justifications for their views

The skills of information retrieval that are taught should be applied, for example, in reading history, geography and science textbooks, and in contexts where pupils are genuinely motivated to find out information.

In writing, use further organisational and presentational devices to structure text and to guide the reader [for example, headings, bullet points, underlining].

DfE (2013)

Chapter overview

This chapter explores the main concepts, ideas and learning that children in Key Stage 2, especially in meeting and exceeding national expectations, need to develop in non-fiction. The chapter draws on the 2013 National Curriculum and exemplifies ideas in context from the 'Creative approaches to ...' chapters, specifically with regard to reading skills, scaffolding the writing process, and creative ways to present non-fiction texts that make them relevant, meaningful and purposeful for the children to engage in.

Whilst exploring creative approaches to all non-fiction text types, the chapter focuses in more depth on persuasion and discussion texts and how dramatic techniques can greatly enhance children's use of these types of text. As part of the planning process in this case study, formative assessment and record-keeping will be addressed. A list of recommended alternative texts will be given in Appendix 9.1 at the end of this chapter, with ideas on how to use them.

Introduction

As stated in the previous chapter, children will encounter non-fiction texts in their daily lives into adulthood. They will have to interpret instructions, leave instructions and interpret and understand reports, either in the popular press or in digital text. They may well have to write them, too. In other words, children need to become conversant with the form, features and purposes of the different types of text which they will meet. They must be able to crack the code of structure, language and layout. But, also having the tools to crack the codes and the keys to unlock meaning in addition helps them, as Myers and Burnett state, to: 'be aware of the exciting and extensive opportunities to increase their knowledge of topics that interest or intrigue them' (2004: 105). There is also the need to read critically: to be able to distinguish between fact and opinion and to weigh up what is read, and to make decisions and use a variety of sources to form opinions. Being able to access a range of non-fiction texts will assist in this very important skill. A television highlights show may give a very different perspective on a football match to the sports pages write-up and this again may be very different from an eyewitness observer. How does one make decisions about how the football match played out? It is by understanding bias, interpretation and perhaps even political spin, and developing non-fiction comprehension skills which can help.

Embedded in non-fiction are the skills of information literacy. Information literacy is not just about the written word but is also about a wide variety of sources. Information can be disseminated through artwork, video, photographs, or physical evidence. It can also be represented through numbers, statistics, graphs and databases. Toyn (2013) highlights the work of Kellner and Share (2005), who suggest that information is often filtered according to where power resides in society. For example, news, which is information, is filtered by the media, which, it could be argued, are organised to gain power and profit. Being able, therefore, to distinguish between fact and opinion and understand the 'spin' placed on the story is vital. It is often said that history is written by the winners.

I was privileged to be a part of a wonderful history lesson in a Year 5 class which exemplified this point beautifully. The children were asked to work in pairs and move around the room where various sources of information about King Henry VIII were displayed. The teacher had chosen paintings, cartoons, extracts from biographies, letters, eye-witness accounts, songs and poems for them to explore. At each source, the children were asked to determine what information was being given, whether the source was valid and whether the information creator thought positively about the king or not. Immediately, the children were interpreting the sources, reading for information and discussing the important point that angering the King of England, particularly this king, in the sixteenth century was probably not very advisable.

This example also helps 'mythbust' a common misconception: that critical thinking and creative thinking cannot coexist. This example proves that both of these skills are vitally important. In order to examine the texts fully, the children needed to read critically: to detect bias and weigh up the words and images. They also needed to think creatively as there was no one right answer because all the sources were open to interpretation. What they did need to do was justify their views.

So what other opportunities are there for creative approaches to critical reading in other non-fiction text types? In the previous chapter, I focused a little more on non-chronological reports and recounts, so below are some thoughts and ideas for exploring instructions, explanations, persuasion and discussion. Further examples of persuasion and discussion, exploring the writing process in more depth, will be considered later on in the chapter.

Creative Opportunities for ...

Instruction texts

Instructions lend themselves perfectly to writing across the curriculum and give teachers the opportunity to plan for the application of knowledge, skills and understanding. Children therefore have the opportunity to demonstrate their ability to transfer their knowledge and demonstrate a deeper understanding. Corbett and Strong provide some ideas for this such as: 'How to put on a toga; How the Vikings crossed the seas; How to stay healthy' (2011: 71), and the list goes on. Children can work together and write in-role. For example, children could be in-role as a Viking chief leaving the chiefdom to his son and leaving him instructions for sailing, trade routes and bartering skills. Corbett and Strong go on to suggest that a clear sense of the needs of the audience is crucial to successful instructions. The audience in the brief example given above is the

Viking chief's son, so his style and words would need to take that into account. This approach can utilise dramatic skills. As Clipson-Boyles (2012) argues: not only can drama be motivating for children and provide contexts for them to write in, but it can also assist in the understanding of the needs of the reader.

Instructions also lend themselves to possibility thinking and facilitate the use of story as a context. Using the text *The Bully* by Jan Needle, (a text already encountered in Chapter 4), children could write in-role as lead character Simon, writing instructions to his friend to find his hiding place in the chalk pits. Children could use reversal thinking, writing a 'How to Bully Guide for Oppressing Others'. This technique is a particularly powerful tool as it turns a problem on its head and facilitates the children to think about it differently. There are many different contexts in which this notion of writing instructions for characters in stories could be used. In traditional tales, for example, a 'wolf-catching tool' can be devised and instructions given for Little Red Riding Hood to use it. A burglar alarm and instructions created for the three bears to keep any more porridge thieves and house-wreckers out could also be devised. Many creative ideas that capture children's imagination are possible.

Explanation texts

Have you ever wondered how a teacher's mind works? Have you ever wondered why children like to be glued to screens? What about why Vikings have beards? Perhaps you have considered why Roman men of a certain age have a particular haircut. Explanation texts can facilitate the creative responses to some of these questions. Like instructions, there is plenty of scope to make cross-curricular links across a range of topics.

One of the dangers to fall into when writing explanation texts is making sure that they do not become recounts. Wray (2006) draws on the theoretical framework of scaffolding as he suggests that children need access to models, demonstrations and guidance during writing and access to pro formas. These tools should be at the writer's disposal as a support but should not be deemed to be the only way to do it. Cremin (2009) suggests that the goal is to help children make non-fiction texts their own, to avoid them merely parroting information in a form that is the same as that which has been read. There is a danger that providing too many prompts and grids, sentence starters and writing frames can restrict the children and support them getting the writing right, but this leads to a procedural knowledge of the text, rather than a deep understanding of what the text is for, how it functions and how to manipulate it.

Writing an explanation text does need some scaffolded support and I have drawn attention to some ideas from Wray (2006). However, talk is crucial to planning writing and this is particularly important with explanation writing. Harris (1989), in Corden, states that writers need to 'plan flexibly and review constantly' (2000: 119) and talking first – orally rehearsing text – facilitates this beautifully. Speaking the sentences and text first and then revising the speech against explanation features, allows text-shaping, flexibility and review before the committal to paper or screen.

Explanation texts can be developed creatively very effectively through role-play, much like instructions. It is again possible to use story as a vehicle for this type of writing and to use characters and situations from stories. For example, the web-based text, *The Peanut Butter Princess* by M K Grassi, has a 30-minute gap towards the end of the story, where the princess seems to have a personality change. Children can creatively explain how this happened? Who did she meet, and what did they say/do?

Again, working across the curriculum, there are opportunities to deal with a key feature of explanation: cause and effect, explaining why something is. Anderson (2014) suggests children taking on the role of a historical figure such as Winston Churchill, talking about the reason for his decisions and speech content and the effect that these had. Not only does this approach support the oral rehearsal, as stated earlier, but it also builds thinking skills and supports transferability of understanding.

Discussion texts

Table 9.1, adapted from the Department for Education and Employment's (DfEE, 2000) document *Grammar for Writing*, provides a very helpful guide as to what a discussion text is, what it is for and some of the key features. However, it is important to note that these features should not be seen as rigid and should not stop teachers and children from being creative with them. Cremin (2009) notes that creative teachers do not see these textual boundaries as unalterable or unbridgeable, and she recommends that boundary crossing between genres is often helpful and where appropriate should be encouraged. I would argue that the idea should come first, and concern over which specific genre it should fit into is of secondary importance. For example, if the class is looking at King Henry VIII (see a previous example in this chapter) and the teacher decides to ask the class to do a newspaper report on, for example, the execution of Anne Boleyn, there will be elements of reporting, discussion, explanation and perhaps persuasion in the report. Cremin goes on

Table 9.1   Features of discussion texts

Text type: Discussion texts

Purpose	Key features	What else the writer needs to know
To present arguments, information and debates from different viewpoints	*Structure* Statement of issue + preview of main arguments Arguments for + evidence Arguments against + evidence (or for/against, for/against) Recommendation/summary *Features* Present tense Logical connectives Direct speech (quotation) Statistics can be used Moves from generic to specific	The title can be a question Think about who the audience is as formal language may well be used Why is the issue important? Check that you have been fair to both sides so as to produce a balanced argument

Source: Adapted from DfEE (2000: 154–5)

to suggest, and she cites the work of, among others, Kress and Knapp (1992) and Lewis and Wray (1995), that underlying theories around genres state that genres are actually created by the author's purpose. As there are many purposes for creating text, then genres can also be very varied and often mixed.

Exceeding expectations

Adapted from the *National Curriculum Level Descriptors* (QCA, 2010), the points below detail what would be defined as 'exceeding expectations' in speaking and listening, reading and writing for Key Stage 2 children in relation to discussion texts.

Speaking and listening

Pupils adapt their talk to the demands of different contexts, purposes and audiences with increasing confidence. Pupils take an active part in discussions, taking different roles and showing understanding of ideas and sensitivity to others. They demonstrate their knowledge of language variety and usage effectively and use Standard English fluently in formal situations.

Reading

Pupils give personal responses to literary texts, referring to aspects of language, structure and themes in justifying their views, and making connections between texts from different times and cultures and their own experiences. They summarise a range of information from different sources.

Writing

Pupils show some adaptation of style and register to different forms, including using an impersonal style where appropriate. Pupils use a range of sentence structures and varied vocabulary to create effects. A range of punctuation is usually used correctly to clarify meaning, and ideas are organised into paragraphs.

Adapted from the *National Curriculum Level Descriptors* (QCA, 2010: 16–18)

As you read and reflect on the case study below, identify how the class teacher facilitates children to achieve these higher levels as stated above.

Case study

Steve is working with his Year 5 class on discussion texts. His topic is looking at the local area and he has been working with his class on looking at the history of the school. They have been to the local records office and have found various documents, including the first school logbook from the Victorian era that made very interesting reading. This gave Steve a great opportunity to develop critical reading skills with his class. They became 'history detectives' and created an assembly, using actual historical sources to take the rest of the school back in time to what it would actually have been like. Steve is now keen to develop this topic of the local area into the present-day and is interested in what their views are on local town developments. Over the weekend, Steve set his class the challenge to find out what is happening in their local area: building developments, road improvements and conservation projects and discuss any of them with whoever is at home. The task was to report back the issue and some key points on Monday morning.

Unanimously, the children had picked the new bypass that was being built to take traffic from the busy port straight to the motorway rather than through the town. Many of them, it seems, faced lots of traffic jams and congestion just to get to school as a direct result.

Many points were brought for and against and Steve jotted them all down ready for the shaping of a text the next day. Steve had decided that the class's texts would be sent to the local paper and MP and hopefully published on the local council website.

The children arrived the next day to find a long table set up at the front of the classroom, with the words 'Local Council Debate' displayed on the whiteboard with the council logo attached. Steve had created five characters, each with a vested interest in the issue and, using the children's ideas, had created some character viewpoint sheets to help add fuel to the debate. Each group would discuss their character's viewpoint and one person would come and play the role in the debate, giving their character's views and responding to questions. Steve chaired the debate. As the cut and thrust of debate continued, another class member scribed further information given by the characters onto the board to assist with writing the discussion text later.

The following day, the children entered the classroom transformed into a newspaper office. Steve was in-role as the editor and greeted his class as junior reporters given the task of creating the story. Later, the children would go out with cameras and take still photos but also live reports from the construction site. Steve had set this up earlier in the week.

Steve modelled the first few lines of the report and he used meta-cognitive discussion as a tool to show the children what was going on in his mind as he wrote. The children then created a structure for the discussion text. He modelled the editing process and the use of formal language. Using laptops, the children worked in pairs, writing a section of the report on the bypass using the notes from the board. Steve used mini-plenaries to draw out from the children how to make the discussion more emotive and the children, after discussion, arrived at the use of direct quotations and statistics: evidence.

By the end of the week, the children had put together a discussion text that Steve sent to the the local newspaper and MP. The edited live reports later went up on the school's website.

Reflecting on the case study

- How did Steve facilitate the development of those 'exceeding expectations' skills from the National Curriculum?
- What was the impact of the role-play? Winston states that: 'Children feel they have lived through or actually witnessed the

(Continued)

(Continued)

experience. As a result their talk can be situated within the experience as well as being reflective of the experience' (2004: 21). How was this important for their writing?

- Steve encouraged the children to devise the structure and some of the language features? Why was this important?

Stop and think

How could you use a meaningful and relevant context to develop children's writing?

How can you align home literacies with school literacies to facilitate children having a voice to speak out on local issues that affect them?

How can you give the writing real purpose (e.g., school website, letter to a newspaper, letter to an MP)?

Persuasive writing

Table 9.2, adapted from the DfEE's document *Grammar for Writing* (2000), provides a very helpful guide as to what a persuasive text is, what it is for and some of the key features. However, as with the earlier section on discussion texts, it is important not to be limited by the boundaries. Within this section, I want to focus on planning persuasive writing using one of Robin J. Fogarty's models for curriculum integration and the learning (introduced in Chapter 6) that can be gained through the process of creating and shaping text, as opposed to just the assessment of the end product.

Figure 9.1 draws on Fogarty's (1991) 'threaded approach' to curriculum integration. This approach is not about subjects but supersedes subjects. The skills identified in the model transcend subjects and the advantage of thinking and planning in this way is that the process of learning is at the forefront of planning.

As you read and reflect on the case study below, think about how the class teacher threads the skillsets through her unit of work. The work draws on learning from the National Curriculum for History KS2, exploring the changing power of monarchs with a focus on Queen Elizabeth I.

Table 9.2 Features of persuasion texts

Text type: Persuasive writing

Purpose	Key features	What else the writer needs to know
To argue the case for a point of view and attempt to convince the reader	*Structure* An opening statement Arguments in the form of the point, followed by elaboration and evidence Restating the position + summary *Features* Present tense Logical connectives Direct speech (quotation) Statistics can be used Moves from generic to specific	Use good reasons and evidence to convince the reader Use facts not just persuasive language Provide incentives to agree Use other devices such as humour, alliterative slogans and emotive language Think about who the audience is as formal language may well be used

Source: Adapted from DfEE (2000: 154–5)

Thinking skills | Social skills | Study skills

Source bias:
Possibility thinking – what was the author's intent?
Synthesis of ideas

Discussion
Negotiation
Collaboration
Delegation and teamwork

Investigating sources
Critical reading
Note-making
Skimming and scanning

Figure 9.1 Using Fogarty's (1991) 'Threaded Approach' to Curriculum Integration Persuasive Writing – Queen Elizabeth I was a good queen

Case study

Sasha and her Year 6 class were exploring the changing power and role of the monarchy, charting highs and lows of England's kings and queens and their contribution to its history. Sasha had arrived at a huge turning point for Britain, its first female monarch. Sasha had been exploring

(Continued)

(Continued)

the significance of a female ruler for the country and the impact that would have had on sixteenth-century England. Sasha had shown her class film extracts from several interpretations of Queen Elizabeth I. They had watched the BBC's (1986) *Blackadder II* starring Miranda Richardson, and Glenda Jackson's 1971 portrayal in *Elizabeth R*, again from the BBC. They had also watched excerpts from Cate Blanchett's 1998 portrayal in Michael Hirst's *Elizabeth* and again in 2007 *Elizabeth: The Golden Age* also written by Michael Hirst with William Nicholson. Todd reminds us that:

> images are so accessible [and that] children from an early age already have experience of them ... If children are already 'switched on' to the world of images, then by examining, interpreting what they see, we can begin to explore comprehension at increasingly sophisticated levels. (2013: 107)

Tasked with exploring the different portrayals of Elizabeth and identifying aspects of her character, the children interrogated these visual texts expertly. They were engaged, enjoyed the costumes, discussed together and were able to share different viewpoints, drawing on evidence. Their key question asked: 'Was Elizabeth I a good queen and did she influence the country for good?' Later, Sasha laid out information packs on Elizabeth, with a variety of sources for the children to interrogate. Character comments using 'Role on the Wall' (see Chapter 6) have been added to the working wall for this unit of work from discussion of the film extracts and now the children would be comparing evidence. Using letters, paintings, extracts from biographies and evidence from people who knew her, the children, in groups, developed and practised their critical reading skills, comparing the evidence to film interpretations.

Sasha then challenged the children to position themselves: those who believed, from the evidence, that Elizabeth had influenced the country for good; and those who believed she hadn't. How would they persuade the others that they were right?

Sasha grouped the children, mixing those with different opinions. Using a tablet and voice recorder, the children shared their viewpoints, trying to persuade the others.

After several minutes, each group listened to and evaluated another group's work and gave feedback. Sasha asked who was convinced and those who affirmed that they were, shared what was most persuasive and what convinced them. Answers ranged from emotional pleas, to facts and figures, incentives, other source evidence, decisions she had made and her impact on the poor, and Sasha drew these together into some 'Key Features of Persuasion' onto the working wall.

The children's task was to write a speech to persuade Elizabeth's Privy Council either to take some of her power away from her because she was not doing a good job, or to give her more power and trust her more as she is clearly a very good queen. They researched some Elizabethan language and Sasha modelled an opening. The children worked in pairs to create their speeches and presented them to the head teacher, in-role as Lord Burghley, the Queen's chief advisor.

Reflecting on the case study

- Reflect on how thinking skills, social skills and study skills were threaded through this unit of work. Why are they important for the process of learning?
- Reflect on Sasha's use of visual literacy through the film extracts and paintings. How did this enhance the children's comprehension and develop their critical reading skills?
- Reflect on the use of the working wall to chart the process of learning and ensure that none of the valuable discussion is lost. Why was this such a good tool to use?

Planning this unit of work

Fogarty's 1991 'threaded approach' provides a tool to make skills explicit. However, Table 9.3 shows how this unit might be visualised alongside the writing process shown in chapter 6. The case study above focuses mainly on the pre-writing and ideation stages and Table 9.3 demonstrates how this might be taken forward in stages towards publishing work.

The case study above utilises some key elements of visual literacy, which have been considered in earlier chapters. But what this case study particularly emphasises is the work of Kress and Van Leeuwen (1996/2006), who look at ways in which images communicate meaning. Bhojwani (2015) draws on this and pulls out some key principles, some of which I think the above case study illustrates. They also illustrate the importance of connecting skills and using other subject areas as a context for writing. These are: 'Texts can be read in more than one way; the design of the text facilitates

Table 9.3   The Writing Process and Persuasive Writing – Queen Elizabeth I was a good queen

Writing process stage	Unit of work stage
Pre-writing	Watch film extracts and look at a variety of source material to gather evidence to form opinions on whether Elizabeth I was a good queen. Work in mixed groups to persuade each other and discuss what conventions were the most persuasive and why
Ideation	Using the notes from the working wall, children pull together their key arguments and evidence to respond to whether Elizabeth I was a good queen and influenced the country for good
Writing	Teacher models the opening of the text, children contribute in pairs and evaluate against style and features. Children work in pairs to draft their persuasive argument
Responding	Children work with writing partners to evaluate work – could the text be more persuasive? Are there any anachronisms that would be inappropriate for an Elizabethan privy council?
Revising	Reorganise structure to give the most persuasive effect. Clarify precise language, using Elizabethan terms, check emphasis of facts and evidence
Editing	Correct against conventions of persuasive language: tense, connectives
Publish/share	Read speech out in role as a privy councillor, the audience being the rest of the privy council

this process; the author may have indicated a particular "heirarchy" by drawing attention to particular features' (Bhojwani, 2015: 146). Visual texts certainly do this through image size and background elements. This is particularly seen through *The Ditchley Portrait* of Elizabeth I, painted *c.*1592 by Marcus Gheeraerts the Younger. This painting depicts Elizabeth standing on a very small England, showing a half-sunny sky and half-stormy sky. One cannot miss the image of power.

Try this

Activity 1: Instructions for fictional characters

When you are next planning a unit of work on instructions, think through what fiction work you have just done or what else is going on in the curriculum. Invite children to create something requiring instructions for a character to use to solve their problem in the story.

Activity 2: Give children a voice

When planning a unit of work on discussion, make it relevant for the children. Connect it to a local area study and explore what is happening in their lives out of school. Get them reading the local press and council websites and discussing with whoever is at home. How can you bring home literacies into school so that the children can make connections?

Activity 3: Reading 'text' in its broadest sense

Reading is not just about the printed word. Facilitate critical reading through the use of film, paintings, artefacts, cartoons. What is the creator of this source trying to convey? How can you motivate children by this different approach to reading?

Summary

Non-fiction texts provide a great opportunity to make English real and give it a tangible relevance to everyday life. The main purpose of this chapter is to deliver that message. If children can see the purpose and relevance to the work they are doing, then they are more likely to engage with it and more likely to learn.

In both case studies, the teachers have been facilitators, creating environments for children to learn and develop understanding. The first case study emphasises the importance of working in-role and using talk to develop writing. It focuses on the use of a relevant and real context for them to give them a voice in their local community.

The second case study focuses more explicitly on the process of learning. Threading skills through the unit of work ensures that they are learnt and developed, rather than hoping that the children may develop them by some vague chance. It also explores the power of visual literacy and how this can motivate and also enhance comprehension without what can sometimes be the barrier of the printed word.

Both of these case studies also show how children can be facilitated to 'exceed expectations' and understand what is required to do this. Non-fiction reading and writing is very motivating for children as it is concrete and usually deals with fact, opinion and bias and provokes debate. Seize the opportunities that a non-fiction unit brings and see how many skills will develop.

Appendix 9.1 Text resources

- Key Stage 2 Human Body pack from Oxford Literacy Web. *Exploring the Human Body* provides a great stimulus for thinking about other ways to present information for other audiences.
- *Ocean* by Sean Callery. Dive into this book and use it to make connections between other texts.
- *Bollywood* by Cathy West. Explore the world of Bollywood. Evaluate the information and discuss which is fact and which is opinion?
- *A Dream of America* by Dee Phillips. Read the illustrations in this book. What do they add to the text? What do they emphasise?
- *Alone in the Trenches* by Vince Cross. This powerful non-fiction text can be read alongside some classic Michael Morpurgo texts such as *War Horse* and *Private Peaceful* to explore the tragedies of the Great War.
- *Anglo-Saxons* by Bob Fowke is a great text, which aims to give 'what they never told you about the Anglo-Saxons'. This is also a great text to use alongside other evidence sources when writing discussion texts.

Further reading

Clipson-Boyles, S. (2012) *Teaching Primary English through Drama*. London: David Fulton.

This is a very important text as it not only provides a theoretical underpinning for the use of drama in English but also helps with managing the classroom environment and links specifically to how drama supports reading and writing.

Metcalfe, J. Simpson, D., Todd, I. and Toyn, M. (2013) *Thinking through New Literacies for Primary and Early Years*. London: Learning Matters.

This very informative text covers a huge variety of literacies that can motivate children with their learning. The text also supports teachers to think more widely about literacy, including information fluency and visual texts.

Palmer, S. (2011) *How to Teach Writing across the Curriculum, Ages 8–14*, 2nd edn. London: Routledge.

This practical and readable text provides a lot of useful subject knowledge for non-fiction genres as well as excellent practical suggestions for developing learning across the curriculum. There are links to some excellent speaking frames, which develop the talk for learning approach, advocated through this book.

References

Anderson, K. (2014) 'Non-fiction', in D. Waugh, W. Joliffe and K. Allott (eds), *Primary English for Trainee Teachers*. London: Learning Matters.

Bhojwani, P. (2015) 'Multi-modal literacies can motivate boys to write', in D. Waugh, A. Bushnell and S. Neaum (eds), *Beyond Early Writing: Teaching Writing in Primary Schools*. Northwich: Critical Publishing.

Clipson-Boyles, S. (2012) *Teaching Primary English through Drama*. London: David Fulton.

Corbett, P. and Strong, J. (2011) *Talk for Writing across the Curriculum*. Maidenhead: Oxford University Press.

Corden, R. (2000) *Literacy and Learning through Talk*. Buckingham: Oxford University Press.

Cremin, T. (2009) *Teaching English Creatively*. London: Routledge.

Department for Education (DfE) (2013). *The National Curriculum for England*. London: Crown Copyright.

Department for Education and Employment (DfEE) (2000) *Grammar for Writing*. London: DfEE.

Fogarty, R.J. (1991) 'Ten ways to integrate curriculum', *Education Leadership*. Available at: www.ascd.org/ASCD/pdf/journals/ed_lead/el_199110_fogarty.pdf (accessed 20 July 2015).

Harris, J. (1989) *Writing in the Classroom: Drafting*. Sheffield: Sheffield Hallam University.

Kellner, D. and Share, J. (2005) 'Toward critical media literacy: Core concepts, debates, organisations and policy', *Discourse: Studies in the Cultural Politics of Education*, 26 (3): 369–86.

Kress, G. and Knapp, P. (1992) 'Genre in a social theory of language', *English in Education*, 26 (2): 2–11.

Kress, G. and Van Leeuwen, T. (1996/2006) *Reading Images: A Grammar of Visual Design*. London: Routledge.

Lewis, M. and Wray, D. (1995) *Developing Children's Non-fiction Writing: Working with Writing Frames*. Leamington Spa: Scholastic.

Myers, J. and Burnett, C. (2004) *Teaching English 3–11*. London: Continuum.

Needle, J. (1995) *The Bully*. London: Puffin.

Qualifications and Curriculum Authority (QCA) (2010) *The National Curriculum Level Descriptors for Subjects*. Coventry: QCA.

Todd, I. (2013) 'Visual literacy', in J. Metcalfe, D. Simpson, I. Todd and M. Toyn, *Thinking through New Literacies for Primary and Early Years*. London: Learning Matters.

Toyn, M. (2013) 'Finding things out: Information fluency', in J. Metcalfe, D. Simpson, I. Todd and M. Toyn, *Thinking through New Literacies for Primary and Early Years*. London: Learning Matters.

Winston, J. (2004) *Drama and English at the Heart of the Curriculum: Primary and Middle Years*. London: David Fulton.

Wray, D. (2006) *Teaching Literacy across the Curriculum*. Exeter: Learning Matters.

10

Reading into writing

Key Stage 1 Poetry

Learning outcomes

By reading this chapter, you will have:

- Developed an understanding of how to engage Key Stage 1 children with poetry
- Developed an understanding of some poetic forms that are effective for Key Stage 1 children
- Developed your understanding of the writing process in the context of poetry
- Developed your understanding of the importance of the writing environment and of the teacher as writer

National Curriculum links

From Key Stage 1 Year 1

Develop pleasure in reading, motivation to read, vocabulary and understanding by:

- listening to and discussing a wide range of poems, stories and non-fiction at a level beyond that at which they can read independently
- learning to appreciate rhymes and poems, and to recite some by heart

Pupils should be taught to:
  write sentences by:

- saying out loud what they are going to write about
- composing a sentence orally before writing it
- re-reading what they have written to check that it makes sense
- discuss what they have written with the teacher or other pupils

In addition, from Key Stage 1 Year 2

develop pleasure in reading, motivation to read, vocabulary and under-standing by:

- listening to, discussing and expressing views about a wide range of contemporary and classic poetry
- recognising simple recurring literary language in stories and poetry
- continuing to build up a repertoire of poems learnt by heart, appreciat-ing these and reciting some, with appropriate intonation to make the meaning clear

make simple additions, revisions and corrections to their own writing by:

- evaluating their writing with the teacher and other pupils

DfE (2013)

Chapter overview

This chapter draws on the 2013 National Curriculum and exemplifies ideas in context from the 'Creative approaches to …' chapters. The chapter pre-sents a wide variety of approaches to teaching poetry and utilises a range of creative techniques, such as Morphological Forced Connections, to help stimulate children's imagination. The chapter will consider approaches that are transferable across a variety of poetic genres but will have a case study using 'The Sea in the Trees' by Kit Wright (2009) as its focus. As well as developing engagement with poetry, this chapter will also look at exem-plifying the teaching of the writing process, through creative planning, developing language comprehension skills by focusing on the writer's use of language and creative ways to respond to poetry. As part of the planning process in the case study, formative assessment and record-keeping will be addressed. A list of recommended poems and anthologies will be given in Appendix 10.1 the end of this chapter, with ideas of how to use them.

Introduction

In my experience of talking to teachers and of working with student teachers and children, I have discovered that poetry is a bit like Marmite. People either like it or hate it. However, I have also discovered that the haters often hold some very narrow views about what poetry is. Poetry must rhyme? Poetry must be funny? Poetry is one of those things that you have to analyse at school! However, I think that the author Michael Rosen has it right. Horner and Ryf quote Rosen as saying that: 'Central to poetry is play' (2007: 187). Poetry is surely about playing with words, playing with grammatical structures to convey meaning. Poetry has the power to make us cry. Seamus Heaney's 'Mid-Term Break' (1966) never ceases to do this for me. Poetry can make us laugh. T.S. Eliot's 'Macavity the Mystery Cat' (1939) often does this for me, too. Poetry has the power to comment on life with humour and irony, and can often make the reader, or listener, understand some of the complexities of life in a way that makes them sit up and take notice much more effectively than a news programme. The best comedians and authors also have the power to do this. They are the ones who play with language, play with words and structures for the effect they wish to create, and do it with artistry.

So, why should such young children be exposed to poetry? What does the learning and teaching of poetry give children? Faulkner states that poetry: 'allows freedom of expression and creativity ... and allows children to be creative and explore the use of words in the written language' (2014: 143).

Poetry can also be used to develop grammatical understanding. Faulkner goes on to state that poetry can help children (especially young children): 'explore word classes and literary devices including simile and metaphor' (ibid.: 143).

Poetry also supports phonemic understanding, especially through rhyme. Children love to play with language and make up new words that rhyme. My own daughter, when playing around with the sounds of a new word, would often make up rhyme around it. We were discussing our visit to Russia and my youngest daughter, then a toddler, exclaimed: 'Rusher, rusher, rusher!' followed by 'Rusher tusher, crusher, lusher!' (those phonics experts amongst you will here notice the opportunity to teach the concept of same phoneme, different grapheme!). Bryant et al.'s (1990) longitudinal study demonstrated that children who encounter rhyme at a young age and play with sounds in this way, are often more successful in reading and writing.

Exploring poetry does not have to be reserved for the 'poetry unit of work'. Developing children's understanding of rhyme can take place at any time during the school day. Teachers whom I have worked with use a rhyming register, which they sing in 'performance poet' mode at the start of the day: 'Morning Claire, How's your hair? Morning Peter, is your car a seven-seater?' That is just one example of how I have seen this work. Martin et al. (2004) exhort the use of nursery rhymes to develop this. Rhymes such as 'Humpty Dumpty' are much loved and encourage the emphasis of 'wall' and 'fall'. They go on to support Bryant et al.'s conclusions (1990) and draw on the work of Goswami (2002), who states that, through these songs and rhymes, children do develop their phonological awareness and do take this into their reading and writing.

Creative thinking and poetry

Before exploring creative approaches to teaching poetry, it is important to look at a sample range of poetic forms that are good to teach in Key Stage 1. This is not exhaustive and I would be in favour of using all forms across all Key Stages, dependent on the learning of the children. However, the sample in Table 10.1 gives a flavour and some opportunities that the forms present.

Table 10.1   A sample of poetic forms

Poetic form	Opportunities
Traditional stories in simple rhyme	Developing phonological awareness through these well-known poems such as 'Humpty Dumpty' and 'Baa, Baa, Black Sheep'. Using the rhyming opportunities to play with language and develop their own traditional stories
Action verses	Predictable and patterned structures that again support phonological awareness but the actions help children 'concrete' their understanding, for example: 'One, Two, Buckle my Shoe' and 'Incy Wincy Spider'. The links between recitation and action develop reading skills
Chants	Predictable and patterned structures that again support phonological awareness but the actions help children 'concrete' their understanding. The rhythmic patterns in these chants, often used for skipping or ball games, help children with the rhythm and metre of words and phrases
List poems	Children love to make lists: shopping lists, to do lists and lists of what they have been doing. This poetic form facilitates the bringing of these lists together into an order to perform and share
Performance poems	It could be argued that all poems should be performed. But this form of poetry includes repetition, emphasis and audience participation. Children should think about which sections of the poem to emphasise
Alphabet poems	Within this poetic form, the letters of the alphabet start each word or line. This reinforces knowledge of the alphabetic code but also allows immense creativity and freedom within a framework

Creative teachers of poetry, as Cremin (2009) states, enable children to respond to poetry and represent it in a variety of ways. They may paint a response, freeze-frame a response, draw a response, dance a response, respond through music. Children should also have the opportunity to share their work through class blogs, web-based forums, children's anthologies and with each other. However, one of the most important things that creative teachers of poetry should do is have knowledge of a wide variety of poets and poetic texts. This is an area that has caused me concern while working with teachers and student teachers over many years. The 'classic' poems that teachers use remain the same: 'The Magic Box' by Kit Wright (2009), for example, is a wonderful poem that I have derived much delight from through teaching it – it is wonderful and I have seen it on displays in Year 2 classes across a variety of counties. Cremin goes on to state that: 'primary practitioners' marked lack of knowledge of poets is restricting children's access to poetic voices in all their energetic and reflective diversity' (2009: 117). Teachers must keep up to date with poetic work that has appeal and use it in the classroom, whilst drawing on an ever increasing diverse range of more established and classic poets such as T.S. Eliot, Benjamin Zephaniah, Michael Rosen and Kit Wright.

Playing with language

Brownjohn (1994) states that children need to be allowed to play with language for its own sake, not for any specific end, or to tick a box, but simply to enjoy playing around with words. They need to manipulate words and see them as pieces that they are in control of moving around, rather than as rigid shapes that cannot be moved and have to fit in a certain order.

So, as teachers, how can we stimulate this use of language? How can we facilitate this playing, which is, of course, at the heart of creativity?

Case study

Adam had been working with his Year 2 class, using the 1980 text *The Paper Bag Princess* written by Robert Munsch and beautifully illustrated by Michael Martchenko. He was looking at traditional stories and

(Continued)

(Continued)

this alternative traditional story was hugely enjoyed by his class. Adam decided that as he wanted to tackle some poetry, stimulated by one of his class sharing some poems at the end of the previous week, he wanted to move his class to the next level of language use, moving from verbs to adding adverbs. He decided to use *The Paper Bag Princess* as a context. In order to generate creative ideas for the poetry and give the children a starting point, he decided to use a creative technique called 'morphological forced connections' (Cave, 1996). This technique allows the invention of new ideas and, through the random selection of attributes, forces the user of the technique to make meaning.

Adam wanted to create some new characters for his story, so he worked with his class to draw up some lists of six characters who could appear, six adjectives, and six verbs for what they would do, and six physical attributes. He would discuss the six adverbs later. Then the dice would be rolled to make some connections. The lists are shown in Table 10.2.

Table 10.2   Morphological Forced Connections grid – character descriptions

Dice roll	Character	Adjective	Verb	Physical attribute	Adverbs
1	Wolf	beautiful	gardening	big head	angrily
2	Grandma	hideous	crying	warty nose	noisily
3	Woodcutter	hungry	fishing	fat tummy	quietly
4	Little Pig	clumsy	sleeping	skinny legs	loudly
5	Goldilocks	wise	eating	big bottom	sadly
6	Wicked Stepmother	ferocious	helping	messy hair	fiercely

The first dice for character, rolled 3: woodcutter

The second for adjective, rolled 1: beautiful

The third for verb, rolled 2: crying

The fourth for physical attribute rolled 5: big bottom

The fifth for adverb, rolled 2: noisily

So, this meant that the first poem would be about a beautiful woodcutter with a big bottom who was crying noisily. What could he be doing in the story?

Reflecting on the case study

- Reflect on Adam's use of the traditional story. Why did he use this for the context and why add more characters to the story?
- Reflect on the use of the creative thinking tool – morphological forced connections. What is the impact of this on children's creativity?

The opening for Adam's class story might be developed in the following ways around poetry. There might be a writing frame such as:

I am a .... and I have ....

I am .... because ....

And the children could insert the words and play around with them to build a rhyme or even add more about what they are doing in the story.

Children could create lists of rhyming words – for example: crying, flying, buying, trying, sighing – and this could be used to develop phonological awareness.

Children could also create a song for their character: How would the woodcutter announce his arrival? 'Fee-fi-fo-fum, I am crying and I have a big bum!'

All of these ideas are about children playing with language and developing their enjoyment of story whilst building up their toolbox of linguistic devices to develop their written and verbal communication skills. What could be more enjoyable than watching a five-year-old boy, wearing a hat and checked shirt, stomping into the classroom chanting rhythmically, 'Fee-fi-fo-fum, I am crying and I have a big bum!' Whilst enjoying himself, he is demonstrating great awareness of rhythm, metre and rhyme and the connection between movement and language.

'The Sea in the Trees' by Kit Wright

The next part of this chapter unpacks possible creative approaches to responding to and creating poetry. We will be exploring and deconstructing a unit of work based on the brilliant 'The Sea in the Trees' by Kit Wright (2009) for a Key Stage 1 class. This will form the mix of case study, deconstruction, analysis and reflection on the approaches used by class teacher Nazeera.

Case study: Part 1 – Pre-writing

Nazeera's class is a mixed Year 1 and Year 2 class. The class has children of varying abilities, varying levels of engagement with learning and varying phonological understanding. Nazeera is looking at how the same phoneme can have different graphemes in her phonics work this term, and she is doing a local geography study as well as landscape painting. Nazeera loves Kit Wright's poetry and thought the poem 'The Sea in the Trees' was evocative, thought-provoking and presented plenty of creative opportunities for her children. (A full version of the poem can be found at: http://www.poetryarchive.org/poem/sea-trees and in Kit Wright's 2009 poetry collection, *The Magic Box*.)

Nazeera took her class outside to the playing field. She sat them underneath a tree and invited them to listen to what was around them. What could they hear? When they closed their eyes and listened, what pictures came into their minds? Nazeera had brought large sheets of paper for the children to respond in drawing or words and these would form the background for her working wall. The paper began to fill with describing words, pictures of trees, birds, castles, wind, God, hands and clouds.

Nazeera then read the poem 'The Sea in the Trees' quietly to the children. She invited them to stand up and close their eyes as she read the poem again and asked the children to shout out what images were in their minds. Nazeera recorded this on her tablet for later use. The children shouted out describing words such as calm, happy, peaceful and quiet, and other words such as boat, sea, trees, birds and fish. Stills of this recording were printed off and prepared to be added to the working wall.

Reflecting on the case study (part 1)

- Reflect on the importance of Nazeera's creative approach to bringing the children into the world of the poem. How much more effective was this approach than just reading it aloud in class? If so, why? If not, why not?
- Reflect on the different ways in which Nazeera encourages the children to respond to the poem. Were these important stages? Think about what the children were learning and how these activities will support later work with the poem.
- Reflect on the use of the working wall. Why did Nazeera bother to keep the responses and then display them?

Deconstruction and analysis

Creating an environment for poetry is very important. Poetry should not just be read or heard but also experienced. Glazzard and Palmer (2015) state that creating a good context for writing will enable the children to be hooked into learning. Nazeera's class were hooked into the place of the poem, the park and the idea of images in their minds as the old man in the poem had. The pre-writing stage, and even this pre-reading stage, is vitally important for poetry. Children need to feel the timbre of a poem and can far more quickly respond to its rhythm and mood without the barrier of the printed word. Through his document, *Building a Poetry Spine* from *Talk for Writing*, Pie Corbett (2013) states that, for babies and young children, sounds and forming tunes into rhythms help name their worlds and bring their worlds into being.

Case study: Part 2 – Ideation and writing

After the children had left for the day, Nazeera covered a large display board with their responses from the previous day. She printed out some still photographs from the film she had recorded and attached those to the display board, too.

Nazeera began to laugh and looked a little embarrassed as the children arrived the next day and settled down. They instantly quietened, wondering what was going on. Now the children were hooked and Nazeera revealed that late last night, when she got home from school, she was so tired that she fell asleep on the sofa. She looked very embarrassed and the children laughed. One little girl said, 'Did you dream about us Miss?' Nazeera looked surprised and told the children that she did have a dream but it was a bit silly. She said she had dreamed that the classroom walls had turned into the walls of a castle tower and that she was the princess, trapped inside it, waiting to be rescued. This gave license for the children all to start talking at once about their dreams. Nazeera let them. As the children were engaged in other activities that afternoon, she had attached a large sheet of paper to the working wall – with 'Dreams' written out at the top. She invited the children to come and write what some of their dreams were.

(Continued)

(Continued)

The next day, Nazeera began to write, and on one side of the page she had a sentence about her dream and on the other side she had a brief writing frame:

The .... fell asleep on the ....

And dreamed of ....

Underneath she had left a blank space and told the children that this was to describe what it was like where she fell asleep.

Then Nazeera read the first verse of 'The Sea in the Trees' and asked the children to work in pairs to discuss what they noticed about the words, and she said that her poem was going to be the same. As she read it again, she tapped her foot to help with the rhythm and the children joined in.

Nazeera started to model the opening sentence of the poem, discussing her thoughts with the children, encouraging them to join in with her emphasising the rhythm as she reread. She modelled thinking through word choices and discussed how to make the poem like Wright's original poem in order to get the rhythm right. She settled on this:

When the cool rain was falling

On the tiles, on the roof of the house.

She asked the children to finish the poem, using the writing frame from earlier.

Reflecting on the case study (part 2)

- Reflect on how Nazeera creatively hooked her class into the writing. What impact did it have on the children's idea creation?
- Reflect on how Nazeera scaffolded this stage of the writing process through modelling. How did this help the children? Was the writing frame necessary? If so, why? If not, why not?

Deconstruction and analysis

Nazeera started off with a writing hook. By using her own experience, she hooked the children into the lesson, rather than the more traditional,

'Right, children, let's do some writing.' Bearne (2002) makes the distinction between being a writing teacher and being a teacher of writing. Nazeera was clearly a writing teacher: a teacher who thinks, writes and models for her pupils. In this sense, she was also modelling the creative process. By hooking the children in, she was giving relevance and purpose to their writing and the children could relate to what she was doing and to the ideas she had. As a result, their ideas were vast and varied. The role of the teacher is crucial.

Bearne and Warrington's (2003) research into motivation and writing identified a number of key characteristics of effective writing teaching. One of these was about the teacher demonstrating the writing that should be undertaken using verbal commentary to make the decision-making process clear. The power of Nazeera's modelled writing should not be underestimated. However, what gives it its power is the verbal commentary that she gave while she wrote. Nazeera helped her children to see that the teacher has to think, too, and if she thinks like that, then I should, too. Nazeera empowered the children to get it wrong first time, and not always find the perfect word at the first attempt, and also that crossing something out is fine, too. This approach is very freeing for children and helps create that environment for creative expression within the genre-specific parameters, rather than fearing getting it wrong.

Case study: Part 3 – Respond, revise, edit, publish

As Nazeera worked with her class, the children used the writing frame to pull together their ideas from their dreams and pictures in their heads onto a framework. Nazeera encouraged flexibility with the framework at this stage so as not to dissuade the children from giving their ideas and recording their thoughts. Revising the text would come later. She particularly noted the two responses below and stopped the children to share this work:

The little girl fell asleep on the bed.

And dreamed of fish swimming on a mouse

(Continued)

(Continued)

> The tired boy fell asleep on the big, huge bed
>
> And dreamed of a massive castle with knights killing everyone ...

After she had read them to her class, Nazeera asked the children why they thought she had chosen these two particular examples. There was silence. So Nazeera read the first one again, alongside her example. She tapped her foot and read it rhythmically:

> When the cool rain was falling
>
> On the tiles, on the roof of the house.
>
> The little girl fell asleep on the bed.
>
> And dreamed of fish swimming on a mouse

Then she read the second one. The children immediately noticed the rhyming of house and mouse. Some of the more able children also noticed how it sounded right. The words fitted the rhythm, or as one child said: 'when we tapped, it all went in the right place'. Nazeera praised the second one for its great use of describing words but now the challenge was to make it all fit together 'in the right place'. She encouraged the children to read their work to each other, tapping their feet to check that it would all scan effectively. Those children who had finished and edited their work so that it scanned were then to add a second verse in the style of Wright, describing more about their dream. The children were pointed to the work from phonics sessions on the use of different graphemes for the same phoneme and this supported their thinking of a wider variety of alternative words.

They performed these poems to another class in a 'Poetry Reading' event, and parents were invited. All the poems appeared on the class blog and the final versions were on display in an anthology in the school foyer, with copies sent to Wright.

Assessment of the unit

As the unit progressed, Nazeera was formatively assessing the children's progress. She observed their discussion, their responses to her writing and worked with guided groups during the process.

Examples were placed on the working wall to support the children and she noted who was using them. She made notes in plenary sessions of children who had understood the rhyme and rhythm, and notes of how the children had responded to the task. Nazeera also wrote about who had found it difficult and why. These notes were then used to support planning for later units and guide the interventions that she would need to put in place. Essentially, Nazeera used the skills of noticing what was going on and what impact her teaching was having.

Reflecting on the case study (part 3)

- Reflect on the notion of Nazeera as a writer as well as a teacher. How was this important for the children's learning at this stage?
- Reflect on the ways in which the children were asked to share their work and the opportunities that Nazeera created. For what purpose did she make this effort?

Deconstruction and analysis

This revision and editing stage of the writing process can often get missed out as there is never enough time and you are always battling with those who say, 'but, I've finished'. However, this stage is crucial. It could be argued that Nazeera wasn't being particularly creative because she used a structure and writing frame and did what is usually regarded as good teaching, nevertheless let's look more closely.

Nazeera fostered self-direction and agency for her children as writers. Cremin (2015) states that these are central to creative pedagogic practice. Nazeera also involved the children as co-participants, she was writing with them, not doing it to them and this, Cremin goes on to say, is also central to creativity and is very inclusive. There is also the ethos to consider. The positive relationships that Nazeera had developed with her class and the emotional safety they felt was essential to success. Having their work read out and scrutinised was all part of their work as a community of learners. This was modelled by Nazeera, who, as a writer, was willing to have her work scrutinised, too. In fact, she shared her work as part of the poetry reading and it was included in the anthology, too. This trust, as Shayer and Adey (2002) state, is necessary to ensure a creative ethos.

Stop and think

How can you become a writing teacher and a writer, rather than just a teacher of writing? What impact could this have on your children's learning? Try it!

Try this

Activity 1: Morphological forced connections

When you are next planning a unit of work that requires some creative design or invention, try out this creative thinking technique to force the children to make connections between ideas that may not, at first sight, go together. If children are given no structure or framework to create with, they will often fall back on tried-and-tested ideas. Use this as a framework to stretch their thinking.

Activity 2: Change the environment

Do you have to teach every lesson in the same room? Could you take the children outside if it will enhance their learning? Could you change the room layout? Change their perspective on learning? Take them into the hall? Essentially, your environment will shape your lesson and impact heavily on learning, so only change it when it will enhance learning and engagement. For poetry, living the poem or experiencing the poem is crucial to engagement and creative responses. How can you get the children to live it?

Activity 3: Be a writer

When you are next planning a unit that involves writing, try writing alongside the children. Not only will it help you understand the challenges they face as they write, but, as a co-writer, you would also be setting yourself up to walk the journey with them. Nazeera, in the second case study, was prepared to have her writing scrutinised and this facilitated the ethos of collegiality and support for the children. Model writing, model thinking about writing and walk the journey with the children as they create and edit. It can be a powerful tool.

Summary

Throughout this chapter, I have focused on the notion that poetry is about playing with words and structures. Being playful is an essential part of being creative. Desailly states that: 'many a great discovery has been the result of playfulness with ideas or materials' (2012: 14). One of the ways in which we learn is through discovery, exploration and play, and the examples and ideas given in this chapter demonstrate how effective playing can be in developing children's engagement with and creation of poetry. The ideas in this chapter and approaches to poetry can be transferred across to other poems and forms, and the planning framework can be used across other genres. The writing process used in Nazeera's case study was first introduced and explained in Chapter 6 and other concrete examples of its application can also be found in Chapter 9.

Appendix 10.1 Great poetry collections to get to know

The Magic Box by Kit Wright (2009)

The Works: Key Stage 1, poems chosen by Pie Corbett (2006)

Magic Poems by John Foster and Korky Paul (1997)

Commotion in the Ocean by Giles Andreae (1998)

Second Big Book of Poetry selected by John Foster (1999)

A Child's Garden of Verses by Robert Louis Stevenson (1885)

The Oxford Nursery Rhyme Book collected by Iona and Peter Opie (1963)

Collected Poems for Children by Charles Causley (1996)

Umpteen Pockets by Adrian Mitchell (2009)

An Imaginary Menagerie by Roger McGough (1988)

I am a Potato by John Hegley (2014)

Further reading

Waugh, D., Bushnell, A. and Neaum, S. (eds) (2015) *Beyond Early Writing.* Northwich: Critical Publishing.

This great text covers all types of writing in the primary classroom, but the chapter by the editors on writing poetry makes good links to the teachers' own knowledge of poetry and the impact this has on children. It has some very clear case studies to contextualise the ideas.

Waugh, D., Joliffe, W. and Allott, K. (2014) Primary English for Trainee Teachers. London: Learning Matters.

Holly Faulkner's chapter on poetry in this text is really clear and focused. She emphasises how rhythm and rhyme support phonemic understanding and how poetry develops reading skills.

Wilson, A. (ed.) (2015) *Creativity in Primary Education*, 3rd edn. London: Learning Matters.

Teresa Cremin's chapter on creative teachers and creative teaching is great for getting your classroom ethos right. She unpacks the importance of play and trust relationships. Liz Chamberlain's chapter on creativity and literacy explores this further as she looks at creating language landscapes and the importance of the purpose and relevance of writing contexts.

References

Bearne, E. (2002) *Making Progress in Writing*. London: Routledge Falmer.

Bearne, E. and Warrington, M. (2003) 'Raising boys' achievement', *Literacy Today*, 35 (18): 18–20.

Brownjohn, S. (1994) *To Rhyme or Not to Rhyme*. Abingdon: Hodder and Stoughton.

Bryant, P., MacLean, M., Bradley, L. and Crossland, J. (1990) 'Rhyme and alliteration, phoneme detection and learning to read', *Developmental Psychology*, 26 (3): 429–38.

Cave, C. (1996) *Morphological Forced Connections*. Available at: http://members.optus net.com.au/charles57/Creative/Techniques/morph.htm (accessed 30 December 2015).

Corbett, P. (2013) *Building a Poetry Spine*. Available at: www.talk4writing.co.uk/wp-content/uploads/2013/09/Poetry-spine.pdf (accessed 30 December 2015).

Cremin, T. (2009) *Teaching English Creatively*. London: Routledge.

Cremin, T. (2015) 'Creative teachers and creative teaching', in A. Wilson (ed.), *Creativity in Primary Education*, 3rd edn. London: Learning Matters.

Department for Education (DfE) (2013) *The National Curriculum for England*. London: Crown Copyright.

Desailly, J. (2012) *Creativity in the Primary Classroom*. London: Sage.

Eliot, T.S. (1939) 'Macavity the mystery cat'. Available at: http://allpoetry.com/Macavity:-The-Mystery-Cat (accessed 31 December 2015).

Faulkner, H. (2014) 'Poetry', in D. Waugh, W. Joliffe and K. Allott (eds), *Primary English for Trainee Teachers*. London: Learning Matters.

Glazzard, J. and Palmer, J. (2015) *Enriching Primary English*. Northwich: Critical Publishing.

Goswami, U. (2002) 'Rhymes, phonemes and learning to read', in M. Cook (ed.), *Perspectives on the Teaching and Learning of Phonics*. Leicester: United Kingdom Reading Association (UKRA).

Heaney, S. (1966) 'Mid-term break', in Death of a Naturalist. Available at: www.poemhunter.com/poem/mid-term-break/ (accessed 31 December 2015).

Horner, C. and Ryf, V. (2007) *Creative Teaching English in the Early Years and Primary Classroom*. London: Routledge.

Martin, T., Lovatt, C. and Purnell, G. (2004) *The Really Useful Literacy Book*. London: Routledge.

Munsch, R. (1980) *The Paper Bag Princess*. Manitoba: Annick Press.

Shayer, M. and Adey, P. (2002) *Learning and Intelligence: Cognitive Acceleration Across the Curriculum from 5–15*. Buckingham: Open University Press.

Wright, K. (2009) 'The Sea in the Trees' and 'The Magic Box', in K. Wright, *The Magic Box*. London: Macmillan Children's Books.

11

Reading into writing

Key Stage 2 Poetry

Learning outcomes

By reading this chapter, you will have:

- Developed an understanding of how to teach form and rhyme creatively
- Developed your understanding from previous chapters of how to use guided writing effectively to develop writer's skills, knowledge and understanding
- Developed an understanding of multi-sensory approaches to teaching poetry
- Developed an understanding of how to use poetry to teach higher-order reading skills

National Curriculum links

From Key Stage 2 Years 3/4

develop positive attitudes to reading and understanding of what they read by:

- preparing poems and play scripts to read aloud and to perform, showing understanding through intonation, tone, volume and action

- discussing words and phrases that capture the reader's interest and imagination
- recognising some different forms of poetry [for example, free verse, narrative poetry]

From Key Stage 2 Years 5/6

maintain positive attitudes to reading and understanding of what they read by:

- learning a wider range of poetry by heart
- preparing poems and plays to read aloud and to perform, showing understanding through intonation, tone and volume so that the meaning is clear to an audience

draft and write by:

- selecting appropriate grammar and vocabulary, understanding how such choices can change and enhance meaning

evaluate and edit by:

- assessing the effectiveness of their own and others' writing
- proposing changes to vocabulary, grammar and punctuation to enhance effects and clarify meaning

DfE (2013)

Chapter overview

This chapter draws on the 2013 National Curriculum and exemplifies ideas in context from the 'Creative approaches to …' chapters. Here, the focus is poetry, reading and writing. Using as a focus Ian Serraillier's 'The Visitor', from Wilson's 1988 book *Every Poem Tells a story*, dramatic approaches to teaching poetry will be explored as well as exploring how to teach form and rhyme. Guided writing will be considered here as a powerful tool to develop language richness and teach form and structure. Within the theme of 'A Graveyard Meeting', cross-curricular links to a local history topic will also be explored, drawing on the use of primary sources to find out about the past. This chapter will also explore teaching higher-order reading skills and focus on Assessment focuses 5–7: exploring writers' use of language, writers' intent and cultural aspects of the writing. As part of the planning process in this case study, formative assessment and record-keeping will be addressed. A list of recommended poems and anthologies will be given in Appendix 11.1 at the end of this chapter with ideas of how to use them.

Introduction

Having taught in Years 5 and 6 for many years and then having spent a lot more time observing lessons and working with Years 5 and 6 teachers, there are a couple of classic narrative poems that all the children in all the classes explore. For those reading this chapter with experience at this end of the school, you can probably name them without reading on. For those who do not have this experience, I will tell you about this.

These famous narrative poems are Alfred Noyes's 1906 classic, 'The Highwayman', telling the story of the landlord's daughter, Bess, falling in love with the handsome roguish highwayman and being used as bait by the king's men to bring him to his death. The other is Walter de la Mare's 1912 classic, 'The Listeners', an eerie tale of a traveller keeping his promise to arrive at a house, no one answers but someone or something is listening. Both of these poems are brilliantly written, wonderfully phrased and tell incredibly compelling stories that engage the reader. But, despite their brilliance, they are overdone and probably by me, too. In fact, it was only last month I took the opportunity to set up a murder scene in a lecture theatre, dress up in a highwayman's outfit and enact the poem for my Primary PGCE students.

In this chapter, I want to focus on classic narrative poetry but present some alternative resources, new approaches and fresh choices that still engage the reader but also use language creatively to increase children's choices as they write.

Drama and poetry

I have considered the role of drama and shared some dramatic techniques throughout this book, but mainly in Chapter 4. Here, I suggest that drama is not just about getting into character and motivation but also about supporting specific elements of poetry. Bearne (2003), cited by Grainger (2005), suggests that the process of writing needs considerable investment: the process of composition needs to be extended through a lot of discussion, exploration, talk and drama. Drama is an essential part of the writing process. However, with poetry, particularly narrative poetry, drama can provide different support and really help children, not just with the narrative element but also with the form and structure. McNaughton's (1997) empirical work suggests that children who engage in drama prior to writing use a greater range of vocabulary choices, and whilst the later empirical work of Cremin et al. (2006) focuses on children's motivation and engagement with writing, there is still the vision of authorial intent, structure and language choice to create certain effects.

In the case study below, the class teacher uses a dramatic approach to support an understanding of the poem, which will then lead to some writing. As you read the case study, reflect on how the physical approach to the poetry reading supports the children's understanding of the writer's intent, the mood created and the story.

Case study: Part 1 – Bringing a poem to life

Roxanne was planning a unit of narrative poetry alongside the theme of local history. She chose Serraillier's poem 'The Visitor' (in Wilson 1988) as she felt that it would engage the children, provide a way into local history through the graveyard and also develop their understanding of form, metre and rhyme. The poem also has a humorous overtone.

Roxanne began by having the tables and chairs pushed back to leave a big open space. She arranged the furniture and put in some benches at different heights and called for some actors: a man and his wife (to many titters from her class!), and a skeleton to lie on the ground. The players took their places. Roxanne split the class into four parts for her orchestration of the poem: wind in the trees sounds, werewolf sounds, waves crashing onto the rocks sounds, and owls hooting. She would conduct these sections whilst reading the poem and the children would act out whatever she read with some help. Roxanne invited each group in turn to take their places on the benches at different heights to form the backdrop scene to their play. They each in turn practised their noises and were ready to begin. Roxanne used different voices for the man, the wife and the skeleton and read with expression and drama, conducting the sounds to create the effect. At the end, she asked each person to take a 'still photo' in their mind of an image from the play, return to a table and sketch it out in whatever way they wanted.

Reflection, deconstruction and analysis

Why did Roxanne go to all that trouble? Why not just read it out normally? Grainger states that:

> [creative teachers of writing] find inspirational and involving ways forward that build on the children's interests, capture their imaginations and energise their emotions so that a desire to write is developed and their voices are activated through deep creative engagement and considered reflection. (2005: 88)

This summarises what Roxanne was doing here. She was using a creative and involving approach to the reading of the poem that the children said made it come alive, in other words it turned the abstract words on the page into a concrete experience. A buzz of excitement, laughter in the right places and enjoyment of the interplay between the man, wife and skeleton happened because Roxanne brought the words to life and made the children active participants in their own learning. Ansell and Foster (2014) state that physical engagement in learning such as that described above, provides a necessary supplement to what can be quite a formulaic approach to teaching writing. Children who are more engaged will often learn more effectively and therefore it is part of our jobs as teachers to ensure that engagement as far as we can. Helping children become actively involved in their learning, rather than them being spectators, is a very good start.

In the next part of the case study, Roxanne moves the class on into developing their understanding. They are now familiar with 'The Visitor' in terms of the story and characters, but as you read this next section of the case study, reflect on how Roxanne develops the children's reading skills, especially inference, questioning and clarifying from the text and getting inside the mind of the author.

Case study: Part 2 – Higher-order reading skills

Roxanne began the next stage of this unit of work by posing some questions. She opened her lesson with: 'As I was rereading this last

(Continued)

(Continued)

night, there's some things in this poem which really puzzled me.' She stated the first questions: 'Why was this man walking alone? Who was he?' and the children began to speculate. Roxanne gave pairs of children a copy of the poem with a wide margin and encouraged them to speculate about what was happening and asked them to fill in some details.

Roxanne then asked the children why they thought that Serraillier might have written this poem, were there any messages that he was trying to convey? Was there any commentary on life he was trying to make and was this consistent with other writings of his. Roxanne had compiled a display of more of his work: *The Silver Sword*, a wartime children's novel; and his five-line poem, 'The Tickle Rhyme'; as well as another poem, 'First Foot', with a similar rhyme scheme, form and content to 'The Visitor'; and two other books *There's No Escape* and *The Enchanted Island*. The children had an opportunity to look at these and to get a sense of Serraillier's approach. After much discussion as to what the author was trying to do, a couple of groups arrived at the idea of humour within a scary setting and this also came out in 'First Foot' and *The Enchanted Island*. It provided a very good line of enquiry. The children were then given pictures of Serraillier working at his desk and some thought bubbles to stick on, write in and capture his thoughts whilst writing the poem.

The class decided that the rhyming couplets and rhythm added some of the humour and some of the nonsensical replies from the husband as the skeleton appears. They decided that this was like something from a children's adventure cartoon, rather than a serious poem. Instinctively, the children had considered the impact of tone.

Reflecting on the case study (part 2)

- Inference is all about reading between the lines and, as Kispal (2008) states, is about taking two pieces of information from the text and using knowledge and ideas gained to arrive at a third piece of information that is not explicit. How did Roxanne support the children to do this?
- Why was it helpful for the children to see a range of the author's work? What support did it give to the children in understanding authorial intent for 'The Visitor'?

> • Think about the progression in children's responses, from specu-
>   lating about the text and asking questions, to arriving at the idea of
>   humour in a scary setting, to form and structure. How did Roxanne
>   facilitate this? This is very high order thinking but Roxanne did not
>   explicitly teach it. How then did it happen?

Deconstruction and analysis

Warner (2014: 56) cites the work of Pardo (2004) and Lewis and Tregenza
(2007) as she identifies some key strategies for developing comprehension.
These strategies are:

- Activating prior knowledge
- Prediction
- Questioning and clarifying
- Visualisation and imagination
- Summarising
- Drawing inferences
- Monitoring understanding

In the case study above, we saw a number of these strategies employed to
help children arrive at a deeper understanding of the text. Better and more
experienced readers bring their understanding of the world to a text.
Graham (2010), also cited by Warner (2014), suggests that children need to
make connections between their own lives and texts so that texts become
a fundamental part of their lives and not just a peripheral one. In the case
of 'The Visitor', do children know what a graveyard is? Have they visited
one? Perhaps a retelling of this story in a graveyard might be a good idea?
A colleague of mine once borrowed a skeleton from his doctor brother-in-
law, wrapped it in a cloak and used that for this poem's retelling: it certainly
caused some screaming amongst his class as the skeleton rose from the
ground on strings. Children do need to understand what is going on and
have their knowledge activated and enriched if they are to understand text.

In the first part of the case study, children were visualising and using
other senses to respond to the poem. Warner (2014) explains that this strategy is very valuable to develop understanding. She suggests that it challenges
and extends thinking, surprises the reader and helps add a greater depth to
children's understanding of the story. I will also add that I think it helps them
see how the form and structure of the text impacts on understanding, too,
especially if the children are actively involved in the reading.

Stop and think

How will you activate children's prior knowledge and allow them to bring their knowledge and experience to a text? How will you start their reading journey for them? How will you facilitate the kinds of discussions Roxanne had with her class?

Teaching poetry writing creatively

To some, it could certainly appear that writing poetry, fitting into a particular rhyme scheme and structure, fitting in a certain number of beats per line and using the right stresses, is not very creative. However, I would argue otherwise. I see writing poetry as problem-solving, an essential creative skill. The key aim is to try and solve the problem of which words to use to give the desired effect, which rhyming words give the best options. Bushnell et al. (2015) suggest that poetry is about using words with precision and, in poetry, each word counts. Each word must do exactly what the writer wants it to do, there is no room for anything extraneous. This requires the essential creative skills of exploring language, playing with sounds and ordering words playfully to communicate meaning, all within the enabling constraints of the poem's form and structure. Bushnell et al. also discuss the importance of prosody in writing poetry. Prosody is the collective word for other elements of poetry that we have touched on earlier in the chapter: rhythm, metre, volume and pitch, all that Roxanne had to take into consideration – as shown in the case study – and as she moves into writing, she will have to pay attention to how she teaches it.

In this third part of the case study, reflect on how Roxanne approaches teaching children to write with the same form and structure in a sequel to the visitor.

Case study: Part 3 – 'The Skeleton Returns'

Having now scaffolded her children's understanding of the poem through questioning and exploration, Roxanne introduces the next task. She is keen for her class to explore the form and structure of 'The Visitor' and use it as an opportunity to select precise language to create humorous episodes in a dark setting, as Serraillier does. Since her class has discovered that the form and structure does that through rhyming couplets, she is keen to keep the rhythm, metre and rhyme scheme the same. So, she introduces the idea of a sequel: 'The Skeleton Returns'. In order for the children to understand the rhythm and metre of the poem, she reads the first and the fourth couplet placing the stresses so there are four in each line:

<pre>
    /   /   /   /
'It's the loveliest ring in the world', she said
      /   /   /   /
As it glowed on her finger, they slipped off to bed
</pre>

Roxanne invited her class to clap the rhythm on the stresses and then rap the poem with her. They made a recording to listen to while they were writing to support their understanding of the form.

The children were then asked to explore ideas for how 'The Skeleton Returns' could go. Did he lose the ring again? Did he want revenge for the wife throwing the ring away? Was there something else? Did he just want to be friends, or was he wishing for others to join him in the land of the undead? Following these questions, the story had to be thought through: would they start and finish with three lines, the same as in part one in Serraillier's poem? What would the interplay between the characters be this time? Was there a new character? Perhaps the man and wife's child? So many questions to explore, problems to solve and decisions to make.

Roxanne invited the class to reinvestigate the poem for any other structural features to take into account. They noticed the repetition of couplets 6 and 8 and the first half of couplet 11, and also some changes of pitch denoted by capitals. There was also the use of ellipsis to show the necessity for pausing whilst reading. Roxanne explained how these were essential for the overall effect. In pairs, the class began to start composing part 2 of 'The Skeleton Returns'. The rap they had made was playing to support their understanding of rhythm and 'The Visitor' was displayed for children to be reminded of the rhyme scheme.

Reflecting on the case study (part 3)

- Reflect on Roxanne's use of rap to support the metre and rhythm of the poem. Why was it important to record it and play it while the children were composing part 2?

(Continued)

(Continued)

- Roxanne doesn't explicitly teach the different form and structure but facilitates the children's understanding through investigation and exploration. Why is this more effective?
- A big part of being creative is encouraging children to solve problems. How does Roxanne use this approach whilst maintaining some high-level problem-solving around rhythm, metre, pitch and tone? I have called these 'enabling constraints'. Why is seeing structural features such as rhythm and rhyme 'enabling', rather than 'constraining', important for the concept of creativity?

A guided intervention

In Chapter 3, and later in Chapter 8, we explored guided writing in some detail, but here I want to look at it again in the context of poetry and also in the context of developing children's editing skills. Guided writing should take place at any and every stage of the writing process and it is an essential scaffold to support children's ability to engage effectively but also for teachers to assess understanding.

Rooke's (2012) report on transforming writing highlights the importance of guided writing to respond to children's needs as the assessment takes place during the process of writing, rather than after the event. Misconceptions can be addressed and teachers can respond in a timely and effective way. Rooke cites a teacher from his research, who states that:

> Guided writing is so much more than just the writing. It's the thinking that's going with it and it's getting that in a small group and getting children to bounce ideas off each other and discuss it and even if at the end of a session where it's been guided writing the children haven't written anything, that talk can be most powerful and you can see it in their writing the next day. (2012: 36)

Guided writing is a very powerful tool, not only to support putting the words down on the page in the most appropriate order and form for the task set, but also to support the thinking and discussion that goes alongside it.

Roxanne had targeted a small group of children from her class who she had noticed from her observations of their earlier work, discussion with groups of children writing and responses in mini-plenaries to support with their composition. Her plan is found in Figure 11.1.

Date:	Grp/chn: (6)

Focus/objectives

To use the form, rhythm and structure of a rhyming couplet from Ian Serraillier's 'The Visitor' so as to compose their own couplet for a sequel, 'The Skeleton Returns'

National Curriculum: From Upper Key Stage 2 Year 5/6

draft and write by:

- selecting appropriate grammar and vocabulary, understanding how such choices can change and enhance meaning

evaluate and edit by:

- assessing the effectiveness of their own and others' writing
- proposing changes to vocabulary, grammar and punctuation to enhance effects and clarify meaning

Success criteria

Children to create these at the start of the session – based on objective and shared work

Structure and approaches	**Resources**
Listen to the rap of 'The Visitor' created earlier by the class using the four stresses. Look at the words written down and where the stresses are and note how it is stressed iambically. Rap together Teacher models a line of a new couplet for 'The Skeleton Returns': *He ran up the hill towards the cottage* - Does it fit the stresses? - Is the rhyming word effective at the end? - Does it convey the same tone? - Can we change the language Edit together Using mini whiteboards, write the next line Evaluate together Work in pairs to check stresses and rap the lines Collect ideas for the rest of the sequel	Whiteboards and pens

Plenary

Each pair raps their new line in turn whilst showing it with the stresses for evaluation by the rest of the group

Discuss and amend as appropriate

Assessment and comments

Names	

Action needed

Figure 11.1   Guided Writing Plan: 'The Visitor'

A word about assessment and feedback within this context

Effective assessment comes out of effective planning and it is a core teaching skill, which is all part of the teaching and learning process and not an add-on. In the case study sections in this chapter, our teacher, Roxanne, has utilised a lot of different formative assessment techniques. As she has been in the role of a facilitator, she has enabled herself to observe the children's understanding and also join in with discussions. Here, Roxanne is beginning to build a picture of what her children can do. As Anderson (2014) states, effective assessment is about gathering a range of evidence. It is not enough just to assess a product. Creative approaches are all about valuing the process of learning and valuing the thinking and word that leads up to the product as well as the product itself. Using a range of approaches during the process of writing is crucial to gaining a clearer understanding of what your children can do.

In terms of assessing composition, reading work and giving feedback as one-to-one, in guided writing or during mini-plenaries is helpful, but is this the most helpful approach? I would argue that facilitating opportunities for pupils to support each other in this is not only useful to free up the teacher but it also means, as Anderson (2014) also states, that children will be much more able to consider the purpose of their piece and what is required for the audience as they work independently and in pairs. Notice how, in the case study above, Roxanne always asks the children to write in pairs, this is so that they can support each other and help each other evaluate their work.

This is not to say that summative assessment and marking work is unhelpful. If done effectively, it is phenomenally valuable. Responding in your feedback, either verbally or in writing, to the learning outcome, how the child has performed, recognising strengths and areas for development and then giving them a chance to read it afterwards, is great practice.

Case study: Part 4 – 'A Graveyard Meeting': a cross-curricular local history study

Roxanne chose 'The Visitor' because it set the scene for some exploratory primary-source investigation for a local history project on 'Who am I?' This was stimulated by a visit to the graveyard at the local church next to the school and an opportunity for the children to look at some of the names and make some connections with their own personal history. Roxanne had invited the curator of the local archives into the school to meet the children and support them in tracing some of their own family histories.

This began by starting a family tree at home and talking to parents and grandparents to get it started. Cremin states that: 'creative teachers ... make frequent references to and integration with other subjects and to the world beyond the school gate' (2015: 39). For Roxanne, the poem 'The Visitor' gave her an opportunity to enthuse children about the past, their own past and also the past life of the school. Looking through the school's old Victorian logbook, they found some names that were then traced to the graveyard and into the archives and records of births and deaths. The children from the Victorian period who had previously trodden the floorboards of the school, then started to come to life for the children investigating and they decided to have a 'Victorian Day' to celebrate, inviting past pupils back to see all they had found out. Cremin goes on to say that:

> Such teachers encourage children to link their learning between subjects and within subjects and often prompt connections with the children's lives outside school. This appears to increase the relevance of the curriculum to the learners. (2015, 39)

Reflecting on the case study (part 4)

- Notice how Roxanne capitalises on the opportunities that 'The Visitor' poem presented. She took some risks in bringing in the local curator, taking a trip to the archives and using the graveyard, not only as a setting for a poem but also to capitalise on the primary source of gravestones there for a local history study. Was this a bit too much? What learning could the children have done from this?
- Roxanne made learning purposeful and relevant to the children and also to the children's families. Why is this a good idea?
- What learning opportunities can you see in putting on a themed day such as a 'Victorian Day', inviting past pupils and displaying work on the history of the school? How does learning become relevant here?

Try this

Activity 1: Performing a poem

When you are next planning some work on poetry, think about how to perform it. Poems should not be confined to words on a page but should come alive. You may not need to go to the lengths that Roxanne did to create an almost human stage set but do think about how you can turn often abstract words into a contextual experience for the children.

Activity 2: Poetry as problem-solving

Why not frame your next unit of work on poetry as a puzzle or problem to solve. See the form and structure as enabling constraints and encourage the children to explore and play with language to fit the gaps which the puzzle offers. Constraints are important because they often mean that children have to be more creative, rather than just giving them free rein.

Activity 3: Cross-curricular opportunities and text choice

Roxanne chose the poem of 'The Visitor' because it provided a great context for her work on local history. The graveyard provided a rich source of primary historical data for her children to use and become history detectives. Think through as you plan, what texts you will use and how they can fit into your overall plans and vision for learning so that it becomes relevant and connected for children.

Summary

This chapter takes a different approach to poetry, looking at how to teach a narrative poem creatively and in a way that engages children. Using rap to help with rhythm not only helps children see the structure but it also helps children see that poetry is not just about words on the page but about performance. By considering the author's intent, often speculating, there is an opportunity to consider why the author would have written it and helps in the understanding of the content. Serraillier, as 'The Visitor' shows, was clearly interested in humorous interludes within quite a scary context. For children, seeing how writers think and understand their approach and their purpose for writing, helps them see themselves as writers, rather than just school children writing in a book for the only purpose of it being marked by the teacher.

Facilitating opportunities for children to discuss, share and rehearse writing, as discussed in other chapters, especially comes to the fore here because, for children to get rhythm, metre and structure right, they need to rehearse out loud, share with a partner and be in a classroom environment where this is encouraged. In our case study, Roxanne does exactly that. Finally, making the learning connected and relevant is crucial to children seeing how learning opportunities are present in everything we do. This is something so inherent to effective Early Years practice that seems to disappear as children move through school, where subjects become compartmentalised and learning is often reduced to written exercises. The process of learning should be valued and discussed and assessed, just as Roxanne did.

Appendix 11.1 More great classic narrative poems and poetry collections to get to know

The Highwayman by Alfred Noyes

The Listeners by Walter de la Mare

The Lady of Shalott by Alfred, Lord Tennyson

The Charge of the Light Brigade by Alfred, Lord Tennyson

Ozymandias by Percy Bysshe Shelley

Inchcape Rock by Robert Southey

The Owl and the Pussycat by Edward Lear

On the Wings of Peace: In Memory of Hiroshima and Nagasaki by Sheila Hamanaka

Poetry Speaks: Who am I? edited by Elise Paschen, Dominique Raccah and Joy Harjo

Because a Fire was in my Head edited by Michael Morpurgo

101 Poems for Children chosen by Carol Ann Duffy

Further reading

Brownjohn, S. (1994) *To Rhyme or Not to Rhyme?* London: Hodder and Stoughton.

This classic text by a great writer gives everything you need to know about how to teach children to write poetry. It covers all aspects of subject knowledge, some great poems and lots of excellent practical ideas.

Phinn, G. (2009) *Teaching Poetry in the Primary Classroom.* Carmarthen: Crown House.

Well-known former teacher, inspector, author and speaker Gervase Phinn presents a practical and easy-to-read guide to how to get children writing poetry. He also focuses on the importance of the classroom environment, a recurring theme throughout this book.

The Poetry Trust, (2010) *The Poetry Toolkit: Foolproof Recipes for Teaching Poetry in the Classroom.* Halesworth: The Poetry Trust. Available at: www.thepoetrytrust. org/images/uploads/pdfs/Toolkit%20for%20Teachers.pdf (accessed 3rd Jan 2016).

This is a very practical toolkit that provides a lot of exciting and engaging ideas to use and adapt to get children into poetry. There are some great resources in it, too, that can kick-start ideas and prompts for planning.

References

Anderson, K. (2014) 'Assessment: An invaluable classroom resource', in D. Waugh, W. Joliffe and K. Allott (eds), *Primary English for Trainee Teachers.* London: Learning Matters.

Ansell, C. and Foster, T. (2014) 'Talking and learning through language and literacy', in A. Vickery (ed.), *Developing Active Learning in the Primary Classroom.* London: Sage.

Bearne, E. (2003) *Making Progress in Writing.* London: Routledge.

Bushnell, A., Neaum, S. and Waugh, D. (2015) 'Writing poetry', in D. Waugh, A. Bushnell and S. Neaum (eds), *Beyond Early Writing.* Northwich: Critical Publishing.

Cremin, T. (2015) 'Creative teachers and creative teaching', in A. Wilson (ed.), *Creativity in Primary Education,* 3rd edn. London: Learning Matters.

Cremin, T., Goouch, K., Blakemore, L., Goff, E. and Macdonald, R. (2006) 'Connecting drama and writing: Seizing the moment to write', *Research in Drama Education: The Journal of Applied Theatre and Performance,* 11 (3): 273–91.

Department for Education (DfE) (2013). *The National Curriculum for England.* London: Crown Copyright.

Graham, J. (2010) 'Small children talking their way into being readers', in P. Goodwin (ed.), *The Literate Classroom,* 3rd edn. London: Routledge.

Grainger, T. (2005) 'Motivating children to write', in P. Goodwin (ed.), *The Literate Classroom.* London: David Fulton.

Kispal, A. (2008) *Effective Teaching of Inference Skills for Reading: Literature Review.* DCSF Research Report No. 031 (DCSF-RR031). London: Department for Children, Schools and Families (DCSF).

Lewis, M. and Tregenza, J. (2007) 'Beyond simple comprehension', *English 4–11,* 30: 11–16.

McNaughton, M.-J. (1997) 'Drama and children's Writing: A study of the influence of drama on the imaginative writing of primary school children', *Research in Drama Education*, 2 (1): 55–76.

Pardo, L. (2004) 'What every teacher needs to know about comprehension', *The Reading Teacher*, 58 (3): 272–80.

Rooke, J. (2012) *Transforming Writing: Interim Evaluation Report*. London: National Literacy Trust and Esmee Fairbairn Foundation. Available at: www. literacytrust.org.uk/assets/0001/6090/TW_Interim_report_FINAL.pdf (accessed 4 January 2016).

Serraillier, I. 'The Visitor'. In Wilson, R. ed (1988). *Every Poem Tells A Story: A Collection of Stories in Verse*. London: Viking Kestrel Books.

Warner, C. (2014) 'Learning to comprehend', in D. Waugh and S. Neaum (eds), *Beyond Early Reading*. Northwich: Critical Publishing.

Wilson, R. (ed.) (1988) *Every poem Tells a Story: A Collection of Stories in Verse*. London: Viking Kestrel Books.

Creative approaches

Transition Key Stage 2–3

12

Learning outcomes

By reading this chapter, you will have:

- Understood the importance of transition of curriculum and approaches to teaching and learning between Key Stages 2 and 3
- Developed an understanding of how to support transition for children effectively
- Reflected on the importance of creative approaches to teaching and learning in order to develop children as learners
- Explored a range of approaches to planning and teaching English at the end of Key Stage 2 and into Key Stage 3

National Curriculum links

Key Stage 3

Section 6: language and literacy. All areas: spoken language, reading and writing and vocabulary development.

However, there is a particular focus on reading critically, writing polished scripts for presentations, improvising and rehearsing and performing play scripts, using role, intonation, tone, volume, mood, silence, stillness and action to add impact.

Upper Key Stage 2

maintain positive attitudes to reading and understanding of what they read by:

- preparing plays to read aloud and to perform, showing understanding through intonation, tone and volume so that the meaning is clear to an audience
- drawing inferences such as inferring characters' feelings, thoughts and motives from their actions, and justifying inferences with evidence

draft and write by:

- selecting appropriate grammar and vocabulary, understanding how such choices can change and enhance meaning

DfE (2013)

Chapter overview

Teaching English post-Standard Assessment Tests (SATS) is always a challenge. Realistically, there will be a lot of preparation to get those all-important attainment percentage targets. So, what can be done to help motivate learners beyond SATs and help prepare for Key Stage 3? Here, the focus is on preparation for the Key Stage 3 curriculum. It focuses on a key text: Philip Pullman's *Northern Lights* (1995) and explores the Personal, Social and Health Education (PSHE) theme of relationships. Here, integration is done through concepts and skills and also looks at embedding strong literature into the curriculum. Thinking techniques explored include the 'Napoleon technique', first introduced in Chapter 4, which involves putting yourself in someone else's shoes, for which *Northern Lights* is perfect as a key text. This case study highlights the importance of reading into writing and supports learning and understanding into Years 7 and 8 expectations.

Transition from Key Stage 2 to 3

Leaving primary school and moving into secondary education is a key transition in a child's life. It is extremely important and fraught with many uncertainties. A child will have a range of different teachers, not one. They will have to negotiate their way around a larger building with limited time between lessons to find the right classroom, rather than go to one room for everything. They will have to negotiate a range of different teaching styles, different homework, a greater complexity of tasks, more children, many of whom they won't know. A lot happens that can stop children from feeling safe. An effective transition is important to ensure that the child progresses into Key Stage 3 towards Key Stage 4 and GCSE level.

Hughes et al. (2013) maintain that a successful transition is crucially important for a child's psychosocial well-being. We know that if a child is feeling safe and happy, then they are more likely to learn.

An important factor to support effective transition is the progression of curriculum, so children are building on what they have already done and know. Therefore, when they go into Year 7 with all the changes to context, they do have something to build on. An empirical study by Rainer and Cropley (2015), within the context of physical education (PE) teaching, suggests that a failure to do this can disadvantage children's ability to engage in lifelong learning. They also suggest that liaison between Key Stages 2 and 3 teachers is vital to ensure successful transition.

Gill Parker's (2011) study explores transition in the teaching and learning of English between Key Stages 2 and 3. She sets the context of teachers having access to assessments, a curriculum continuity document and some transition units that the Year 6 children completed prior to starting Year 7. One of the challenges which she raises is the issue of the six-week holiday and children regressing. She also suggests that the narrowing of the curriculum that can occur as a result of preparing for the end of Key Stage 2 tests (SATS) can have a major impact on Year 7 learning. Galton remarks that:

> the reality is that for many pupils much of Y6, in the run up to the tests, consists largely of revision with an emphasis on whole class direct instruction. This squeeze on the curriculum and the restricted range of pedagogy employed in Y6 has implications for teaching at the lower end of the secondary school. (1999: 14)

So, what can be done to support children's progression from Key Stage 2 to 3? My first suggestion is probably undoable and unthinkable in the current performativity culture of education in England: stop narrowing the curriculum and spending from January to May of Year 6 doing endless practice tests. This will turn children off English, reduce English to knowing how to pass the test and not help them in their learning.

My second suggestion is to maximise the time offered by the latter part of Year 6 with some focused work that supports children's progression to Year 7. The National Literacy Strategy published some Year 6 planning materials in 2002, which supported fiction, non-fiction and poetry towards transition. Until 2010, the primary national strategies published some helpful material using Michael Morpurgo's 2000 novel *Kensuke's Kingdom* and Jacqueline Wilson's 1993 novel *The Suitcase Kid* (the planning for these units are available at: DfES, 2002).

These units are intended to help provide an early introduction to a typical Year 7 lesson structure and teaching approach. They are intended to help inform teachers' understanding of children's strengths and areas to develop immediately prior to Year 7 and support transfer and liaison through shared work with secondary providers through a Year 7 unit. The planning utilises objectives from the Key Stage 3 English curriculum.

What I am not saying is that these transition units are the answer to effective transition. What I am saying is that some learning and teaching that takes on the aims as outlined previously can support engagement with English, help children develop their learning, not just of the content, but also of learning how to learn. Children need to develop in their confidence as learners and know how to learn in order to smooth the transition into Key Stage 3.

The Key Stage 3 curriculum for English

The National Curriculum for English Key Stage 3 (DfE, 2014) demands that children read whole books, that they read for pleasure and purpose, in simple terms, that they enjoy reading. But alongside this, the curriculum demands that teachers develop children's understanding of authorial intent, looking at nuance in the texts and developing use of figurative language. Children are expected to develop their understanding of writing for purpose, taking into account the audience and the differences between written and spoken language. As this book has shown, these demands follow on progressively from those in Key Stage 2. In fact, having done some primary English taster sessions for secondary English teachers and student teachers, they are all surprised by some of the complexity and expectations demanded in Upper Key Stage 2 and the level of knowledge, skills, concepts and understanding that children in Years 5 and 6 can demonstrate.

Teaching English creatively at Key Stage 3

In this section, I want to draw some parallels with other concepts I have pulled out through this book. There is perhaps a misconception that English teaching in secondary school is 'chalk and talk' and endless essays preparing for GCSEs, where, yet again, teachers and schools are judged by the grades achieved. However, Pike (2004) refers to English teaching as an art, not just about the transmission of information. He refers to Dickens's 1854 novel *Hard Times*, where the aptly named teacher Mr Choakumchild is being introduced through all the knowledge he has accumulated. The comment at the end of the section suggests that more knowledge does not always make a better teacher. The inimitable Mr Keating from Peter Weir and Tom Schulman's 1989 film *Dead Poets Society*, quite literally rips up the textbook with the desire to see his boys get underneath the language, rather than read the textbook and answer the questions which the author has set.

Pike's earlier (2000) work applauds responsive teaching of English, where the teacher manipulates the curriculum so that it starts from where the child is, and not from where the teacher or scheme of work is. This is picked up by Dymoke (2009), who suggests a helpful structure for a Key Stage 3 English lesson but goes on to say that variety is a key feature of a successful lesson. Why? So that learners can be engaged.

Dymoke goes on to connect this with engagement with texts and writes that children should be encouraged creatively to enjoy their encounters with texts and he cites Ofsted (2005), which states that engaging children in reading could be a way to affect social change. I cannot imagine anything more creative than that. So, how can this be planned? Clarke, Dickinson and Westbrook state that: 'Planning is highly creative' (2010: 34). She goes on to share that children, in terms of Key Stage 3 English, should be active and independent learners, and should be gradually scaffolded to having more control over their own learning. Again, you will see from other chapters in this book how this correlates with teaching English creatively at Key Stages 1 and 2.

So, yes, the demands, complexity and expectations of knowledge, skills, concepts and understanding are higher. The range and complexity of texts are greater but the essence is the same. The job of the teacher is to raise the achievement of the children in their class – not just their attainment but their achievement, too. As I have said many times in this book, children learn more effectively if they are engaged and active in the learning process. They learn more effectively if they are inspired by a creative and enthusiastic teacher who makes learning purposeful and relevant, and if they feel safe in the environment and with the ethos they are in.

The following section is an extended case study, using as a focus text Philip Pullman's 1995 novel, *Northern Lights*, the first of his *His Dark Materials* trilogy. The case study explores creative teaching of English developing transition to Year 7 and demonstrates how to engage and enthuse children and develop their creative thinking whilst exploring the demands of the Key Stage 3 English Curriculum. The class teacher has planned for differentiation using a model of 'All, Most, Some': what he expects all the class to be able to do, most of them and then some of them (see Table 12.1, created for *Northern Lights*). Rather than providing differentiation by asking children to do more, this approach facilitates the same objective being met but at different levels of cognitive challenge.

Table 12.1   All, Most, Some'. Differentiated Outcomes for *Northern Lights* unit

Year 6–7 Transition: *Northern Lights* by Philip Pullman

All	Most	Some
Retell extracts from the story	*Compare* the film, *The Golden Compass*, with the book	*Persuade* merits of the book or film
Select key moments		
Summarise some of these key moments into a story board to demonstrate understanding of the plot structure	*Identify* differences – perhaps look at scenes, characterisation	*Analyse* differences
		Create a scene mentioned but not described in the book
Describe major characters	*Explain* preferences	*Invent* some additional characters and explore how they would impact on the other characters and the action

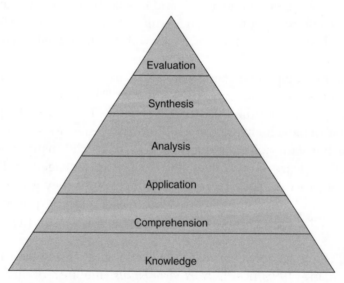

Figure 12.1   A representation of Bloom's Taxonomy

The 'All, Most, Some' approach draws on Benjamin Bloom's et al. (1956) taxonomy of educational objectives. Bloom's taxonomy was developed with several aims in mind. Krathwohl (2002) defines these as: providing a common language for learning goals; providing a basis for determining curricula; a way to determine the congruence of objectives; and to provide a panorama for the range of educational objectives available. I have seen this framework also used by a variety of teachers to support the planning of learning in order to facilitate challenge for those more able learners in class. Krathwohl refers to this as the 'original taxonomy'. A representation of Bloom's six main categories of knowledge is demonstrated in Figure 12.1.

Case study: Part 1

Nick's Year 6 class had just finished their end of Key Stage 2 assessments and were looking forward to a break. He had communicated with the three secondary schools that all his class were going to start attending the following September, and members of all the three English departments had agreed to work with him to meet up and spend time over the half-term break planning some transition work based on Philip Pullman's *Northern Lights*. The week before half-term, the three secondary school English teachers and Nick spent a session with his class introducing the idea and the approaches that would be taken. This was viewed very positively by the children: they were meeting people who might be their English teacher in their new schools and they were doing 'harder' work. Many of them said that it made them start to feel ready for the move to Year 7. During the morning, each one in the class received their own copy of the text *Northern Lights* to have and take with them when they left.

They were then given tasks based on chapter 1, where the context of Oxford University and the main character of Lyra are introduced as well as the concept of Lyra's daemon Pantalaimon. The children were asked to consider the nuance of fantasy elements in a real-world context. They also watched the first section of *The Golden Compass*, Chris Weitz's 2007 film interpretation of the text. Most of the children were asked to compare the film extract with the book, responding to details omitted and the accuracy of character portrayal. Some of the children were asked to create a persuasive argument for the book over

(Continued)

(Continued)

the film and vice versa for some of the other children. All of these activities were about being inducted into Lyra's world. Nick then gave each child a reading journal that they were asked to keep during half-term. The intention was for the child to read the book during the week and respond to various moments in the book through drawing, description, poetry and advice for Lyra in some of the situations she would find herself as the story in the book unfolded.

Reflecting on the case study (part 1)

As you reflect on the first part of this case study notice:

- The teamwork between Nick and his secondary counterparts. Admittedly, Nick had developed a good relationship with the three secondary schools as he is an experienced Year 6 teacher, but the joined-up nature of the transition work prepared certainly helped smooth the transition for the children in English.
- The ownership that the children were given. Each child, funded by the school, was given their own copy of the book and a reading journal, which they had to use in the first term of Year 7 as the unit progressed. The children were also invited to engage in open-ended reader-response activities that looked for their thoughts and opinions and opened up many possibilities. Who's to say what could happen in a fantastic transformation of Oxford? Woods (2001) states that reading is about empowerment and gives readers a voice. He goes on to say that this is all part of creative teaching, characterised by, amongst other things, ownership of knowledge. The activities and learning set allowed the children to respond in their own way and bring their own experiences and ideas to their reading. The tool of a reading journal can aid in this process.

The use of a reading journal is very powerful. Not just for transition to Year 7, but also because it provides an opportunity for the child to respond to the text in some way. However, variety is crucial or, as Clarke, Dickinson and Westbrook advise: 'beware of always insisting they write lengthy reviews as this will dampen enthusiasm' (2010: 170). Providing alternative response ideas for children helps them engage in the story but in a way that makes sense to them. A review of the book can be interesting and an important learning tool, but this does tend to be the first idea for a teacher to help children engage with a reading journal. Children can respond through a cartoon, a short poem, a satirisation, speech bubbles, thought bubbles, opinion or 50-word challenge. The key point is in knowing why you want children to respond in order to develop their learning and is also in knowing how you will do this. Cremin supports this idea as she states that a journal can develop: 'interrogation and reflection upon texts' (2009: 107). Helping children interrogate texts facilitates their deeper engagement, and the interest and their understanding of the inferences and nuances that writers convey. Cremin also suggests a variety of prompts to scaffold the reading work: predicting, picturing, comparing, empathising and responding to issues and evaluating are helpful verbs to support their reading.

Case study: Part 2 – Developing thinking

At the meeting of the four teachers during the half-term break, it became apparent that, in order to help prepare children for secondary school, they needed to develop the children's thinking skills and their understanding of how to learn. Having just come from a term of working towards scoring highly in standardised tests, Nick's class needed to re-find their thinking ability. During the introduction session, Nick had noticed that some of the children were reticent to give answers because they didn't want to get them wrong, make a mistake or look silly in front of the Year 7 teachers or their friends. Nick needed to create a thinking environment. He decided to use the idea of daemons to start with. These are a big feature of the book, *Northern Lights*, and help delineate normal Oxford from fantastic Oxford.

Daemons in Pullman's novel are your soul worn on your sleeve, able to communicate with their human body. They appear as a talking-animal friend that goes with you wherever you go. Nick asked the class to think of what their daemon would be and why. This was open-ended and allowed children to explore this concept of the soul and start asking questions about why certain souls take certain forms. Nick displayed some of the characters from the story and their daemons and asked the class what each character's daemon said about them. What

(Continued)

(Continued)

was being inferred by Pullman? This activity demands a synthesis of the logical elements of critical thinking and the more divergent elements of creative thinking. Nick was not worried about labelling the thinking because he was keen to get children engaged in the concept and just start thinking. The children's ideas developed a level of sophistication that Nick had not seen from his class for a while and he was pleased with the result: a depth of understanding had been gained and one of the many subtexts in the story had been explored. For example, Lord Asriel, the daemon of Lyra's father, is a snow leopard. This prompted a huge variety of responses. Some said that he is calm and calculated because snow leopards always seem to be thinking and planning or stalking their prey. Some asked why a snow leopard as opposed to a normal leopard? The response was simple – it denotes that he is a cold man.

In order to develop this, Nick turned the class's attention to a problem to solve in the story and he wanted the class to have some empathy with Lyra. Lyra is given an alethiometer by the Master of Jordan College. She knows that it is something important but is not sure why or what it is for. Should she keep it safe and give it to her father Lord Asriel or show her mother Mrs Coulter, or keep it to herself? What should she do? No one really knew, so Nick introduced the class to a thinking technique called the 'Napoleon technique'. This technique, discussed earlier in Chapter 4, is often used in the context of business as it helps see a problem through completely new eyes. It removes the key protagonist from the situation, replaces them with someone else and sees how they would solve the problem. It is called 'Napoleon' because the initial intention is to use this key historical figure to become the new protagonist.

Having recently completed a topic on the Tudors, Nick chose Henry VIII for his new protagonist. How would Henry respond, given Lyra's problem? The answers sparked great hilarity amongst the class. The children were asked to create and perform a short scenario. One group also added Anne Boleyn to the scene and had Henry hiding the alethiometer from Anne so that she wouldn't suspect that he had something secret from her. Another group had the bombastic Henry, King and Lord of All he Surveyed, daring anyone to challenge his right to have the alethiometer. Another group played to Henry's sporting prowess and suggested a jousting tournament, where the winner would keep the alethiometer. They decided that context was crucial. What was the purpose? Not to find the right answer, but to discover the process of creation, divergent thought, developing ideas together, building on one another's ideas, understanding the characters, applying one context to another.

Reflecting on the case study (part 2)

- Notice how Nick dealt with authorial intent, nuance and subtext by using a simple creative technique. His use of open questioning allowed the children to explore some key symbolism in the story (daemons, a difficult concept) and create their own interpretations.
- Notice how Nick didn't present different scenarios for Lyra to choose her own adventure and the class had to read the text and find the right one. Nick wanted more than that. He wanted children to explore possibilities. Using the 'Napoleon technique' provided an exciting and stimulating way to do that. Notice that the learning occurred through the process - learning, not just about the story, but about themselves as learners and thinkers, too.

Stop and think

If you are a teacher of Upper Key Stage 2 children or children of a higher ability in other year groups, how will you support their understanding of authorial intent? Nick wanted his class to move away from obvious answers and encouraged a range of possibilities to articulate and then justify their thinking. This approach promotes learning in its widest sense. How will you achieve this in your teaching?

Case study: Part 3 – Writing for a purpose and for drama

Nick turned the class's attention to a scene mentioned in Pullman's book but which was not fully explored. At the end of chapter 12, Lyra and

(Continued)

(Continued)

Pantalaimon come across a little boy with no daemon. It had been severed away by the gobblers. However, the novel does not say how this came about. Nick gave his class the challenge of creating a new scene in the form of a playscript. This would continue to stretch their thinking, but also force the children to consider the development of some of the main characters, especially Lyra. How would she react to a boy with no daemon, no soul? What will she do? They would need to develop the gobblers and create the boy's backstory while still staying true to Pullman's text. For the following week, the children worked collaboratively in groups developing ideas. They brought in some of the other characters: the witch Serafina Pekkala. One group had Lord Asriel paying the gobblers to cut the daemon from the boy because he was a threat. The class developed playscripts through a scaffolded approach, worked on stage directions, Pullmanesque dialogue and rehearsed and performed for the school and parents as part of their leavers assembly. They also did a tour of the three secondary schools, performing for Year 7 English classes and their teachers, who had been part of the developing plan.

Reflecting on the case study (part 3)

As you consider this third part of the case study:

- Reflect on the use of drama. Nick uses drama as performance. Earlier on in this book, I discussed drama as a process of learning through working and writing in-role. This process is important, but drama as enactment of a play is equally as important because it requires interpretation, some improvisation and visualisation. As Connell states: 'Drama approaches allow pupils to explore the meaning, language and structure of texts actively' (2010: 232). This is highly creative because it is all about exploration and therefore multiple perspectives and interpretation.
- Notice how Nick focuses on writing for a purpose and audience(s) through playscripts. This form of writing requires a very different approach to writing prose and poetry because the writer must think about the actor through careful stage direction and communicating meaning through action. The writer must also think about the overall effect through careful dialogue and setting for the

audience to whom the play will be performed. This form of writing requires students to think at a much more sophisticated level than the usual writing required at Key Stage 2 and certainly than for standardised tests. It is this thinking that will support an effective transition to Key Stage 3.

Drama is important. Gardner states that it: 'provides teachers with a wide range of creative and highly flexible techniques, strategies and devices' (2010: 52). It allows children to explore difficult problems and situations vicariously and allows them to walk inside the shoes of other beings and experience other worlds and lives. But what is the significance of writing a script? The Key Stage 3 English curriculum demands it. That is the short answer, but what do children actually learn from script-writing? I believe that they learn to visualise. This is an important skill for writing and planning. As they start to develop dialogue and stage direction, they have to imagine the words being spoken and the action that takes place. They have to decide how the words will be spoken and why, and what the interplay between the characters will be. This is a step up in sophistication. It also means that their writing is purposeful and the audience is for an actor to have to interpret what is being written. Writing a playscript requires accuracy of language, authorial intent to be evident and a significant awareness of two audiences: the actor and those watching the performance.

Try this

Activity 1: Reading journal

In your next planning for a fiction unit of work, and if you feel that it would benefit the learning of your class, try using a reading journal with the class, or even a group. It could also be used for a guided reading group, if this is an approach you use. Think of a variety of skills that you want children to develop and what you want them to interrogate and reflect on. Prepare a variety of weekly activities for them to engage in. Evaluate the learning that occurs as a result.

(Continued)

(Continued)

Activity 2: Secondary English Department liaison

Notice the impact that the teachers working together had on the children's engagement and enthusiasm as well as continuity through into Year 7. This joined-up approach can only be helpful. If you are a Year 6 teacher, get to know your secondary schools – especially those that teach Year 7 – and cultivate some good professional relationships with them.

Summary

This chapter explores the challenging business of transition in English between primary and secondary schools. There are many excellent practices that I have seen from secondary schools, where Year 7 staff go into schools and teach Years 5 and 6, giving them tasters and helping start relationships. Some produce school webpages for Year 6 children preparing to go to their new school, while others have magazines written by Year 7 to help Year 6s to prepare. Many hold taster sessions, open evenings and visit days. However, I think that the approach in Nick's case study is phenomenally effective. Planning a transition unit of work with Year 7 colleagues is a very challenging experience but one that brings many rewards. Nick's class will go into their respective Year 7 classes having experienced the school and met and worked with the teachers and having already started some of the work they will be doing. The approaches that Nick took to *Northern Lights* impacted massively on the development of his class. He focused on thinking and learning through the process of activity, rather than on the end product. Nick recognised that this is the culmination of learning, not the learning itself. This is the main focus of the chapter: the sophisticated thinking and understanding of the text that Nick facilitated through the development activities around daemons, the Napoleon technique, reading journal and playwriting set very high expectations for his class but also engaged and motivated them so that the end of Year 6 was a significant transition experience for them and not just the end of their primary school days.

Further reading

Clarke, S., Dickinson, P. and Westbrook, J. (2010) *The Complete Guide to Becoming an English Teacher*. London: Sage.

This effective text supports all types of English teaching. Mainly rooted in the secondary sector, it does have many approaches that are transferable to Key Stage 2, with lots of practical drama ideas and strong pedagogy. The approaches to teaching Shakespeare, I think, are particularly effective.

Harmer, J. (2007) *How to Teach English*, 2nd edn. London: Pearson.

Harmer's new edition focuses really effectively on skills and attributes of the English teacher. These can also be transferred to other subjects for the primary teacher. It also looks mainly at the learners and the role they play in the learning process. It starts with the learner, not the teacher.

Haworth, A., Turner, C. and Whiteley, M. (2004) *Secondary English and Literacy: A Guide for Teachers*. London: Paul Chapman.

This is a great read. It can be a revelation for a primary teacher to pick up texts aimed at secondary teachers. I find this book to be very helpful in the way that it is divided up, and I especially like the sections on oracy and investigating grammar. This text also supports the development of subject knowledge. A very useful text.

References

Bloom, B.S., Engelhart, M.D., Furst, E.J., Hill, W.H. and Krathwohl, D.R. (1956). *Taxonomy of Educational Objectives: The Classification of Educational Goals. Handbook I: Cognitive Domain*. New York: David McKay Company.

Clarke, S., Dickinson, P. and Westbrook, J. (2010) *The Complete Guide to Becoming an English Teacher*. London: Sage.

Connell, M. (2010) 'Doing drama', in S. Clarke, P. Dickinson and J. Westbrook (eds), *The Complete Guide to Becoming an English Teacher*. London: Sage.

Cremin, T. (2009) *Teaching English Creatively*. London: Routledge.

Department for Education (DfE) (2013). *The National Curriculum in England Key Stages 1 and 2*. London: Crown Copyright.

Department for Education (DfE) (2014) *The National Curriculum in England: Key Stages 3 and 4 Framework Document*. London: DfE. Available at: www.gov.uk/government/uploads/system/uploads/attachment_data/file/381754/SECONDARY_national_curriculum.pdf (accessed 28 Dec 2015).

Department for Education and Skills (DfES) (2002) *English Transition Units*. DfES Publications. Available at: www.wirral-mbc.gov.uk/english/AdminArea/Secondary TeacherFiles/01132002Engtransitionunits.pdf (accessed 22 Dec 2015).

Dickens, C. (1854) *Hard Times*. England: Bradbury and Evans.

Dymoke, S. (2009) *Teaching English Texts: 11–18*. London: Bloomsbury.

Galton, M. (1999) *The Impact of School Transitions and Transfers on Pupil Progress and Attainment*. DfEE Research Report No. 131. London: Department for Education and Employment (DfEE).

Gardner, P. (2010) *Creative English, Creative Curriculum*. London: David Fulton.

Hughes, L., Banks, P. and Terras, M. (2013) 'Secondary school transition for children with special educational needs: A literature review', *Support for Learning*, 28 (1): 25–34.

Krathwohl, D. (2002) 'A revision of Bloom's Taxonomy: An overview', *Theory into Practice*, 41 (4): 212–66.

Morpurgo, M. (2000) *Kensuke's Kingdom*. London: Egmont.

National Literacy Strategy (2002) *Year 6 Planning Exemplification 3*. London: Department for Education and Skills (DfES). Available at: http://dera.ioe.ac.uk/6162/1/nls_y6exunits013502book3.pdf (accessed 20 Dec 2015).

Ofsted (2005). *English 2000-05: A review of inspection evidence*. Available at http://dera.ioe.ac.uk/5476/1/English%202000-05%20a%20review%20of%20inspection%20evidence%20(PDF%20format).pdf (accessed 1 February 2016).

Parker, G. (2011) 'Transition from Year 6 to Year 7 in the English Department', *The Use of English*, 62 (2): 109–15.

Pike, M. (2000) 'Keen readers: Adolescents and pre-twentieth century poetry', *Educational Review*, 52 (1): 13–28.

Pike, M. (2004) *Teaching Secondary English*. London: Paul Chapman.

Pullman, P. (1995) *Northern Lights*. London: Scholastic.

Rainer, P. and Cropley, B. (2015) 'Bridging the gap – but mind you don't fall: Primary physical education teachers' perceptions of the transition process to secondary school', *Education 3–13*, 43 (5): 445–61.

Wilson, J. (2006) *The Suitcase Kid*. London: Yearling Books.

Woods, P. (2001) 'Creative literacy', in A. Craft, B. Jeffrey and M. Liebling (eds), *Creativity in Education*. London: Continuum.

Concluding remarks

One of the main threads running through all the chapters in this book is the classroom environment. Creating an effective environment is vital for the facilitation of creative learning and teaching. There are typically three facets to any classroom environment: the physical environment, the social environment and the cognitive environment. Much of what has been discussed throughout this book relates to the cognitive and social environment, and I want to conclude by pulling together some of the key messages that I have already shared.

In terms of the social environment, there needs to be an ethos of trust and respect and this must be designed by the teacher for creative learning and teaching to occur. Both the teacher and the children must trust each other; and the children must trust each other in order to work together, take risks with learning and explore concepts together. Talk for learning is another key aspect of the social environment, too. Children must be comfortable talking with everyone in their class, learning together and building on each other's ideas in a wide variety of contexts. This will always be challenging because social relationships are one of the hardest aspects of school to have success in. They require significant interpersonal and intrapersonal skills as well as negotiation, emotional intelligence and empathy. But, as a teacher, it is worth working hard to facilitate this as much as possible because relationships are at the heart of effective teaching. When these two elements of trust and working together are in place, they can create a platform for working in-role, which can motivate, engage and enthuse children in learning and can be used as a tool for developing skills, knowledge and understanding.

This leads me nicely onto the cognitive classroom environment. The cognitive environment that we as teachers create arises out of what we believe about learning and teaching and how children learn. If I believe that children learn by constructing knowledge through dialogue, then the activities I facilitate will be characterised by that belief. I may not do so much upfront teaching, but I might do more facilitation of learning. I may more likely guide rather than dictate. Children will play an active part in their learning. If I believe that children learn best through play and discovery, you could expect children in my class to be exploring, thinking, playing, arriving at their own solutions and learning a diverse range of things, beyond my learning intentions for the session. Children learn through the process of learning, rather than by producing a product as proof of learning. Here is where creativity lies and this is what characterises creative learning and, in the context of this book, creative learning in primary English.

As you read this book, you will see lots of connections between English and history. I make no apologies for that as there are so many links that can be made between these two subjects. Skills, knowledge, concepts and understanding in both subject disciplines lend themselves beautifully to using one as a context for the other. However, there will be just as many for other curriculum subjects and I would urge you, as you again read some of the case studies and examples, to use them as a basis for letting your own creative connections develop. One thing is clear, for English to be taught creatively and effectively in primary schools, there needs to be relevance and purpose which a wider topic can provide, but also an appreciation of an audience. Who will your children write for?

Index